Copyright 2022 by Michael W. Rickard II

All rights reserved. Without limiting rights under the copyright reserved above, no part of this publication may be reproduced, stored, introduced into a retrieval system, distributed or transmitted in any form or by any means, including without limitation photocopying, recording, or other electronic or mechanical methods, without the prior written permission of the publisher, except in the case of brief quotations embodied in critical reviews and certain other noncommercial uses permitted by copyright law. The scanning, uploading, and/or distribution of this document via the internet or via any other means without the permission of the publisher is illegal and is punishable by law. Please purchase only authorized editions and do not participate in or encourage electronic piracy of copyrightable materials.

For permission requests, email
mike@michaelrickard.com

ISBN: 9798839519428

MCMAHON'S MESSES AND MISSES: SCANDALS, SHOCKERS, AND SHENANIGANS IN PROFESSIONAL WRESTLING

by Michael W. Rickard II
Copyright 2022 by Michael W. Rickard II
All rights reserved

Other Books by Michael W. Rickard II

Wrestling's Greatest Moments

Laughing All the Way to the Bank (Robbery): How an Attorney Survived Prison

Flunky: Pawns and Kings

Don't Call Me Bush Beans (The Legend of a Three-Legged Cat Begins)

Don't Call Me Bush Beans 2: I'm Not a Scaredy Cat!

Introduction...1

Part One: The Current Controversy...3

Chapter One: The Scandal..5

Chapter Two: What Could Vince McMahon Lose

from the Scandal?...18

Chapter Three: #MeToo McMahon Style.......................................27

Part Two: From the Outhouse to the Penthouse......................47

Chapter Four: What Makes McMahon Tick?...................................49

Chapter Five: The Road to the Top...59

Chapter Six: Vince McMahon's Trials by Fire..........................69

Chapter Seven: Shooting for the Stars.......................................81

Part Three: Ruthless Aggression...91

Chapter Eight: Black Saturday..93

Chapter Nine: Business, the Vince McMahon Way..............108

Chapter Ten: Move Along, Nothing to See.........................121

Chapter Eleven: Is There Systemic Racism in Wrestling?.........154

Chapter Twelve: Financial Opportunity or Blood Money?.........161

Chapter Thirteen: The WWE Concussion Lawsuit................175

Part Four: Turning a Blind Eye...199

Chapter Fourteen: Did Jimmy Snuka Get Away with Murder?...201

Chapter Fifteen: The Fall of Hulk Hogan..........................215

Chapter Sixteen: The Frightening Legacy of the Fabulous Moolah
....239

Chapter Seventeen: The Plane Ride from Hell 258

Chapter Eighteen: Warrior Wackiness: The Twisted History of the Ultimate Warrior..269

Part Five: McMahon and Super McMahon............................291

Chapter Nineteen: A McMahon for All Seasons......................292

Chapter Twenty: McMahon's Gracious Giving: Helping Out Other Wrestlers..300

Chapter Twenty-One: McMahon's Sentimental Side................304

Chapter Twenty-Two: The Wit and Wisdom of Vince McMahon...318

Chapter Twenty-Three: Story Weather or Blue Skies?................329

Appendix A: The World Bodybuilding Federation: Bigger Isn't Always Better..335

Appendix B Inglorious Bastards: The Story of the XFL............353

Appendix C The Montreal Screwjob: Turning Chickenshit into Chicken Salad 375

Wrestling has seen many great brother tag teams including The Briscos, Owen and Bret Hart, The Steiners, and The Usos. This book is dedicated to my Irish Catholic twin brother Dave who is not only the world's greatest brother but a true connoisseur of the grappling game.

Introduction

The saga of WWE (World Wrestling Entertainment) owner Vincent Kennedy McMahon is a true American success story. McMahon risked everything he owned when he purchased his father's wrestling company, the WWF (World Wrestling Federation) in 1982. McMahon took more risks when he changed the way wrestling was promoted. Originally, promoters ran their shows in specific geographical areas, staying out of competitors' territories. Vince McMahon broke this long-standing unwritten rule by promoting wrestling across the country, encroaching on other wrestling organizations' territories and eventually putting the majority out of business. Over time, McMahon turned the small WWF into the global entertainment company, the WWE which airs and tours internationally.

Like most people, McMahon has faced many challenges and obstacles in his life (arguably, some by his own making). Just like the larger-than-life world of professional wrestling he promotes (or sports entertainment as he prefers people call it), McMahon's trials and tribulations are anything but ordinary. These include lawsuits, a federal criminal trial, bitter business battles (including an all-out war for his wrestling company's survival), and an upbringing that reportedly led to him contemplating suicide.

Now, the latest scandal in McMahon's life threatens to take everything he's spent four decades building up. As we'll see, McMahon's life has been one fight after another. This book isn't a detailed biography of Vince McMahon but an overview of who he is, where he came from, how he built his wrestling company into a global juggernaut, and what the future could hold for him and his company. We'll look at his humble beginnings as a trailer park kid and the road that led to him controlling a billion-dollar empire. This includes his fight to the top of the wrestling industry and how he's dealt with his wrestlers and his adversaries (sometimes one and the same) along the way. There's a lot to learn about Vincent Kennedy McMahon including some lighter moments in his life, his idiosyncrasies, and some touching tales of how McMahon has helped others out. This book will give you a better understanding of the WWE as a business, Vince McMahon the entrepreneur, and Vince McMahon the person.

Note: These chapters are taken from various pieces I have written for several wrestling news sites and *YouTube* channels. I've included the original sources for the articles but in some cases, the links to websites are broken.

Part One: The Current Controversy

The hush money allegations being made against Vince McMahon and his former Head of Talent Relations John Laurinaitis are potentially perilous for McMahon and the WWE because they potentially involve #MeToo allegations and could reveal a corporate culture that turned a blind eye to sexual harassment. This section will look at the current allegations, their potential fallout, and past allegations against Vince McMahon.

Chapter One: The Scandal

Originally published 2022

The scandal rocking the WWE has quickly raised several questions including how it will affect the WWE, Vince McMahon, and wrestling in general. It's also raising an equally important question—is there a power struggle to oust the McMahons from the company they built? The potential fallout from the WWE scandal could impact more than the WWE. It could affect the entire wrestling industry from small promotions to national ones.

The Allegations

On June 15, 2022, *The Wall Street Journal* reported the WWE's Board of Directors uncovered:

> a secret $3 million settlement that longtime chief executive Vince McMahon agreed to pay to a departing employee with whom he allegedly had an affair, according to documents and people familiar with the board inquiry. (Palazzolo and Mann)

The article states the board began its investigation in April and discovered other nondisclosure agreements with other female ex-

WWE employees. These agreements reportedly concerned Vince McMahon and the WWE's Head of Talent Relations, John Laurinaitis.

More Allegations Raised

On 8 July 2022 *The Wall Street Journal* provided further details on the nondisclosure agreements:

> Vince McMahon, World Wrestling Entertainment Inc.'s longtime leader, agreed to pay more than $12 million over the past 16 years to suppress allegations of sexual misconduct and infidelity, an amount far larger than previously known. (Palazzolo et al).

According to the article, McMahon allegedly engaged in sexual harassment and/or sexual misconduct, with the *Journal* article pointing out an allegation that presents a potential pitfall:

> The previously unreported settlements include a $7.5 million pact with a former wrestler who alleged that Mr. McMahon coerced her into giving him oral sex and then demoted her and, ultimately, declined to renew her contract in 2005 after she resisted further sexual encounters, according to people familiar with the matter. The wrestler and her attorney approached Mr. McMahon in 2018 and negotiated

the payment in return for her silence. (ibid)

The article also noted allegations of a 2008 nondisclosure agreement regarding Vince McMahon sending unsolicited nude photos of himself and a 2006 nondisclosure agreement over an alleged sexual relationship.

Additionally, the article commented on the WWE's Head of Talent Relations John Laurinatis and the WWE Board of Directors investigating a:

> $1.5 million nondisclosure agreement reached in 2012 with an employee involving misconduct claims against Mr. Laurinaitis (ibid).

This incident may have been related to Laurinaitis stepping down as Head of Talent Relations in 2012:

> His demotion came around the same time as the $1.5 million deal with the employee, who alleged she had an affair with Mr. Laurinaitis and that he demoted her after she broke it off, people familiar with the nondisclosure agreement said. (ibid)

Laurinaitis eventually returned to his former role but is currently on leave after the current allegations surfaced.

The Great Unknowns

There are several factors concerning the allegations that remain unresolved. The first is whether Vince McMahon used any WWE funds to pay for the settlement (his attorney denies this). If so, this could expose McMahon to a claim that he breached his fiduciary duties to the WWE as CEO. The second is the WWE's articles of incorporation and any corporate policies regarding a situation such as this. The #MeToo movement has not only heightened awareness of people using roles of authority to sexually harass and/or assault those in roles of less authority, but also established higher standards for those in authority. Finally, there is the question of what the misconduct was that individuals were compensated for and for which they signed nondisclosure agreements. If any of these incidents involved criminal activity (such as sexual assault) they would obviously have worse consequences than sexual harassment.

At this point, the scandal is being investigated by an independent law firm which will hopefully uncover more details.

How It Could Affect the WWE

The WWE has been performing well as a stock, despite many other stocks suffering in the current bear market. However, the news of the current scandal could lead to a decline or even sharp decline in its value. This depends on two things: 1) what the investigation of the payouts uncovers; and 2) how the WWE handles the problem. If the investigation reveals the WWE knew about the alleged misconduct and ignored it, the stock will likely drop. If the WWE's higher-ups didn't know about the allegations yet chooses to do nothing to resolve any documented problems, the company opens itself up for future litigation and faces a potential decline in its stock value due to the negative publicity.

A related matter is the WWE's image as a family-friendly corporation. Professional wrestling has often been regarded as trash TV, even during wrestling's peaks in popularity. If the investigation reveals a corporate culture that looked the other way at misconduct, it could harm the WWE's reputation; leading to advertisers pulling out and TV partners passing on airing the product or offering less for rights fees.

Vince McMahon

Mr. McMahon stands to lose a lot right now including his position as CEO and control of the company he's spent four decades building up from a regional promotion to a global entertainment empire. Worse, Mr. McMahon could even be forced to sell his stock. On a personal note, McMahon could face a divorce.

McMahon losing his role of CEO seems like a strong possibility unless the stories of so-called hush money payouts turn out to be inaccurate.

There doesn't seem to be any question that the nondisclosure agreements were executed. The question now is whether the allegations of misconduct are accurate.

McMahon could fight to stay as CEO but the WWE's board (not to mention its stockholders) would see him as a liability if the allegations are confirmed, particularly the one alleging coerced sex.

The WWE seems to be making the right moves in terms of protecting its image. A tweet from the news source *WrestleVotes* noted:

> According to WWE Corporate, Vince McMahon has voluntarily stepped back from his responsibilities as CEO & Chairman of the Board until the conclusion of the investigation. Stephanie McMahon will serve as interim CEO and interim Chairwoman.

The embattled McMahon could lose control of his company. Again, a finding that he engaged in misconduct (particularly if it is related to him abusing his role as CEO of the company) would all but force the WWE's board of directors to relieve him of any power whether it is in creative or as the CEO. McMahon might try to use proxies to influence decisions but if this surreptitious control was somehow uncovered, it would damage the WWE's reputation and renew questions about the corporation's dedication to correcting past mistakes.

Worst of all, McMahon could lose ownership in his company. While there are many factors in this possible outcome (including the ones discussed earlier), the WWE's board of directors could force Vince to sell his stock. While this might seem extreme, it is possible and there may even be one or more individuals in the WWE trying to usurp control of the corporation.

The scandal could affect McMahon's personal life as rumors have been circulating for some time that Vince and Linda McMahon have lived apart for some time. Dave Meltzer, the editor of *The Wrestling Observer Newsletter* (a long-running newsletter that covers professional wrestling and mixed martial arts) recently commented on the couple's relationship, "Technically, they're married. I mean, they haven't been together in a long, long time though" (qtd. in Perry). Does this mean that Vince and Linda are one step away from divorce? If so, the McMahons may have decided not to divorce due to financial considerations, this latest scandal could convince Linda to divorce Vince (particularly if the scandal gives her a better standing in court).

A Power Play in the WWE?

With both Vince McMahon and John Laurinaitis coming under fire for the hush money scandal, there are whispers of a possible power struggle in the WWE. *WrestleVotes* posted a timeline which suggests either a series of unfortunate events for anyone with the last name of McMahon or evidence an individual or group have worked to help the McMahons out of the WWE:

> Jan 29: Vince & Shane Rumble spat; Shane removed from further plans
> March 25: Triple H reveals health details, announces in ring retirement
> May 19: Stephanie announces she is taking leave of absence from company
> June 15: WSJ drops allegations on Vince of $$ secret hush pact.

Some critics believe this timeline suggests a pattern of McMahons being eased out of the company and while patterns should be rigorously examined, there are other factors to consider including: 1) who has been leaking the information that is detrimental to the McMahon family; and 2) who stands to gain from disparaging the family and possibly the company itself.

There are rumors that someone in the WWE leaked the details of the WWE Board of Directors' investigation to the *Wall Street Journal* with *The Wrestling Observer Newsletter's* Dave Meltzer speculating it may have been a WWE board member:

"Obviously, there's the big question of, 'Who on the board of directors leaked it?' You know, whatever. I mean, it's a question, but I think it was probably somebody on the board. It may have been, the person who leaked it to the board and then leaking it and The Wall Street Journal finding out the dates and everything and then being told that from the outside."

There are a number of individuals besides board members who might have leaked the story. Individuals looking to get ahead in the corporate world have been known to use whistleblowers to take out a rival. With whistleblower laws providing more protection for employees who reveal misconduct i.e., protecting them from being fired or allowing compensation for unlawful termination, an individual may be persuaded to help out a higher-up looking to take someone else out.

This isn't the first time someone has leaked a story to the press casting the McMahons in a bad light. Not too long ago, someone leaked a story to *Business Insider* that suggested Stephanie McMahon wasn't performing up to expectations, hence her decision to walk away from her role as Chief Brand Officer. While there have been denials that Stephanie left for any reason other than her stated reason (to spend time with her family), some pundits and fans have asked why Stephanie did not do this when Triple H faced life-threatening health problems last year.

Meltzer continued his analysis of the leak:

> "The fact of the investigation and everything seems to indicate that somebody on the board did [leak the news]. And, so, you've got twelve people there. Obviously, Vince didn't, so you've got eleven people there that you can look at and, whatever, it could be one of those but we don't have that answer, obviously."

As for how the WWE's Board of Directors learned of the alleged hush money, the *Journal* noted:

> Board members learned of the $3 million agreement in a series of anonymous emails they received from someone who said the former WWE paralegal was a friend.

The email pulls no punches about the allegations. The *Wall Street Journal* reports:

> The first email, sent to board members on March 30, alleged that Mr. McMahon, 76 years old, initially hired the woman at a salary of $100,000 but increased it to $200,000 after beginning

a sexual relationship with her. The email to the board also alleged that Mr. McMahon "gave her like a toy" to Mr. Laurinaitis. The board is investigating the allegations in the email, the people familiar with the inquiry said.

The evidence needs further analysis before concluding someone (or more than one person) is out to remove the McMahons from the WWE. Nonetheless, it's something which needs to be explored. Motives for an ouster include someone who believes they can operate the WWE better than McMahon, someone looking to buy the company at a lower price (by damaging the stock during the scandal and hoping it goes up), or someone looking to sell the company, but who sees a sale as unlikely as long as Vince McMahon is in control.

There have been rumors of the WWE being sold for the last few years and it's believed the company could command top dollar due to its vast inventory of content. This content would appeal to streaming services. In 2021, the Peacock streaming service acquired the distribution rights to the WWE Network, a reminder of how valuable content is for streaming services.

Exit Vince McMahon, Enter Stephanie McMahon

Thing took an interesting turn with the appointment of Stephanie McMahon as interim CEO and Chairwoman. If someone is trying to oust Vince from the company, is it possible he had Stephanie appointed in order to protect his interests? Stephanie has gained an image as a friendly face for the company and someone who has championed the WWE's self-proclaimed "women's movement" (spending more time promoting women's wrestling). The board may feel she is a good look (and even an eventual replacement) for the company while it waits for its investigation into the hush-money scandal. Stephanie McMahon could reassure stockholders who feel the WWE is better-represented as a family-run business.

The Harm to the Wrestling Industry

Finally, this scandal could hurt the entire wrestling industry, as the public reexamines some of wrestling's more sordid stories. Even if wrestling continues to provide good ratings, its perception by advertisers is what matters and if advertisers aren't willing to pay top dollar for wrestling, a network is less likely to carry it whether it's the WWE, its rival All Elite Wrestling (AEW), or smaller promotions.

Works Cited

Palazzolo, Joe and Ted Mann. "WWE Board

Probes Secret $3 Million Hush Pact by CEO Vince McMahon, Sources Say." *The Wall Street Journal.* 15 June 2022. https://www.wsj.com/articles/wwe-board-probes-secret-3-million-hush-pact-by-ceo-vince-mcmahon-sources-say-11655322722?page=1. Accessed 15 June 2022.

Palazzolo, Joe et al. "WWE's Vince McMahon Agreed to Pay $12 Million in Hush Money to Four Women." *Wall Street Journal.* 8 July 2022. https://www.wsj.com/articles/wwes-vince-mcmahon-agreed-to-pay-12-million-in-hush-money-to-four-women-11657289742. Accessed 8 July 2022.

Perry, Michael. "Vince McMahon & Linda McMahon No Longer Living Together." *Ringside News.* WWE News. 16 June 2022. https://www.ringsidenews.com/2022/06/16/vince-mcmahon-linda-mcmahon-no-longer-living-together. Accessed 16 June 2022.

@WrestleVotes. "According." 17 June 2022. https://twitter.com/WrestleVotes/status/1537761233197322241?s=20&t=6Dqk84D0QbnKJU8CxKWi_Q.

Chapter Two: What Could Vince McMahon Lose from The Scandal?

Originally published 2022

Vince McMahon faces the potential loss of many things depending on the outcome of the WWE Board of Directors' investigation and any disciplinary action that follows. Chapter one discussed how McMahon could lose his company but there are many other things at stake.

His Wealth

Is Vince McMahon going to end up on the streets as a homeless man? While this is highly unlikely, he could lose a good chunk of his wealth. The first way is through the WWE stock taking a tumble. While the WWE's stock hasn't dropped much after this latest scandal, it could take a substantial hit if the investigation confirms the current allegations against McMahon, and even more if the WWE's higher-ups are shown to have turned a blind eye to it (particularly if current or former employees file suit alleging sexual harassment or worse). If McMahon is forced to sell his stock, he may fight the move, incurring additional costs in legal bills. McMahon could also face lawsuits from people who allege misconduct and are not bound by nondisclosure agreements.

His Freedom

One of the most intriguing aspects of the WWE scandal is the developing story suggesting there may have been insider trading as WWE stock was sold right before *The Wall Street Journal's* expose of the hush money scandal in the WWE. As the WWE Board of Directors continues its investigation into Mr. McMahon's payouts to women for possible misconduct, the WWE may be facing another scandal. *Wrestlenomics'* Brandon Thurston tweeted on June 16, 2022:

> 2.1 million $WWE shares changed hands yesterday, about 1.5 million more than an average day, all before the WSJ story broke just after the market closed. It may be worthwhile to read the paragraph from the code of conduct headed, "Prohibition Against Insider Trading".

To sum things up, it's unknown who made this sales transaction but it could lead to criminal prosecution for whoever was involved. This is not to say that Vince McMahon was involved (and again, it remains to be seen if the transaction even counts as "insider trading"). Nonetheless, the federal government has a long memory and prosecutors will likely be happy to get another crack at prosecuting Vince McMahon, the man who beat federal prosecutors during his 1990s steroid trial and bragged about it.

His Netflix Documentary

Speaking of Mr. McMahon's battle against the federal government, it appears the documentary about Vince's battle with the media and the federal government in the early 90s, i.e., the steroid scandal and trial against Vince McMahon, could be shelved. First announced in 2020, the Netflix program was reportedly going to be a four-part series which painted the WWE kingpin in a favorable light. However, Dave Meltzer discussed the project's shaky future in light of the allegations against McMahon:

> "The other thing, too, is the television show, you know, the Netflix show that they've been working on. That changes a lot of the dynamic of that show, too, because the whole show is about portraying Vince McMahon as this babyface and Phil Mushnick and others as these giant heels out to get him for all the stuff in the 90s, and it was always a weird one to me, the trial and the Justice Department and everything like that" (qtd. in Perry "Netflix").

People may have trouble sympathizing with a man accused of paying women to sign nondisclosure clauses for alleged misconduct against him. Meltzer continued:

"With this hanging over Vince's head, I don't know that Netflix wants to put a show like that on the air. It's kind of, even if Vince doesn't have to leave with the sexual allegations and everything against him, that becomes a very tricky little thing there."

Of course, should McMahon find a way to extricate himself from this latest scandal, Netflix could always make it into a five-part documentary.

His Autobiography

Recent news suggested Vince McMahon was shopping an autobiography around. This followed news of an upcoming biography of Vince McMahon by Abraham Riesman, the author of the controversial Stan Lee biography, *True Believer, The Rise and Fall of Stan Lee* (Miles). *The New York Post* reported that Vince was shopping an autobiography to various book publisher. Does McMahon want to produce a sanitized version of his life to not only counter Reisman's book but to cut into its sales? While the Vince McMahon autobiography has not been confirmed, it's likely going to be difficult to sell unless Vince pulls a Karma Houdini with his current scandal, in which case he could have a best-seller on his hands.

His Marriage

Rumor has it that Vince McMahon and his wife Linda have been living apart for some time. The specifics are unknown but it doesn't sound like an ideal marriage and a very public revelation of Vince doling out hush money to an alleged ex-lover may be enough to push Linda to file for divorce.

His Family

Vince could see his relationship with his children deteriorate. No one knows the inner workings of the McMahon family but the reports of son Shane McMahon butting heads with his father are well-known to wrestling fans. Things heated up again earlier this year when Shane reportedly clashed with his father over Shane's plans for *The Royal Rumble* (a wrestling event where Shane wrestled in the match and according to some critics, made himself look better than the WWE's wrestlers). Rumor has it Vince dismissed Shane's plans for wrestling over the next few months (including a big match at the WWE's Super Bowl-esque *WrestleMania*) and relieved Shane of any further role in the WWE's creative department. As for Stephanie, her recent exit from the WWE led to speculation whether she wanted to step down or was asked to. Her return as interim CEO and Chairwoman has some thinking Stephanie might be on good terms with her father. In Stephanie's case, only time will tell.

His Legacy

Vince McMahon has never shied away from his image as a self-made multi-millionaire who went from a trailer park to the head of a billion-dollar global entertainment empire. He's also admitted being cocky, street-smart, and someone willing to fight it out in the business world as well as in the streets. While McMahon has admitted to extramarital affairs, he's always depicted them as consensual, also seeming to imply that women were attracted to him and that there was no sexual harassment (or worse). Indeed, McMahon has denied past claims of sexual assault and sexual harassment (although it bears mentioning that the WWE settled out of court with former WWE female Superstar Sable after she filed a $110 million lawsuit alleging sexual harassment and unsafe work conditions) (Dickinson).

His Social Standing

As trivial as this may sound, Vince McMahon could lose his social standing. Not only is McMahon wealthy, but he has many high-powered social and political connections. This could change if the hush-money allegations against him are confirmed. If the #MeToo-like accusations against McMahon are proven, he'll likely be persona non grata in many social circles. Even people who might support him will think twice of socializing with him as he'll be seen as a liability.

It Ain't Over 'Til It's Over

Regardless of the current scandal, some fans and pundits feel that Vince McMahon's legendary ability to escape scandal, criminal prosecution, and certain business failure means he'll find a way out of this mess.

Whether history repeats itself depends on the results of the investigation and how it affects the WWE as a corporation. It's all about assets and liabilities when it comes to Vince's future with the company. If he is seen as a liability, it's difficult to imagine the board keeping him as CEO and Chairman lest the WWE risk shareholder suits for a breach of the company's fiduciary duty. Obviously, any alleged criminal activity would lead to a temporary ouster depending on the outcome of any criminal prosecution.

Don't expect Vince McMahon to back down from the allegations or the possible repercussions. McMahon, who rarely appears on WWE TV any more shocked many fans when he showed up on the June 17, 2022, episode of *SmackDown* and the June 20 and 27 2022 episodes of *RAW*. Although he didn't address the allegations, some industry observers familiar with McMahon's history believe this is his way of showing he'll fight things tooth and claw, the same as he's done throughout his life.

Works Cited

@BrandonThurston. "From." *Twitter*. 16 June 2022. https://twitter.com/BrandonThurston/status/1537424119003856898?s=20&t=fgCp9THVuFLnv2ZLqptFLA.

Dickinson, Martin James. "Sable's Lawsuit Against the WWE, Explained." *The Sportster*. WWE. 3 May 2022. https://www.thesportster.com/sables-lawsuit-against-the-wwe-explained. Accessed 17 June 2022.

Miles, Joe. "RAW TALK Explosive new Vince McMahon biography book on WWE boss to be written by Stan Lee author gets release date." *The U.S. Sun*. Sport. 1 June 2022. https://www.the-sun.com/sport/914491/vince-mcmahon-biography-wwe-author. Accessed 16 June 2022.

Mohan, Sai. "Vince McMahon Autobiography Reportedly in the Works." *Wrestling Inc*. News. 10 June 2022. https://www.wrestlinginc.com/news/2022/06/vince-mcmahon-autobiography-reportedly-in-the-works. Accessed 12 June 2022.

Perry, Michael. "Netflix May Cancel Planned

Vince McMahon Biography in Wake of Scandal." *Thirsty for News*. Sports News. 16 June 2022. https://www.thirstyfornews.com/2022/06/16/netflix-may-cancel-planned-vince-mcmahon-biography-in-wake-of-scandal. Accessed 18 June 2022.

Chapter Three: #MeToo McMahon Style

Originally published 2019

Vince McMahon has long been considered a trendsetter in professional wrestling, taking the industry to unparalleled heights with his unique vision for sports entertainment. However, behind the scenes McMahon developed a reputation for scandalous behavior, behavior which would incur harsh repercussions if it was proved today

No Stranger to Controversy

Vince McMahon has never been shy about parts of his past, but his braggadocio has sometimes come back to haunt him. Vince McMahon has admitted to extramarital affairs during his marriage to Linda McMahon, something some people would find objectionable. More importantly here, Vince McMahon has been accused of sexual harassment and sexual assault. What should we make of these accusations and what if any effect would they have on the WWE, a publicly traded business?

I Have Always Been...Loyal. Not Necessarily Faithful

In order to examine the allegations against Vince McMahon, one must understand Vince's past including his adulterous behavior. During his

1999 interview with *Playboy* magazine, McMahon was candid about his adultery. In it, he discussed his infidelities, telling the interviewer that while he was loyal to wife Linda, when it came to fidelity, he was:

> Not necessarily faithful. I probably lied to myself, thinking she knew who I was when we got married. The wild guy. But I never, ever threw anything in her face. I was discreet. And Linda never suffered from a lack of attention, physical or emotional. But one day she asked me, point-blank, "Are you having an affair with so-and-so?" And I've never lied to her. "Yes." It crushed her. Then she asked, "What about such and such?" "Yes. "It went on. More names. I said, "Yes, yes and yes."

When asked about whether his affairs happened at different times or at the same times, McMahon answered:

> "Different times. Some were concurrent, but I didn't think she had to know that. She didn't ask that question or I'd have had to say yes to that, too. It's not something I'm proud of. I just didn't realize the impact of messing with other people's lives. Notwithstanding the impact on my

wife. I'm talking about the havoc you create in other lives, just from wanting to have a good time. There's no such thing as an innocent fling. When a woman commits to a sexual encounter, it's generally with a great deal of emotion. With very few exceptions, it's not just, 'Let's have sex! Boy, that was great. OK, see you.' Women don't do that. So I guess, maybe . . . I hurt a lot of people. The sex was terrific, but from an emotional standpoint, I regret it." ("Playboy Interview: Vince McMahon)

The reason McMahon's past infidelities are important is because his lax standards concerning his marriage might be seen by some as evidence of a person who lives by his own standards, rather than that of society. McMahon's morals can certainly be called into question and may play a role in assessing claims of criminal behavior.

There are a number of reasons why a man may be unfaithful including insecurity, sex addiction, being sexually abused, or a combination of these and other factors (Weiss). One distinct factor for McMahon could be his self-disclosed history of physical abuse at the hands of his step-father and hinted sexual abuse by someone else. According to a 2013 article in *Psychology Today,* which discusses why someone might be unfaithful and/or promiscuous:

> Perhaps he is acting out early trauma experiences, such as physical abuse, neglect, or sexual abuse. His formative wounds have left him unable or unwilling to fully commit himself to another person. He may also seek sexual intensity outside his relationship as a way to self-medicate (escape from) his emotional and psychological pain" (Weiss).

During his *Playboy* interview, McMahon hinted at possible being sexually abused by his mother. If so, this might explain his infidelities.

One question to consider is whether Vince McMahon was an adulterer or a womanizer. Although the two may seem synonymous, there is a distinction. The website "Help for Adult Victims of Childhood Abuse" distinguishes between:

> …adulterers and womanizers. Adulterers (males) usually have one affair, typically during a crisis—when passed over for a promotion or when his wife is very busy—and then feels guilty. Womanizers compulsively seduces women as a full-time avocation and hide this from their wives. They often claim to have a high

sex drive and a lust for sexual variety. Their therapists say such men often don't like women or even sex. Womanizers have a disease or an addiction, in which they see women as the enemy. They think of "being a real man" as escaping a woman's control and as being someone who can powerfully manipulate and deceive women. Like a rapist, he seeks power and superiority.

Is it inconceivable that McMahon crossed the line in seeking power over a woman by sexually abusing or assaulting her?

A Voracious Appetite

Keep in mind that the authors are using Vince McMahon's own words here. In 2014, the WWE kingpin told *Forbes,* "I have a voracious appetite, for life and everything in it. To a certain extent I will die a very frustrated man because I didn't do this or accomplish that" (qtd. in Shoemaker). Two years later, he told the *Orlando Sentinel*:

"Some would say I'm still a teenager as far as certain aspects of my brain. It's like I refuse to grow up. I don't want to grow up. Now I'm old enough to say I'm not going to grow up. So what are you going to do about that?" (qtd. in Shoemaker).

In a 1998 interview with *New York Magazine* McMahon talked about his "Mr. McMahon" wrestling character (a role he played on the air as part of WWE storylines):

> "My god. Some of the things I have said and have done. [Mr. McMahon is] the most reprehensible individual on the planet. … Uncaring, a powermonger, manipulative, very manipulative, always trying to get what I want and being very clever about it. Art imitating life and vice versa. It's fun because some of it's true, you know what I mean?" (qtd. in Shoemaker)

Consider McMahon's comments while we present the accusations made against him.

The Accusations

It's important to note that: 1) Vince McMahon has never been criminally convicted of any crimes; 2) these accusations have gone no further than allegations; and/or 3) in some cases we do not know the exact details of what transpired due to the matter being settled through a settlement and an accompanying nondisclosure agreement. A nondisclosure agreement bars all parties from discussing the case.

Referee Rita Chatteron

In the 1980's the WWF hired Rita Chatteron, a single mother who'd struggled at a dead-end job as a bookkeeper at Frito-Lay (Assael 115). According to the book, *Sex, Lies, and Headlocks,* "Vince turned her into one of his cheesecake girls, giving her a layout in the WWF's pulp magazine and a job as his first female referee" (115). Working as Rita Marie, this referee officiated various matches with male Superstars and appeared on the WWF's *Tuesday Night Titans.* Then in 1986, she was gone from WWF television (a subsequent lawsuit alleged Chatteron was fired for "incompetence"). In 1992, Chatteron appeared on Geraldo Rivera's *Now It Can Be Told,* alleging:

> "He made me have oral sex. And he started to get really excited and I pulled away and he got really angry and said that's worth half a million dollars a year. And when I said no, he said I better satisfy him and he pulled off my pants and he pulled me on top of him and he satisfied himself through intercourse" (Assael 116)

In 1993, Linda and Vince McMahon's attorney Jerry McDevitt filed a federal lawsuit against Chatteron, Geraldo Rivera, the Tribune Entertainment Co., and the Investigative News

Group (Bellantoni). According to the website *Talking Points Memo:*

> The 18-count lawsuit claimed that Chatterton and Shults conspired in 1992 to make an audio recording of the former referee leveling accusations against Vince McMahon, designed to sound as if it had been made in 1988. It also claims that Chatterton's counsel demanded $5 million in exchange for agreeing to "waive her First Amendment right to speak out."

The Hartford Courant reported on the story in 1993, noting:

> Through a spokesman, Rivera denied the suit's allegations. "It's a mark of honor to be sued by the WWF," Rivera said. He vowed, "I will body slam them in court."
>
> "We stand by the story," said Jeff Erdel, Rivera's spokesman. "We repeatedly asked Mr. McMahon to appear on the program to counter the allegations. He repeatedly refused." Shults, through his lawyer, Eileen McGann, called McMahon a "well-known bully" and said the charges are "bizarre" and "hysterical." (Ewing)

McDevitt claims no police report was filed by Chatterton and according to McDevitt, the statute of limitation lapsed on any lawsuit (Bellantoni). Interestingly, the case resurfaced in 2010 during Linda McMahon's first campaign for the United States Senate. *Talking Points Memo* was threatened with a lawsuit when they raised the issue.

Sable

Rena Mero took the wrestling world by storm when she debuted as Marc Mero's valet, Sable. By some accounts, Vince McMahon was smitten with her and saw her as a bonus when he hired Marc Mero. This was because Sable could appear at ringside during Mero's matches, adding sex appeal to his act, which some fans and critics felt was bland compared to other wrestlers. Working as "Sable," she quickly eclipsed her husband's career, becoming a huge success and the company's top female attraction. Sable appeared in the April 1999 issue of *Playboy* and became a featured attraction on WWF programming. However, her ego reportedly grew out of control as she made, "…a slew of new demands. One was that she no longer wanted to work house shows. Another was that she didn't want to wrestle on *RAW* [the WWE's flagship weekly TV series]. The only times she'd get down and dirty was, she said, was on a pay-per-view where she stood to get a cut of the gross" (Assael 225). Behind the scenes, Sable was seen by many of her colleagues as a prima donna who also made trouble for anyone she perceived as a threat. Things spiraled out of control and despite Sable's popularity, she quit the company. On 23 February 1999, *People* magazine reported:

> Rena Mero, known to wrestling fans as Sable, has filed a $110 million lawsuit against Titan Sports Inc., better known as the World Wrestling Federation, alleging the WWF sought to intimidate her into performing obscene and dangerous acts. The suit alleges the WWF forced Mero to give up her championship belt after she repeatedly refused to have her gown torn off and her breasts exposed on national TV. April's Playboy magazine ran a cover shot and topless photos of Mero. (People Staff)

In a 2011 article, website *Bleacher Report* printed an excerpt from Rena Mero's lawsuit against Titan Sports. In her pleadings, Rena Mero alleged that she:

> "…bitterly complained about her concerns and the humiliation that she was constantly facing, which was not only interfering with her well-being,

but with her safety and state of mind. For example, men would routinely walk into the women's dressing room as if by accident; men would cut holes in the walls to watch the women dressing; extras were hired as WWF regulars to expose their breasts; big nipple contests were engaged in; men regularly bragged about their sexual encounters without regard to the women present; WWF produced catalogues and tee-shirts depicting Mrs. Mero In a degrading fashion offering sexual favors; Mrs. Mero was requested to display affection to women to promote a "lesbian angle"; Mrs. Mero was asked to have her gown ripped off repeatedly (notwithstanding promises to the contrary), and Plaintiff was asked to expose her breasts by 'mistake' on national television during a wrestling contest." (qtd. in Bixenspan "5 Most Interesting")

The lawsuit was settled mere months after it was filed and per the terms of a nondisclosure agreement, no dollar figure is known. Sable would return to the WWE in 2003 before leaving again in 2004, albeit on good terms.

The Tanning Salon Incident

In 2006, a Florida woman filed a criminal complaint that Vince McMahon sexually assaulted her while she was working at a Boca Rotan tanning salon. The woman claimed that Vince showed her nude photos of himself before sexually assaulting her. The complaint was dismissed. Was there any substance to the case, however?

In 2018, *The Daily Beast* revisited the case, publishing the woman's police report. According to *The Daily Beast,* the then 22-year-old woman was working at the tanning salon when McMahon asked to rent a bed:

> Before he got on the bed, McMahon asked the woman to take a photo of him with his phone so he could send it to his girlfriend in New York, she told police. When she handed the phone back to him, he began showing her nude and semi-nude photos of himself that were on it, she said. She then asked him to stop and said it was inappropriate behavior, according to the documents. McMahon then tanned for 20 minutes and chatted with the salon attendant and another customer after he was done. She then went to clean a tanning bed, but McMahon followed her into the room and shut the door behind him, she told police.

There were no surveillance cameras in the tanning rooms at Tanzabar, which is now permanently closed. Then, according to the documents: McMahon grabbed her and tried to kiss her. She said she put both of her hands on his chest and tried to push him away. McMahon continued to grab her, touching her waist and butt and attempting to lift up her button-down shirt while rubbing her breasts with the back side of his arms, she told police. (Feuerherd)

The complainant was reportedly unable to identify McMahon and the case went no further when it was presented to the State Attorney General for prosecution. A spokesperson for the Attorney General's Office stated, "The filing standard for the state is above and beyond a reasonable doubt," Mike Edmondson, a spokesperson for the Palm Beach County State Attorney's Office said. "Prosecutors have to file at a higher standard, which is proof above a reasonable doubt. It's a much different standard than probable cause." And "A misdemeanor that is not done in the presence of a law enforcement officer in Florida generally is not a prosecutable case unless there is an independent witness and or physical evidence as in photos — that kind of thing," (qtd. in Feurerherd).

Anything More than Allegations?

Through the years, gossip and innuendo has been thrown around that certain WWE Superstars engaged in sexual relations with Vince McMahon in exchange for a push i.e., being promoted as a bigger star. However, nothing has ever been verified. With McMahon heading a multi-million-dollar corporation, it is possible that opportunistic individuals might manufacture charges against him. At the same time, McMahon has a powerful legal team that aggressively defends him from court action, a policy which seems to reflect McMahon's personality and his need to protect himself and his family.

The Sable case is the only known case involving sexual harassment to come to any sort of settlement. It's impossible to discuss the case without knowing the details of the agreement, but if the allegations made by Sable were made today and proved in court, the WWE could face substantial damages. A corporate culture involving sexual harassment and/or discrimination would have to be established and while that may have existed during Sable's tenure in the WWE, its current climate is unknown.

As for Vince McMahon the individual, he is a self-admitted adulterer who it can be inferred was (and may still be) a womanizer. Whether he crossed the line into criminal behavior has never been substantiated and readers can only assess the evidence and decide for themselves whether they believe there is anything to the allegations.

The recent revelations that Vince McMahon signed multiple nondisclosure agreements changes everything as people what ask whether any misconduct occurred in the past and if so, whether it was covered up.

The Rita Chatteron case could be reopened, even though the statute of limitations has expired. The July 4, 2022, edition of "The Wrestling Observer Newsletter" noted that:

> *New York Governor Kathy Hochul signed the Adult Survivors Act. It essentially eliminates the statute of limitations for claims of sexual assault for a one-year period that starts in November 2022. Chatterton's allegations occurred in New York State. So legally she could file suit until November 2023.*

Works Cited

Assael, Shaun and Mike Mooneyham. *Sex, Lies, and Headlocks: The Real Story of Vince McMahon and World Wrestling Entertainment.* Three Rivers Press, 2004.

Bellantoni, Christine. "FLASHBACK: McMahons

Sued Geraldo for Airing Rape Claims By Former WWE Referee." *Talking Points Memo.* DC. 12 Oct. 2010. https://talkingpointsmemo.com/dc/flashback-mcmahons-sued-geraldo-for-airing-rape-claims-by-former-wwe-referee. Accessed 25 Mar. 2019.

Bixenspan, David. "WWE: The 5 Most Interesting Excerpts from WWE-Related Lawsuit Filings & Case Law." *Bleacher Report.* WWE. 7 Oct. 2011. https://bleacherreport.com/articles/883214-wwe-the-5-most-interesting-excerpts-from-wwe-related-lawsuit-filings-case-law#slide0. Accessed 25 Mar. 2019.

Bixenspan, David. "Politico brings the 1992 WWE sex scandals back into the limelight." *Cageside Seats.* WWE. 2 Aug. 2010. https://www.cagesideseats.com/2010/8/2/1601193/politico-brings-the-1992-wwe-sex. Accessed 27 Feb. 2019.

Damage, Brian. "On the Brink of Redoing History: The Story of the WWE's First Ever Female Referee." *Ring the Damn Bell.* 28 July 2018. https://ringthedamnbell.wordpress.com/2017/07/28/on-the-brink-of-redoing-history-the-story-of-the-wwes-first-ever-female-referee. Accessed 27 Feb. 2019.

Donofrio, Craig. "How Wrestling King Vince McMahon Fought to the Top." *Work and Money*. View from the Top. 16 Jan. 2018. https://www.workandmoney.com/s/vince-mcmahon-bio-a975aea833484eca. Accessed 25 Mar. 2019.

Ewing, Jack. "PROFESSIONAL WRESTLING CZAR SUES OVER ALLEGATIONS IN RIVERA SHOW." *Hartford Courant*. 12 Feb. 1993. https://www.courant.com/news/connecticut/hc-xpm-1993-02-12-0000106026-story.html. Accessed 25 Mar. 2019.

Feuerherd, Ben. "She Said Vince McMahon Sexually Assaulted Her in a Tanning Booth. Police Found 'Probable Cause.' Prosecutors Shrugged." *The Daily Beast*. Memory Hole. 26 Jan. 2018. https://www.thedailybeast.com/she-said-vince-mcmahon-sexually-assaulted-her-in-a-tanning-booth-police-found-probable-cause-prosecutors-shrugged. Accessed 25 Mar. 2019.

George, Sarah. "15 Divas Who Got Too Intimate with Vince McMahon." *The Sportster*. Wrestling. 30 Mar. 2017. https://www.thesportster.com/wrestling/15-divas-who-got-too-intimate-with-vince-mcmahon. Accessed 27 Feb. 2019.

Harris, James Kamala and Kenny Casanova. *Kamala Speaks (eBook Editor's Edition): Official Autobiography of WWE wrestler James KAMALA Harris.* Amazon Digital Services, 2015.

Harris, Scarlett. "Has #MeToo Reached the Wrestling World?" *Huff Post.* Opinion. 12 Feb. 2018. https://www.huffingtonpost.com/entry/opinion-harris-wwe-metoo_us_5a7c804de4b044b3821a868d. Accessed 27 Feb. 2019.

Jones, Patrick. "Top 15 Shocking Accusations Made Against Vince McMahon." *The Sportster.* Wrestling. 18 Sept. 2015. https://www.thesportster.com/wrestling/top-15-shocking-accusations-made-against-vince-mcmahon. Accessed 27 Feb. 2019.

Marie, P.J. "15 Of the Most Shameful Things Stephanie McMahon Has Done." *The Sportster.* Wrestling. 10 Oct. 2017. https://www.thesportster.com/wrestling/15-of-the-most-shameful-things-stephanie-mcmahon-has-done. Accessed 27 Feb. 2019.

Muchnick, Irvin. *Wrestling Babylon: Piledriving Tales of Drugs, Sex, Death, and Scandal.* ECW Press, 2007.

Observer Staff. "July 4, 2022. Observer Newsletter:

Forbidden Door review, Logan Paul signs with WWE." *Wrestling Observer Newsletter.* 4 July 2022. https://members.f4wonline.com. Accessed 1 July 2022.

People Staff. "Sable Blows Her Top." *People.* Celebrity. 23 Feb. 1999. https://people.com/celebrity/sable-blows-her-top. Accessed 25 Mar. 2019.

"PLAYBOY INTERVIEW: VINCE MCMAHON." *Playboy,* Feb. 2001 56-68. https://assets.documentcloud.org/documents/3237167/Vince-McMahon-Playboy-Interview-OCR.pdf.

Rangarajan, Aditya. "7 Scandals the WWE just don't want you to know about." *Sportskeeda.* WWE. https://www.sportskeeda.com/wwe/7-scandals-the-wwe-just-dont-want-you-to-know-about. Accessed 27 Feb. 2019.

Shoemaker, David. "The Story of Vince McMahon." *The Ringer.* Fights. 2 June 2016. https://www.theringer.com/2016/6/2/16040702/the-story-of-vince-mcmahon-958f3274f5ce. Accessed 25 Mar. 2019.

Snipes, John Lucas. "15 Wrestling Scandals Vince McMahon Tried to Cover Up." *The Richest.* Sports. 20 Oct. 2017. https://www.therichest.com/sports-entertainment/15-wrestling-scandals-vince-mcmahon-tried-to-cover-up. Accessed 27 Feb. 2019.

"10 Most Shocking Vince McMahon Controversies." *Whatculture.* WWE. http://whatculture.com/wwe/10-most-shocking-vince-mcmahon-controversies. Accessed 27 Feb. 2019.

"Unfaithfulness." *Help for Adult Victims of Childhood Abuse.* https://www.havoca.org/survivors/relationships/unfaithfulness. Accessed 25 Mar. 2019.

Weiss, Robert. "The 10 Reasons Why Men Cheat." *Psychology Today.* 30 Oct. 2013. https://www.psychologytoday.com/us/blog/love-and-sex-in-the-digital-age/201310/the-10-reasons-why-men-cheat. Accessed 25 Mar. 2019.

Part Two: From the Outhouse to the Penthouse

Horatio Alger would be hard-pressed to tell a story as fantastic as Vince McMahon's rags-to-riches story (Some might even call it a Horatio Alger on steroids story). Here is a look at McMahon's personal and professional quest to become the Walt Disney of wrestling.

Chapter Four: What Makes McMahon Tick?
Have you wondered what Vince McMahon was like growing up and what shaped his life? McMahon has revealed a surprising number of anecdotes into his life. Here are several that may cast light into his mindset.

Originally Published 2018

He Grew Up in a Trailer Park: Although Vince McMahon's dad was the famous wrestling promoter Vincent James McMahon, the future WWE leader lived with his brother and mother in a trailer park in Havelock, North Carolina after Vince Sr. remarried. In a 2001 interview with *Playboy* magazine, McMahon described his early years:

> A New Moon trailer, eight feet wide. Trailer park isn't poverty. You don't have much privacy, but there are nice things about it. Everything is compact. And it beats some other places. Prior to that I lived in Manly, North Carolina, in a house with no indoor plumbing. That could get a little disconcerting in the wintertime… and the summertime wasn't much better, sitting on the privy with the heat and humidity and stench. Oh, man, the

flies! So when we moved to the trailer park, it wasn't so bad."

Eventually, Vince's dad would take him for the summer, exposing him to a much different lifestyle and showing him the money to be made promoting professional wrestling.

He Regrets He Wasn't Able to Kill His Stepfather: Vince McMahon's mom Vicki lived with Leo Lupton, an electrician who McMahon claims had a violent streak. According to McMahon, Lupton began beating him when McMahon was six years old, sometimes using tools such as a pipe wrench. McMahon would recall trying to defend his mother from Lupton's physical abuse:

> I was the only one of the kids who would speak up, and that's what provoked the attacks. You would think that after being on the receiving end of numerous attacks I would wise up, but I couldn't. I refused to. I felt I should say something, even though I knew what the result would be… First time I remember, I was six years old. The slightest provocation would set him off. But I lived through it." (qtd. in Talk)

Nonetheless, McMahon persevered, surviving the beatings, but never getting the opportunity to revenge himself on Lupton. In his *Playboy* interview, McMahon would express his regret, "It's unfortunate that he died before I could kill him. I would have enjoyed that."

He Considered Killing Himself: In addition to his physical abuse, there have been suggestions that McMahon may have been sexually abused as well. Consider the following questions and answers from McMahon's Playboy interview:

PLAYBOY: Was the abuse all physical, or was there sexual abuse, too?

MCMAHON: That's not anything I would like to embellish. Just because it was weird.

PLAYBOY: Did it come from the same man?

MCMAHON: No. It wasn't...it wasn't from the male.

PLAYBOY: That's so mysterious. It sounds like a difficult thing for a kid to deal with.

PLAYBOY: We can leave that topic, but one thing first. You have said that the sexual abuse in your childhood "wasn't from the male." It's well known that you're estranged from your mother. Have we found the reason?

MCMAHON: [Pauses, nods] Without saying that, I'd say that's pretty close.

According to two of McMahon's friends, the future WWE kingpin contemplated suicide, at one point "...flirting with the idea of drowning himself by walking into the sea along the Carolina coast" (Assael 23).

McMahon credits his experiences with his never surrender attitude:

> "Like I said, I grew up in a very volatile environment. My view was that if I took a beating and lived, I won. I still have that view. It gives me a tremendous advantage, because I'm not afraid of failure. Don't get me wrong--I hate falling. But I'm not afraid to take chances and fall on my ass, because if I live through it I'll be better off, and I'll win." (qtd. in Talk)

McMahon has fallen on his ass in business endeavors but he has yet to give up.

He Considers Himself a Street Fighter:

McMahon has discussed his teenage years during interviews, including how he was on his own for the most part by age 14. McMahon claims to have run with a local group of street toughs that fought with Marines from Cherry Point Station, a nearby military base. According to the book, *Sex, Lies, and Headlocks*, Havelock's "...native kids would hang out at the local drive-in, The Jet, waiting for them in the hope of starting fights" (Assael 22). McMahon recalls, "majoring in badass" (qtd. in Talk) as a teen, fighting with the local Marines.

"On Friday and Saturday nights it was time to get it on with the Marines. It was a challenge. Most of them were in great condition, but they didn't know how to pick a fight. I'm not saying they were easy pickings. They got their testosterone going and they were all liquored up. Some of them were real tough. But me and my guys were street fighters. I mean, maybe you've been through basic training and you know how to operate a bayonet. That's different from sticking your finger in somebody's eye or hitting a guy in the throat, which comes naturally to a street fighter. And they can't believe you're not "fighting fair." Suddenly they can't breathe and/or see, and they realize: "Oh my God, am I in for an ass-kicking." (qtd. in Talk)

However, McMahon's account differs from that of one of his contemporaries. Douglas Franks recalls Vince's attempts to prove his toughness, "He tried to be one of the gang kids, but he never quite made it…He was a wannabe" (Assael 22). **He Was Forced to Choose Between Going to Military School or Reform School:** While Vince McMahon's tales of badassery may be unreliable, it is known that he was a hellion as a teenager, repeatedly getting into trouble on a regular basis. According to McMahon, he stole cars, got into fights, and even ran moonshine on at least one occasion. Eventually, his dirty deeds caught up and he was given the choice of attending reform school or military school. With Vince's mom unable to pay for military school, McMahon's father intervened, paying for it, a gesture that paved the way for a stronger relationship between Vince Sr. and Vince Jr. Military school was a tumultuous time, with McMahon claiming he was court-martialed, the first cadet with that dubious distinction. The offense—feeding a laxative to the commandant's dog who proceeded to defecate in his master's apartment could have led to McMahon expulsion. Instead, the teenage prankster beat the court-martial, perhaps an omen of his eventual victory against the federal government when he was indicted in his infamous steroid trial. McMahon played football in military school, both as an offensive and defensive tackle. Unfortunately, the scrappy Southerner proved to be a poor player, recalling:

> "But all I really knew how to do was fight. So it was, 'Bring it on!' But when you've got bare knuckles and you're hitting a guy with a helmet on, it's not good. I was used to gouging eyes and going for the throat. A big kick in the

nuts is always primo--you hear the guy go "Huhhh!" and you think, His ass is mine. But you can't do that on the football field. Football is all about technique, and I was a lousy football player. In one game I was personally penalized more yardage than our offense gained. (qtd. in Talk).

Vince would graduate military school, showing his ability to get through anything, a trait he would show many times during his life.

He Filed for Bankruptcy: Vince McMahon's business ventures have not all been spectacular successes, especially when they are outside the realm of professional wrestling. Early in their business careers, Vince and Linda McMahon found themselves in a financial hole, filing for bankruptcy in 1976. The McMahon's problems are believed to involve their closed-circuit broadcast of daredevil Evel Knevel's failed Snake River Canyon jump, the Antonio Inoki vs. Muhammad Ali closed-circuit fight, and other failed ventures. In 2001, Vince explained to *Playboy*:

> "It was visions of sugarplums. It was, `Look how successful I am! I guess I really am somebody.' I got involved with people who weren't that bright and let them tell me that I needed tax shelters. There was a construction

company, a horse farm, a cement plant, and it all went belly-up. I felt bad about the bankruptcy. I wanted to pay what I owed, but there were other people involved, and finally the banks wrote it all off." (qtd. in Lockhart)

During her Senate campaign, Linda McMahon elaborated further, noting her and Vince invested in a construction company:

> "We signed personally on some loans from the bank to float that business for a while, and we didn't understand [the industry]…It went belly up. … We tried for over a year to pay off the loans and we just couldn't do it anymore, so we had to declare bankruptcy." (Ginsberg)

Despite these setbacks, McMahon continues to take his company in the direction he wants, trusting the instincts that have led to his success and relying on hand-picked individuals to help him.

Works Cited

Assael, Shaun and Mike Mooneyham. *Sex, Lies, and Headlocks: The Real Story of Vince McMahon and World Wrestling Entertainment.* Three Rivers Press, 2004.

Ginsberg, Leah. "WWE billionaire founder: What bankruptcy taught me about success." *CNBC.* Entrepreneurs. 3 May 2017. https://www.cnbc.com/2017/05/03/wwe-billionaire-founder-what-bankruptcy-taught-me-about-success.html. Accessed 2 Aug. 2018.

Lockhart, Brian. "McMahons' bankruptcy a murky chapter in her rags-to-riches tale." *CT Post.* 1 Oct. 2010. https://www.ctpost.com/local/article/McMahons-bankruptcy-a-murky-chapter-in-her-682114.php. Accessed 2 Aug. 2018.

Race, Harley and Gary Tritz. *King of the Ring: The Harley Race Story.* Sports Publishing, 2006.

Shoemaker, David. "The Story of Vince McMahon." *The Ringer.* 2 June 2016. https://www.theringer.com/2016/6/2/16040702/the-story-of-vince-mcmahon-958f3274f5ce. Accessed 3 Aug. 2018.

Talk Unlimited Online. Forum. 2005. Transcript of *Playboy.* 2001.

https://www.talkwhateveronline.com/threads/vince-mcmahons-playboy-2001-interview.23557 Accessed 3 Aug. 2018.

Chapter Five: The Road to the Top

Vince McMahon's ascent to the top of the wrestling mountain started from humble beginnings. Here's a synopsis of McMahon's journey.

Originally published 2018

A Hardscrabble Life

As we saw in our previous chapter, Vince McMahon was born into wrestling royalty, but you'd never know it looking at his early life. McMahon's father Vincent James McMahon (aka Vince McMahon Sr.) was a second-generation promoter who divorced his son's mother Vicki, leaving Vince to grow up in an eight-foot-wide trailer in Havelock, North Carolina. As McMahon would recall later, it was better than he and his mom's previous residence where they had no indoor plumbing. Vince lived in poverty and he was well aware of how some people perceived him and his family, as being beneath them. McMahon would tell *Muscle and Fitness* that he developed a philosophy that no one was better than him and vice versa (Shoemaker).

Poverty was just one of the future billionaire's problems. He lived in a world of violence, recalling to Matt Lauer in 2001:

> "I grew up in a very aggressive environment to say the least. That includes any number of individuals … beating the hell out of me only because I had a big mouth and had to say what was on my mind." (qtd. in Shoemaker)

By Vince's accounts, one stepfather stood out in terms of physical abuse, an electrician named Leo Lupton who beat Vince with tools including a pipe wrench. The abuse was so bad that McMahon regrets Lupton died before he had a chance to kill him.

As appalling as the physical abuse must have been, McMahon has hinted at being molested by his mother. During his 2001 interview with *Playboy* magazine, Vince revealed he had been sexually molested by a female. Consider this exchange in the interview:

PLAYBOY: We can leave that topic, but one thing first. You have said that the sexual abuse in your childhood "wasn't from the male." It's well known that you're estranged from your mother. Have we found the reason?

MCMAHON: [Pauses, nods] Without saying that, I'd say that's pretty close.

Things began to brighten up for McMahon when he was 12 years old and his biological father Vince Sr. began taking him for the summer. During Vince's summer trips with his dad, he interacted with the many colorful characters who wrestled for his dad, developing a passion for professional wrestling.

When Vince wasn't with his famous father, he spent his time getting into trouble, whether it was stealing cars or wild brawls with whoever wanted to fight. McMahon's brushes with the law eventually led to him being sent to military school (it was that or reform school). McMahon continued his wild ways in military school but learned how to hide his transgressions better and how to keep himself from being expelled (although he came close on at least one occasion).

The teenage Vince would learn valuable lessons for the future during the summers he spent with his father. Surrounded by the larger-than-life wrestlers with equally larger-than-life personas, young Vince marveled at how people gravitated to them. Vince never forgot this, a lesson he saved for the future if he could somehow break into wrestling as his dad and grandfather had done.

At the time though, there was no guarantee of him taking over the family business or even working in it.

Breaking into the Business

Vince found himself in one boring job after another (including selling paper cups and adding machines, as well as working 90 hours a week in a factory). His goal was to work in his father's wrestling promotion, but that was beginning to look more and more unlikely. However, when the aspiring wrestling businessman caught a break, he seized it immediately. He broke into wrestling by becoming an announcer after his father's longtime announcer Ray Morgan requested a pay increase. The younger McMahon analyzed the business and how it operated, learning from one of the industry's best—his father.

Another opportunity arose early on when one of Vince's father's business partners was caught stealing from him. During his interview with *Playboy,* McMahon recalled:

> So my dad tells me, "Look, the guy in Bangor, I just threw him the hell out. Go up there. You can't ever say I didn't give you an opportunity, but this is the first and last opportunity you'll have in this company."

Vince claims he finally got his chance and he ran with it, making money for his dad and helping Vince Sr. expand his business greatly in New England.

Repeated Failures, Repeated Lessons

While the budding businessman found some success, it would be mistaken to say he had the Midas Touch. While Vince Sr. successfully promoted the WWWF (as the WWE was called during the 1960s and 1970s), Vince sought to become successful in his own right. In some respects, Vince was a visionary, and saw how promoters could greatly expand their audience by using closed-circuit television to air a popular event all over the country. Regrettably for Vince, the events he chose to book on closed-circuit TV (stuntman Evel Knievel's failed attempt to jump Snake River Canyon in a rocket sled and a boxer vs. wrestler match between Muhammad Ali and Antonio Inoki that took place in Japan) were failures.

While the younger McMahon had the right vision for expanding the business through closed-circuit broadcasts, the execution wasn't right.

His Biggest Gamble

Despite past failures, Vince McMahon was ready to roll the dice again. McMahon saw that the wrestling industry was changing and he was ready to strike before others did. The expansion of cable television meant that fans from throughout the country could watch one promotion's show on one channel. McMahon knew the days of promoters running shows in one geographic area was about to change and that his father's WWF could promote shows outside the Northeast as it traditionally had, if Vince made the right moves.

Vince offered to buy the WWF from his father, an offer that was accepted, but with a major provision. Young Vince would have to make each payment and if he failed to do so, the company would go back to his father along with every penny the would-be promoter had already paid. Vince agreed to his father's terms and raised the money, becoming the owner of the WWF.

A Bold Vision

Vince McMahon's vision of wrestling depended on him launching a national promotion, something other promoters had toyed with, but who had yet to make successful. McMahon's goal depended on him finding a highly marketable star and an entertaining cast of supporting characters. The promoter raided a number of rival promotions, cherry-picking their best wrestlers, announcers, and other staff. Spearheading the new version of the WWF was the extremely charismatic Hulk Hogan, a Herculean hero who personified everything that Vince wanted in his company—clearly-defined heroes and villains performing in storylines that focused on flash over substance.

Key to Vince's vision was a giant event to capitalize on his investments and planning. That event became known as *WrestleMania*, an all-star wrestling show that featured the WWF's best as well as celebrities like pop singer Cyndi Lauper and TV and film star Mr. T (who wrestled alongside Hulk Hogan in the main event). McMahon was counting on his show being a can't miss event, so much so that people from across North America would watch it in arenas on closed-circuit TV.

Success Leads to More Success

Vince's *WrestleMania* gamble paid off and the WWF's popularity led to an unprecedented number of crossover ventures including a network TV special (*Saturday Night's Main Event*), home video releases of WWF events and profiles on its wrestlers (whom McMahon dubbed "Superstars" to separate them from the competition), expanded merchandise deals including action figures, food products, and even music albums. As the WWF's popularity soared, it crushed many of the other promotions in wrestling until the only major rival was Jim Crockett Promotions (which was saved from ruin when Ted Turner purchased it and renamed it World Championship Wrestling), a distant second to the WWF.

The WWF Stumbles

Although the WWF enjoyed smashing success with Hulk Hogan leading the way, Vince McMahon feared (and rightly so) that the fans would eventually tire of Hogan. However, McMahon's attempts to replace Hogan with a new champion failed as Hogan's would-be successor the Ultimate Warrior, while popular, did not match the Hulkster's success. Even Hogan himself was wearing out his welcome with the fans and the WWF's problems continued as it faced declining business, a steroid scandal that could harm the company, and the loss of major stars. At one point, Vince McMahon himself was put on trial for allegedly distributing steroids, but he would prevail in court.

The WWF began promoting younger stars in a move marketed as "The New Generation," but this couldn't recreate the heyday of the Hogan era. McMahon's problems only worsened when rival World Championship Wrestling's (WCW) new executive Eric Bischoff convinced WCW owner Ted Turner to become more competitive. WCW launched a rival show to the WWF's flagship show *Monday Night RAW* and began an aggressive campaign of signing the WWF's top performers. WCW eventually overtook the WWF in popularity, with some thinking the WWF's days were numbered.

The Competitive Edge

WCW's competition hit the WWE hard, but it also woke up the proverbial sleeping giant. McMahon had always thrived on competition and WCW's threat to his company led to him stepping outside of his comfort zone in terms of how he portrayed his wrestlers. The New Generation transformed into the edgy Attitude Era which saw adult storylines that often caused trouble with TV censors, but which delivered ratings. In one of the wrestling industry's biggest twists, Vince

McMahon went from announcing matches to becoming an on-screen character. Vince's "Mr. McMahon" character proved to be the perfect villain for his promotion's top star "Stone Cold" Steve Austin and business only increased. Eventually, the WWF overtook WCW in the ratings and regained its spot as the number one wrestling promotion.

Going Corporate

Vince McMahon had not only brought the WWF back from the brink of defeat, but he was also ready to take it to greater heights. In 1999, the WWF became a publicly traded company, selling stock that gave it the capital to grow even further. Since then, McMahon has expanded the WWE with its streaming service the WWE Network, its own film production company WWE Studios, its own series of books, and more.

Here to Stay?

At age 77, Vince McMahon maintains a hands-on approach to running his company and he is always eager to find new ways to increase revenue. Not every venture has succeeded (we'll see more about that later). While no business is immune from failure, Vince McMahon has built his empire into a powerhouse that has thrived through ups and downs and is likely to reach new heights. If McMahon can withstand his latest scandal, there's likely no stopping him.

Works Cited

Shoemaker, David. "The Story of Vince McMahon." *The Ringer*. 2 June 2016. https://www.theringer.com/2016/6/2/16040702/the-story-of-vince-mcmahon-958f3274f5ce. Accessed 3 Aug. 2018.

Talk Unlimited Online. Forum. 2005. Transcript of *Playboy*. 2001. https://www.talkwhateveronline.com/threads/vince-mcmahons-playboy-2001-interview.23557 Accessed 3 Aug. 2018.

Chapter Six: Vince McMahon's Trials by Fire

Vince McMahon has been called many things during his career, but one thing that's undeniable is that he's a survivor, having steered the WWE through storms that might have destroyed other businesses and in some cases, emerging stronger from the experience. Here are arguably McMahon's greatest challenges and how he overcame them.

Originally Published 2019

Buying the WWF Under the Gun

Vince McMahon Sr. drove a hard bargain when he and his partners in the WWF agreed to sell the promotion to Vincent Kennedy McMahon. The deal was simple, the younger Vince was to pay his father and his partners back the cost of the WWF (a figure estimated at anywhere from $350,000 to $1 million) within the stated time or they had the option to nullify the deal if "Vinnie missed a single one of the monthly payments" (Assael 32). McMahon hustled his way into paying off the WWF, the first step in his long campaign to become the king of the professional wrestling industry.

Gambling It All on *WrestleMania*: *WrestleMania* was a huge gamble for Vince McMahon and while some argue Vince didn't risk it all on the

"Showcase of the Immortals," the fact is its success was not guaranteed by any stretch of the imagination. According to the book, *Sex, Lies, and Headlocks,* McMahon's advisers recommended he not try his closed-circuit event:

> "the company's cash flow was tight. He was paying out a small fortune—up to $10,000 a week to some stations— to guarantee *All-Star Wrestling* and its siblings had berths on broadcast television in major markets such as Chicago. On top of that, Hogan's novelty was starting to wear off. They were going to need a new star soon. Did Vinnie really want to tie up his energy, not to mention what little cash flow he had, in a single supershow that would involve hundreds of theaters and the inevitable technological hassles that came with closed-circuit broadcasts, not to mention advertising and promotion? "(Assael 53)

Despite the challenges and initial disappointing returns (the event hadn't even sold enough tickets yet to cover the deposits on the theaters showing the event on closed-circuit TV), McMahon threw more money into his event, hiring the public relations firm Bozell and Jacobs to help him out (Rickard). This and savvy promotion of

WrestleMania (including Hulk Hogan and Mr. T appearing on *Saturday Night Live* the day before *WrestleMania*) turned the tide and the first *WrestleMania* thrust the WWF ahead of its competitors.

The Steroid Trial: Arguably Vince McMahon's biggest personal battle, the United States' criminal prosecution against Vince McMahon for steroid distribution also affected the WWF. Although the WWF would have continued without McMahon, it would be hard pressed to carry on with McMahon's day-to-day guidance. Mr. McMahon knew he faced many years in federal prison if convicted and turned control of the WWF over to his wife Linda and had legendary promoter Jerry Jarrett waiting in the wings to help out should he lose his case. Incredibly, McMahon prevailed at trial, astonishing the prosecution when he was found not guilty on all counts. Following the verdict, McMahon was quoted as saying, "I'm elated. Just like in wrestling, in the end the good guys always win," ("Wrestling Promoter McMahon"). The trial was harrowing but it galvanized McMahon's resolve, making him willing to defy anyone and anything to succeed. He would find this resolve helped him as his company faced new challenges.

Charles Austin Injury Lawsuit: In an instance where the hazards of the ring proved real, enhancement talent Charles Austin was hurt during a tag team match against the Rockers. According to *Goliath.com* Austin:

> "who had been training to be a wrestler for a whole six weeks in 1990, when he was put in a tag match against a hot young WWE tag team called The Rockers, made up of Shawn Michaels and Marty Jannetty. During the match, Austin took a Rocker Dropper (you might also recognize the move as Billy Gunn's Fameasser, which is now one of Dolph Ziggler's signature moves) from Marty Jannetty incorrectly, broke his neck, and ended up partially paralyzed. Austin sued The Rockers and WWE for $3.8 million, and the court case dragged on for several years before a jury awarded him an incredible $26.7 million."

The verdict was much more than expected because the jury agreed Austin should not have been put in that position as he told Marty Jannetty he was not trained enough to take the move and "Jannetty, not realizing, just how inexperienced Austin was, assured him it was, 'A piece of cake'" (Dixon 6). As James Dixon detailed in *Titan Sinking:*

> "could hardly have come at a worse time for McMahon what with the millions being pumped into his own trial, business across the board being at its lowest ebb, and the company having just paid Jesse Ventura nearly $1 million. The verdict threatened to sink the entire operation, and potentially the entire business if other enhancement talent injured on the job would have followed suit." (7)

Fortunately, the WWF did not experience a similar problem, but it showed the company's vulnerability in similar situations. According to a 2010 article in the *Wrestling Observer*:

> "Austin wound up getting an out-of-court settlement from WWE for about $10 million. He had only been in about half-a-dozen matches before that one and took the move with his head down, rather than landing flat, which brock his neck on impact. He has since regained some use of his extremities. After the incident, WWE began to use well-trained and experienced guys for enhancement matches on a regular basis." (qtd. in Burnside)

Ringboy Scandal: 1992 saw the WWF facing more bad press when stories surfaced that ring boys (typically teenage boys who helped set up rings at WWF events) and at least one male referee had allegedly been sexually harassed and/or abused by WWF ring announcer Mel Phillips and WWF official Terry Garvin. When Tom Cole alleged Garvin had propositioned him, Vince McMahon appeared on *Larry King Live* to respond to the claims. Wrestler Barry Orton called in, claiming Garvin had "accosted him" (Assael 114) years earlier. However, Cole reportedly worked out a settlement with the WWF for getting his old job back and the controversy disappeared (Assael 115). The WWF dismissed Phillips and Garvin along with Pat Patterson, but only Patterson would return. Further controversy arose when it was alleged Vince McMahon knew of the scandal and turned a blind eye to it. The scandal could have destroyed the WWF's family-friendly image but the WWF seemed to navigate its way out of the potential morass.

The Monday Night War: 1995 was a terrible year for the WWF, especially when WCW executive Eric Bischoff began running *Nitro,* a weekly TV show against the WWF's flagship show *RAW.* Industry analysts wondered whether or not WCW's new show *Nitro* would split *RAW's* audience but it ended up building its own audience. The problem however was that Bischoff's aggressive programming tactics (such as revealing the results of taped *RAW* matches) and the incredibly popular New World Order storyline led to *Nitro* destroying *RAW* in the ratings, with seemingly no end to WCW's dominance. However, luck and experience helped Mr. McMahon develop "The Attitude Era" that turned the tide.

1995: Many people are unaware of how bad a year 1995 was for the WWF, thinking it was a low point, but no worse than other lean years. The truth is that the company was struggling to sell tickets to live events, struggling to keep its stars, and struggling to find a way to fix things. James Dixon's book *Titan Sinking* (which does a great job documenting the WWF's many problems in 1995), The company had operated on cruise control for years after eliminating most of its competition and the product suffered. A number of top stars (including Hulk Hogan and Randy Savage) had also left the WWF for its rival WCW, with more to come. Failed outside ventures such as the World Bodybuilding Federation and ICOPRO (a nutritional supplement the WWF hoped to market alongside its bodybuilding federation) along with the previously mentioned lawsuits and the ringboy scandals created a critical mass that only made matters worse when business hit rock bottom and Eric Bischoff set out to put the WWF out of business. This intense competition this drove

Vince McMahon to figure out a way to not only survive, but prosper, leading to the Attitude Era and the WWF's ultimate victory over its competition. In 1995, this seemed unlikely and wrestling lore has it that McMahon was considering scaling his company back to a regional promotion.

RAW **Almost Being Cancelled:** While legend has it that *RAW* (the WWE's flagship TV show that has aired on Mondays since 1993) was close to being cancelled during the late 90's due to sagging ratings, there's no hard evidence for that. However, the WWF's flagship Monday night show was almost cancelled after the notorious "Pillman's Got a Gun" angle on *RAW*. The use of a firearm on a wrestling program along with Pillman dropping the F-bomb on live TV reportedly led to complaints from parents and more important, complaints from USA Network executives. The USA Network had aired *Monday Night RAW* since its debut, but executives Wayne Becker and Kay Kaplovitz were outraged at what they felt was a betrayal by McMahon (who had been admonished previously for pushing the envelope only to swear it wouldn't happen again). USA executives felt they could cancel *RAW* due to standards and practices clauses in the contract (Assael 171), but instead warned McMahon not to let it happen again. Vince appeared on *RAW* and apologized, but he realized he had stumbled onto something that might win the ratings war against *Nitro*. While the Pillman angle was risky, it cast light on a path for McMahon to take the WWF on, and when the show's rating increased, USA Network executives suddenly couldn't care less about the show's racy content.

The Montreal Screwjob: Arguably the best example of a promoter taking lemons and making lemonade, the Montreal Screwjob saw Vince McMahon vilified for his mistreatment of Bret Hart at *Survivor Series* (and rightfully so). When McMahon. tried to spin things his way ("Bret Screwed Bret"), the fans gave him hell whenever he appeared on WWF TV. McMahon took the fans' vitriol towards him and created the Mr. McMahon character, an over-the-top boss fueled by ego and greed who proved the ultimate foil for the no-nonsense authority-defying wrestler "Stone Cold" Steve Austin. The backlash that threatened to remove Vince McMahon from WWF TV instead led to the creation of one of the WWE's most enduring characters—the villainous "Mr. McMahon" character. This evil authority figure was the perfect foil for the WWF's antihero— "Stone Cold" Steve Austin. (*See Appendix C for more details*)

The Death of Owen Hart: The death of Owen Hart still haunts the WWE, with people still questioning the WWF's decision to continue its *Over the Top* pay-per-view following Owen's horrific fall into the ring. Owen's death was initially investigated by law enforcement and while the WWF avoided any criminal prosecution for criminal negligence, Owen's widow Martha sued the WWF, arguing the WWF knowingly failed to take the proper safety precautions when they had Owen perform a stunt where he descended from the rafters. Had the case gone to trial and Martha Hart prevailed, there's no telling how much the company would have lost. Ultimately, the case was settled out of court for an estimated $18 million. The WWF could have been ruined, but Martha Hart felt satisfied knowing the WWF and Vince McMahon had been held accountable.

Chris Benoit Controversy: The Chris Benoit murder/suicide shocked the world but it also sent shockwaves through the wrestling community as Benoit's horrific crimes put the entire industry under a microscope. Whether it was talk show hosts such as Larry King questioning what happened, or tabloid crime hosts such as Nancy Grace ignorantly spreading misinformation, it seemed that the WWE was a cesspool of drugs and steroids. While that may have been true to a certain extent, the WWE knew things could get even worse thus it worked on enhancing its Wellness Policy (which screens wrestlers for drugs and alcohol as well as providing cardiac testing), eventually developing a concussion protocol for its Superstars.

Works Cited

Assael, Shaun and Mike Mooneyham. *Sex, Lies, and Headlocks: The Real Story of Vince McMahon and World Wrestling Entertainment.* Three Rivers Press, 2004.

Burnside, Ian. "Paralyzed WWE Wrestler Update." *Wrestling Pulse.* News. 15 Mar. 2010. https://insidepulse.com/2010/03/15/paralysed-wwe-wrestler-update. Accessed 7 July 2019.

Dixon, James. *Titan Sinking: The Decline of the WWF in 1995.* Lulu.com, 2014.

Muchnick, Irvin. *Wrestling Babylon: Piledriving Tales of Drugs, Sex, Death, and Scandal.* ECW Press, 2007.

Randle, Stephen. "10 Times WWE Ended Up Fighting Someone…In Court." *Goliath.* 21 Mar. 2016. https://www.goliath.com/sports/10-times-wwe-ended-up-fighting-someone-in-court. Accessed 7 July 2019.

Rickard, Michael. *Wrestling's Greatest Moments.* ECW Press, 2008.

"Wrestling Promoter McMahon Acquitted of Steroid Charges." *Los Angeles Times.* 23 July

1994. https://www.latimes.com/archives/la-xpm-1994-07-23-sp-18991-story.html. Accessed 7 July 2019.

Chapter Seven: Shooting for the Stars

Although Vince McMahon has enjoyed tremendous success with the WWE, many of his other ventures have a lackluster record. Perhaps Vince believes in the words of Robert Brown that "Ah, but a man's reach should exceed his grasp, or what's a heaven for?" or perhaps he doesn't know to stick to what he knows best—professional wrestling.

Originally Published 2017

Evel Knievel Snake River Canyon Jump:
There's little question Vincent Kennedy McMahon was a visionary, but in this case, he had the right idea at the wrong time when he tried to profit off daredevil Evel Knievel's Skycycle X-2 rocket sled jump over Snake River Canyon on 8 September 1974. Knievel had originally tried to sell the event to ABC Sports, but when they refused, Knievel turned to a group of investors, including Vince McMahon. Vince hyped the show for closed-circuit television (the precursor to pay-per-view), only for the event to flop. The idea of broadcasting a spectacular event to a large audience would prove successful (*WrestleMania*), but not here. The stunt was botched when the Skycycle's parachute deployed prematurely. While some stories state Vince's dad was behind the

WWWF's participation, bankruptcy records for Vince and Linda McMahon show them taking a loss for the event (Lockhart).

Cape Cod Buccaneers hockey team: While Vince McMahon worked for years as an announcer in his father's WWWF (and WWF), he would have to wait until 1983 before he purchased Capitol Sports. In the meantime, he purchased minor league hockey team the Cape Cod Buccaneers in 1981 for a reported $15,000. McMahon owned the Cape Cod Coliseum and housed the Buccaneers there. The Buccaneers played in the short-lived Atlantic Coast Hockey League. When the league had financial problems, it cancelled its post-season, leading to McMahon folding his team. Perhaps this explains McMahon creating the character the hockey-themed wrestler the Goon.

The World Bodybuilding Federation (WBF): Given the WWF's roster of apparently 'roided out monsters and Vince McMahon's love of pumping iron, a bodybuilding federation wasn't a stretch. Thus, McMahon created the World Bodybuilding Federation, an organization that would host its own bodybuilding events, but incorporate the WWF's storytelling strengths and showmanship. The WBF's weekly programming (*WBF BodyStars*) would highlight the lives and struggles of bodybuilders, in some ways a precursor to today's reality television. In a perfect world, Vince McMahon could send limited wrestlers like the Ultimate Warrior and Lex Luger there, instead of stinking up WWF rings. Sadly, only Lex Luger worked the WBF, and when it folded, Vinnie Mac put Luger on the WWF roster. (*See Appendix A for more details*)

ICOPRO: When Vince McMahon launched the WBF, he launched his own line of bodybuilding supplements known as ICOPRO, short for Integrated Condition Program. McMahon cross-promoted ICOPRO in the WWF, shoving the products down fans' throats by showing ICOPRO banners at WWF events and featuring vignettes with various WWF Superstars using ICOPRO before work-outs. If what we heard about ICOPRO is true, it had to be shoved down people's throats as no one in their right mind wanted to ingest the near-toxic substance. Wrestler Mr. Perfect's son Curt Axel reportedly drank it during football practice only to get a bad case of diarrhea

XFL: If Vince McMahon is going to do something, he's going to do it big. In this case, his attempt to rival the National Football League turned into one of the biggest fumbles in sports history as Vince McMahon's dream of his OWN football league crashed on take-off. With NBC executive Dick Ebersol reportedly looking for a way to escape the ever-increasing costs of airing the NFL, he partnered with McMahon, giving the upstart league a chance. However, the XFL didn't click with football fans, with some wondering whether the games were as predetermined as WWF matches, and others simply dismissing the athletes as NFL rejects and has-beens. Despite its agreement to give the XFL two seasons, NBC cut its losses. NBC and the WWF reportedly lost $35 million each. *(See Appendix B for more details on the XFL)*

WWF New York/The World: No doubt inspired by the success of themed restaurants and bars such as The Hard Rock Café and Planet Hollywood, the WWF opened WWF New York in late 1999, just months after rival WCW opened its Nitro Grill in Las Vegas. Located at 1501 Broadway in Times Square, WWF New York featured appearances by WWF Superstars and *Sunday Night Heat* aired from the restaurant from late October 2000 to early 2002. WWF New York was even featured in the Invasion angle when WCW's Chris Kanyon took it over for a week, renaming it The Alliance. While WWF New York (later renamed The World) never caught on, it outlasted both the Nitro Grill and WCW itself. In 2003, Linda McMahon announced the WWE was closing the restaurant to focus on global efforts which skeptics saw as focusing on making money instead of losing it.

WWE Niagara Falls: Given Niagara Falls Canada's reputation as a tourist trap full of kitschy wax museums and bars, the thought of a WWE-themed retail store wasn't a bad idea. The store opened in 2002 and featured a slew of WWE merchandise, as well as signing appearances by WWE Superstars. The store is arguably best remembered for its amusement ride, the 220-foot drop tower known as The Piledriver. WWE Niagara Falls closed in 2011.

WWF Casino: In 1998, the WWF was finally on top, winning the Monday Night War and expanding into other businesses. That year, the WWF bought the 193-room Debbie Reynolds Hotel and Casino at a bankruptcy auction, looking to turn it into a WWF-themed resort and casino. However, by 2000, things just hadn't worked out and the company ended up selling the property. In a 2000 interview, WWF spokesperson Judd Everhart said, "After we bought it, we realized it just wouldn't meet our expectations of being able to provide our brand of entertainment on the right scale…So we decided to sell it. We have no immediate plans to purchase other property in Las Vegas, but I couldn't rule that out" ("WWF gives up on Las Vegas casino").

Linda McMahon's Senate Races: Linda McMahon made not one, but two attempts to win a United States Senate seat in Connecticut, running unsuccessfully both times. According to a CNBC article, the McMahon's spent over $90 million dollars for the two campaigns. Linda McMahon's political aspirations ultimately panned out as WWE Hall of Famer and U.S. President Donald Trump appointed her to run the Small Business Administration in 2017.

Not Buying the Ultimate Fighting Championship (UFC): It's difficult to imagine, but the Ultimate Fighting Championship was once available to the WWF for an attractive price. Details are murky, but Shane McMahon is rumored to have lobbied hard for the WWF to purchase the MMA promotion in 2000. Some claim Vince McMahon was uncertain if people would take the UFC seriously given the WWF's worked nature, while others claim Vince didn't see MMA as marketable. History would prove him wrong and the UFC has gone on to eclipse the WWE in terms of popularity.

Works Cited

Lockhart, Brian. "McMahons' bankruptcy a murky chapter in her rags-to-riches tale." *CT Post.* 1 Oct. 2010.

http://www.ctpost.com/local/article/McMa hons-bankruptcy-a-murky-chapter-in-her-682114.php. Accessed 24 Aug. 2017.

"WWF gives up on Las Vegas casino." *SLAM! Sports. SLAM! Wrestling.* 27 Dec. 2000. http://slam.canoe.com/SlamWrestlingArchi ve2000/dec27_casino-can.html. Accessed 24 Aug. 2017.

Works Referenced

Aitken, Robert. "WWE: Ranking Vince McMahon's Non-Wrestling Flops from Least to Most Disastrous." *Bleacher Report.* 5 Mar. 2012. http://bleacherreport.com/articles/1090843 -wwe-ranking-vince-mcmahons-non-wrestling-flops-from-least-to-most-disastrous. Accessed 24 Aug. 2017.

Assael, Shaun and Mike Mooneyham. *Sex, Lies, and Headlocks: The Real Story of Vince McMahon and World Wrestling Entertainment.* Three Rivers Press, 2004.

Frank, Robert. "What Linda McMahon Could Have Done with Her $100 Million." *CNBC.* 12 Nov. 2012. https://www.cnbc.com/id/49725978. Accessed 24 Aug. 2017.

Heitner, Darren. "The XFL's Failure Was a

Success for the Innovation of American Football." *Inc.com.* https://www.inc.com/darren-heitner/the-xfls-failure-was-a-success-for-the-innovation-of-american-football.html. Accessed 24 Aug. 2017.

Joey. "15 Times Vince McMahon Regretted His Decision." *The Sportster.* 17 Apr. 2017. http://www.thesportster.com/wrestling/15-times-vince-mcmahon-regretted-his-decision. Accessed 24 Aug. 2017.

Mueller, Chris. "WWE Weekly 5: The Failed Ventures of Vince McMahon." *Bleacher Report.* 16 Jan. 2012. http://bleacherreport.com/articles/1022003-wwe-weekly-5-the-failed-ventures-of-vince-mcmahon. Accessed 24 Aug. 2017.

Passalalpi, Alessandro. "13 Most Epic Vince McMahon Failures." *The Richest.* 19 Nov. 2015. http://www.therichest.com/sports/wrestling/13-epic-vince-mcmahon-failures. Accessed 24 Aug. 2017.

Reynolds, R.D. and Randy Baer. *Wrestlecrap-the Very Worst of Professional Wrestling.* ECW Press, 2003.

"XFL is Down for the Count." *ABC News.* 11

May 2001.
http://abcnews.go.com/Entertainment/story?id=105329. Accessed 25 Aug. 2017.

90

Part Three: Ruthless Aggression

Vince McMahon once told his wrestlers he wanted them to show "ruthless aggression" in the ring. While this advice was part of a wrestling storyline, the following stories suggest McMahon the businessperson practices what his wrestling character preaches.

92

Chapter Eight: Black Saturday

Wrestling fans have a love/hate relationship with Vince McMahon. While some fans adore him, others blame him for ruining the style of professional wrestling (often known as "Southern Wrestling" or "wrasslin'") by bankrupting these promotions and focusing on a larger-than-life product. During the 1980s, Vince McMahon ruthlessly sought to take out competition, usually succeeding. What follows is McMahon's take on the idiom "you can't make an omelet without breaking a few eggs."

Originally published 2017

Do Not Adjust Your Set

On Saturday 14 July 1984, wrestling fans tuned in to SuperStation TBS to watch their beloved *World Championship Wrestling,* a wrestling show that had aired on WTBS for twelve years, broadcasting matches featuring the stars of Georgia Championship Wrestling. What they got instead was the World Wrestling Federation and Vince McMahon. For fans of southern wrestling this was blasphemy and the day became known as "Black Saturday." "Black Saturday" would change the wrestling landscape, playing a role in the creation of *WrestleMania,* and eventually sparking the wrestling war between Vince McMahon and Ted Turner.

The Importance of Cable Television

Wrestling enjoyed tremendous popularity during the 1950's, an era referred to as Golden Age of Wrestling because of its popularity, a popularity fueled by its appearances on all three television networks at the time. Unfortunately, as often happens with successful programming, wrestling became overexposed, leading to a decline in ratings and its departure from the networks.

With the networks giving wrestling the cold shoulder, promoters had no choice but to air their shows wherever they could. With the advent of the National Wrestling Alliance, many wrestling promoters had agreed on a geographic territory to operate in (thus steering clear of one another) and aired wrestling programs on UHF stations, stations typically independently owned and unable to afford expensive programming.

Wrestling proved attractive for local UHF stations with promoters often paying the stations to air them and getting a few minutes of commercial time to promote arena shows. The promotion often taped its show in a TV studio, then sent the tape to various UHF stations. These shows were in a sense, commercials for the wrestling promotion, introducing fans to stars and enticing them to buy tickets to arena shows to see angles play out to a conclusive finish.

Ted Turner's Relationship with Wrestling

Ted Turner needed cheap programming when he launched his UHF station WTCG (later renamed WTBS in 1979) so he could fill the airwaves. The station was known for airing reruns of various shows but when Turner's friend Ann Gunkel needed a spot for her late husband's wrestling promotion, Turner aired the show. Prior to this, WTCG aired *Georgia Championship Wrestling* beginning in 1972, and providing a two-hour show for wrestling fans. The program helped WTCG with its ratings and Turner would never forget how wrasslin' helped build his empire. By 1981, the show (now renamed *World Championship Wrestling*) was drawing the highest rating on cable, averaging 6.4.

Georgia Championship Wrestling benefited tremendously from its WTBS show. As cable expanded across America, WTBS began to air in a number of markets outside the Georgia area. Unlike most wrestling promotions that had a limited range, Georgia was receiving national coverage. Booker Ole Anderson capitalized on this, running shows outside of the territory's traditional geographic region where fans had access to WTBS.

Vince McMahon Targets WTBS

Vince McMahon's desire to expand the WWF from a regional promotion into a national promotion depended on getting national coverage.

The insightful McMahon saw the possibilities with cable television and bought Southwest Championship Wrestling's spot on the USA Network. Shaun Assael writes, "As Vinnie saw it, the beauty of cable was that it could take the McMahons into every market where the NWA operated, bypassing the czars' control. The cable airwaves could be used like a fighter squadron, providing air support for the live arena wars he was prepared to wage on the ground" (37). The WWF was authorized to sell 60% of the commercial time on its USA programming and McMahon saw WTBS as the next logical step in going national. McMahon approached Ted Turner and pitched the idea of airing WWF programming on the SuperStation. Turner ultimately turned down the offer.

McMahon went to Plan B, buying Georgia Championship Wrestling outright, thus gaining its timeslot. In the book *Sex, Lies, and Headlocks,* Jack Brisco is said to have called Vince McMahon to check on the health of a mutual friend. During the conversation McMahon reportedly asked Brisco, "Would you and your brother consider selling your stock to me?" (Assael and Mooneyham 45). Gerald Brisco's recollection differs. In an interview with WWE.com, Gerald Brisco recalls Vince McMahon contacting him and Jack Brisco about coming to work for the WWF. At that point, the Brisco

Brothers asked McMahon if he'd be interested in purchasing Georgia Championship Wrestling. The Brisco Brothers were reportedly unhappy with payouts from Georgia, blaming booker and co-owner Ole Anderson. According to Gerald Brisco, "We had a very dysfunctional company. Two members of the organization were making all the money. The company was making real good money at events we'd started running in Michigan, Ohio, West Virginia, Kentucky and parts of Pennsylvania, but we weren't getting any good dividend checks" ("Black Saturday: The Unbelievable Story of the Original Invasion").

In his book, *Inside Out: How Corporate America Destroyed Professional Wrestling,* Ole Anderson recounts the events leading up to Georgia Championship Wrestling's sale. According to Anderson, his mother had passed away, resulting in him taking a week off to tend to affairs. Ole had heard rumors McMahon was interested in purchasing Georgia Championship Wrestling but his attorneys had assured him of corporate by-laws which stated, "If a stockholder wants to sell stock in Georgia Championship Wrestling, they must first offer it to another stockholder. If none of the stockholders want to purchase the stock, then they can agree to allow that holder to sell it to someone outside, subject to the approval of the other stockholders" (Anderson 247). If that held up in court, no one could sell the company from under him. However, Anderson also noticed another clause which stated, "If a majority of the stockholders decide to rescind the Buy-Sell agreement, they can do so" (247). Anderson asked his attorneys about this but they assured him the first clause would protect him. They would soon be proved wrong.

The Briscos contacted retired wrestler Paul Jones (not to be confused with Jim Crockett promotions star "Number One" Paul Jones), persuading him to sell his shares. The addition of co-owner Jim Barnett's shares led to Vince McMahon gaining control of the promotion. Ole Anderson took the case to court, but as he feared, he had no case due to the clause in the Buy-Sell agreement.

Despite the circumstances of the Georgian Championship Wrestling purchase, Ole Anderson acknowledges Vince McMahon approached him about working for the WWF. However, Anderson was in no mood to deal with McMahon. In his memoir, *Inside Out,* Anderson recalls, "McMahon said, 'Listen to me, Ole. It's just business. I will make you more money than you ever dreamed of making.' 'Go fu__ yourself,' I replied" (Anderson 254).

Anderson's anger only increased as the court proceedings continued:

The next time Vince came to Atlanta for depositions, he brought his wife with him. He walked over and said, "Ole, I'd like you to meet my wife Linda." By this time, we were really in the heat of the legal battle. I had been raped so badly by those attorneys, I was so mad about everything. As I've always been a man of few words, I said, "Fu__ you," to her, then turned and said, "Fu__ you." To Vince. That was when Vince said, "You'll never, ever work again" (Anderson 256).

With Anderson squeezed out, McMahon put the finishing touches on the deal. He worked with Ted Turner, promising to air live matches in the Georgia Championship Wrestling studio. What happened turned out to be much different.

Black Saturday

On Saturday 14 July 1984, fans saw the familiar opening of *World Championship Wrestling*. From there, Fans tuned in to see the equally familiar face of Freddie Miller, the co-host of *World Championship Wrestling*. Fans were in for a shock though when Miller welcomed the WWF to the SuperStation then introduced Vince McMahon. McMahon promised the viewers to provide the greatest in professional wrestling entertainment in the world today. Given the first match on the show was a squash involving "Special Delivery" Jones and Nick DeCarlo against the WWF Tag Team Champions, Adrian Adonis and Dick Murdoch, it's difficult to imagine fans of Georgia Championship Wrestling being impressed with the new product.

The Difference Between Night and Day

It may be difficult to understand why Georgia Wrestling fans were so outraged but consider these two scenarios- 1) Imagine you're tuning in to *Gotham* and instead of the dark, gritty series you get the *Batman* series starring Adam West; Or to use a wrestling analogy, you're a Ring of Honor fan and you tune in only to see Baron Corbin, the New Day, and Roman Reigns instead of ROH's stars. Your idea of what constitutes good wrestling is much different than what's suddenly being shoved down your throat.

There was more to the fans dissatisfaction than not seeing their favorite stars. After all, the WWF had raided top stars from promotions across the country. The difference between the WWF product and Georgia wrestling was like night and day. Even before Vince McMahon took the WWF into more of a cartoonish style, it's arguable the WWF style was different than southern wrestling which focused more on athleticism and wrestling holds. For fans used to a technically-based world champion like Ric Flair or

Harley Race, the punch and legdrop-based style of WWF Champion Hulk Hogan was much different. *World Championship Wrestling* was known for being an exciting two hours of wrestling. As long-time fan and writer John Molinaro remembers:

> Georgia Championship Wrestling was the holy grail of wrestling TV programs. The first nationally broadcasted wrestling program in the U.S., it revolutionized how wrestling was presented on television and laid the groundwork for shows like Nitro, RAW and Smackdown! to follow: the two-hour format, episodic formatting, well-timed commercial breaks, cliffhanger endings, ring entrances accompanied by rock music, strong main events, major angles that lead to the big payoff matches down the road. A small TV studio. A handful of fans. Three cameras. One ring. One microphone. That brown backdrop with the TBS call letters and the NWA symbol on it that stood behind the interview podium. Gordon Solie. It may sound like just another wrestling show, but to many of us, Georgia Championship Wrestling was more.

Much more. ("End of an era on TBS Solie, Georgia and 'Black Saturday'").

Fans made their dissatisfaction known, phoning the station and sending letters as well. Fans demanded their Georgia Championship Wrestling be brought back, but the reality was it was no longer theirs. Vince McMahon had purchased it and with it, the much-coveted two-hour timeslot. "McMahon got word of the complaints and in an *Atlanta Journal Constitution* news article responded by saying, 'We'll show those complainers the difference between a major league and a minor league production, given time'" ("End of an era on TBS Solie, Georgia and 'Black Saturday.'").

World Championship Wrestling's Woes

World Championship Wrestling's ratings quickly dropped and complaints continued pouring in. Ted Turner acted, airing a one-hour program at 7:30AM *Championship Wrestling from Georgia.* Turner also aired Bill Watts' Mid-South Wrestling and the show quickly became TBS' number-one show.

To no one's surprise, Vince McMahon was upset. He'd counted on exclusive rights to wrestling when he worked the deal out with Turner. Turner felt differently, particularly after McMahon reneged on his promise to produce original programming in the WTBS studio. Instead, WTBS viewers got recycled matches from the WWF's other programs. Ted Turner's frustration mounted to the point where he threatened to sue. Turner reportedly wanted to give Bill Watts the two-hour timeslot. According to the book *Sex, Lies, and Headlocks,* a jubilant Bill Watts purchased an airplane, anticipating trips to Atlanta. Things turned out much differently.

A Timely Intervention

With Ted Turner and Vince McMahon at odds, wrestling executive Jim Barnett proposed a solution. Jim Crockett Promotions was looking to build upon the success of its *Starrcade* pay-per-views and go national. When Barnett informed promoter Jim Crockett Jr. of the chance to buy the two-hour slot on WTBS, he quickly moved into action, purchasing the slot for one million dollars. The result was Jim Crockett Promotions got its national spot and Bill Watts was left out in the cold.

The Aftermath

Vince McMahon had lost his two-hour slot on the SuperStation but he'd rid himself of an unprofitable venture for one million dollars, money he would use to launch the first *WrestleMania.* Wrestling legend has it that Vince McMahon prophetically told Crockett "You'll choke on that million" when he sold the spot, but according to the book *Sex, Lies, and Wrestling,* Jim Crockett recalls Linda McMahon, not Vince was the only one present when the deal was made (Assael and Mooneyham 67).

Vince McMahon and Ted Turner's experience doing business with each other soured them to one another. Ted Turner reportedly was impressed by McMahon when he made his initial offer to buy the *World Championship Wrestling* timeslot. However, that changed after McMahon reneged on his word that he would produce live studio wrestling for his WTBS program.

Bill Watts' Mid-South Wrestling continued through syndicated programming on UHF stations, with Watts attempting to take Mid-South (renamed Universal Wrestling Federation) national. However, overexpansion and an economic downturn in his market forced him to sell the promotion to Jim Crockett Promotions. Many list Crockett's purchase of the promotion as one of the major reasons for the demise of Jim Crockett Promotions, which in turn was bought out by Ted Turner and renamed World Championship Wrestling.

World Championship Wrestling would become Jim Crockett Promotions' flagship show for the next decade, airing some of the promotion's biggest angles over the next few years. Even after Ted Turner purchased the company and rechristened it WCW, the two-hour spot was the place to be. In 1992, *World Championship Wrestling* was renamed *WCW Saturday Night* but it remained the promotion's flagship show until the 1995 launch of *Monday Night Nitro.*

In the meantime, wrestling's popularity saw other cable networks pick up wrestling. ESPN would air the American Wrestling Association and World Class Championship Wrestling. The WWF presence on USA would expand with the creation of *Prime-Time Wrestling* and following the success of *WrestleMania,* the NBC network aired its *Saturday Night's Main Event* specials.

Works Cited

Anderson, Ole and Scott Teal. *Inside Out: How Corporate America Destroyed Professional Wrestling.* Crowbar Press, 2003.

Assael, Shaun and Mike Mooneyham. *Sex, Lies, and Headlocks: The Real Story of Vince McMahon and World Wrestling Entertainment.* Three Rivers Press, 2004.

"Black Saturday: The Unbelievable Story of the Original Invasion." *WWE.com.* http://www.wwe.com/classics/black-saturday. Accessed 29 May 2017.

Molinaro, John. "End of an era on TBS Solie, Georgia and 'Black Saturday.'" *Slam! Sports.* Slam! Wrestling. 3 Apr. 2001.

http://slam.canoe.com/SlamWrestlingFeatu res/tbs1-can.html. Accessed 29 May 2017.

Works Referenced:

Damage, Brian. "30 Years Later: Black Saturday." *Ring the Damn Bell.* 16 Dec. 2014. https://ringthedamnbell.wordpress.com/201 4/12/16/30-years-later-black-saturday. Accessed 29 May 2017.

Hornbaker, Tim. *Capitol Revolution: The Rise of the McMahon Wrestling Empire.* ECW Press, 2015.

Hornbaker, Tim. *National Wrestling Alliance: The Untold Story of the Monopoly That Strangled Pro Wrestling.* ECW Press, 2007.

Reynolds, R.D. and Bryan Alvarez. *The Death of WCW: Wrestlecrap and Figure Four Weekly Present…ECW Press,* 2004.

Rickard, Michael. *Wrestling's Greatest Moments.* ECW Press, 2008.

The True Story of WrestleMania. Directed by Kevin Dunn, performances by Lou Albano, Ken Anderson, and Andre the Giant, WWE Studios, 2011.

Watts, Bill and Scott Williams. *The Cowboy and the Cross: The Bill Watts Story: Rebellion, Wrestling and Redemption.* ECW Press, 2006.

WWE: The Rise and Fall of WCW. Directed by

Kevin Dunn, performances by Terry Allen, Dusty Rhodes, and Arn Anderson, World Wrestling Entertainment, 2009.

Chapter Nine: Business, the Vince McMahon Way

In 2019, the WWE faced competition from All Elite Wrestling (AEW) a new national wrestling promotion that was the first real competition the WWE had faced in nearly two decades. At the same time, the WWE's network partner FOX was reportedly breathing down the WWE's neck about SmackDown's sinking ratings. For some, it appeared Vince McMahon was going to his playbook of dirty tricks to try and sabotage AEW while it tried to placate FOX.

Originally published 2019

A Furious FOX

In 2018, the WWE landed a big-money deal with FOX to air *SmackDown* on the broadcast network, beginning on 4 October 2019. However, months before the WWE's debut on FOX, its new home network was already expressing concern about *SmackDown's* ever-shaky ratings and the WWE's overall problems selling tickets. Journalist Brad Shepard would tweet:

> "According to a source in #WWE, certain folks at Fox are not impressed with this week's numbers (#WWEStompingGrounds included) and are meeting this weekend with Vince, Triple H, Stephanie and a

couple of producers to address any concerns and changes. #SDLive" What the meeting will involve and how it may impact the WWE's pending debut has many people talking already.

While all the details of the WWE's new contract with FOX are unknown, it's believed the WWE has to meet a certain ratings threshold as a requirement of the deal. It's unknown whether FOX could cancel the deal or be allowed to pay less than their current contract states should the ratings go down. Either action by FOX could be devastating for the WWE and undoubtedly damage the value of its stock, which already took a serious hit earlier this year.

According to the news site, *The Wrap*, FOX is keeping *SmackDown* as a 2-hour show (at one point, there were rumors that FOX was interested in expanding *SmackDown* to a 3-hour show):

> "Fox's "SmackDown Live" will debut on Friday, Oct. 4 at 8/7c on Fox. The two-hour series runs until 10 o'clock, which is when Fox's national primetime programming ends. The rest of the Big 4 broadcast networks — CBS, NBC and ABC — have three-hour primetime windows that run until 11 p.m. ET." (Maglio)

FOX announced its fall schedule and *SmackDown* will debut on FOX on 2 October 2019

The deal with FOX is extremely lucrative for the WWE. Consider the WWE's past *SmackDown* deal:

> "NBCUniversal has had rights to *SmackDown* since 2010; at the time, the company is reported to have paid about $30 million for the franchise. The show began airing that year on Syfy, with corporate sibling USA heavily promoting it" (Guthrie).

As multiple sites such as *Forbes* have reported, "*SmackDown's* deal to air Friday nights on Fox is a monumental five-year, $1 billion deal that will see WWE make $205 million per year" (Konuwa). This is quite an increase from the WWE's past deals and naturally, both parties want to meet their respective ends of the bargain.

There is no word on what the meeting between FOX executives and WWE officials will involve so at this point anything is mere speculation. It could be possible FOX will attempt to renegotiate the terms of its contract with the WWE, requesting a lower price. It could be that FOX will simply remind the WWE of its obligations to meet a certain ratings level and strongly suggest it find a way to improve things before the show's 4 October 2019 debut. These suggestions might be something similar to the USA Network's recommendation for a 24/7 Championship or something entirely different. Brad Shepard provided some details on what the focus of the conversation might be, noting:

> "According to a high level source in #WWE, the company's strategy going into Fox isn't just about which WWE show will be the 'A' show (between SD & Raw), but it's about WWE presenting themselves as the 'A' pro wrestling/sports entertainment company, as #AEW airs on TNT." (qtd. in Jenkins "WWE's Reported Strategy")

Vince McMahon is known for being set in his ways but when it comes to a billion-dollar deal, he's likely to make an exception.

Dirty Tricks or Just a Coincidence?

With AEW set to premiere on TNT his fall and the promotion's two consecutive sell-outs for its pay-per-views (as opposed to the WWE's atrocious ticket sales for both its pay-per-view *Stomping Grounds* and the *RAW* the night after), Vince McMahon has cause for concern. AEW is not a small-time operation and although its success isn't guaranteed, it has the backing of billionaire tycoon Shahid Khan. With FOX executives no doubt stressing out Vince McMahon and company, it should come as no surprise that McMahon is looking to do everything possible to hurt AEW's momentum, apparently even if it means opposing a charity show being run by AEW.

The charity show in question is AEW's *Fight for the Fallen,* a live event scheduled for 13 July 2019 in Jacksonville, Florida. The card includes a bout between Kenny Omega and CIMA as well as a tag team match between the Young Bucks and the brother team of Cody and Dustin Rhodes. According to an AEW press conference, "a large portion of the gate would go toward benefiting victims of gun violence."

An announcement by the WWE today is being seen by some as a move to sabotage the charity event. Today it was revealed that:

> "EVOLVE's 10th Anniversary Celebration will air live on the WWE Network at 8 p.m. Eastern time on Saturday, July 13. The show is taking place at the 2300 Arena in Philadelphia, Pennsylvania and is in celebration of 10 years of EVOLVE/Dragon Gate USA. NXT Champion Adam Cole will defend his title against Akira Tozawa at the anniversary event, Matt Riddle is set to face Drew Gulak, and EVOLVE

Champion Austin Theory, EVOLVE Tag Team Champions Eddie Kingston & Joe Gacy, and NXT's Arturo Ruas and Babatunde are also advertised." (qtd. in Currier)

With the event airing on the WWE Network the same night as *Fight for the Fallen,* some see this as a contemporary example of the WWE's past practice of sabotaging competitor's paid events with free shows. At the same time, it might just be seen as a coincidence that both events are being held the same night. We'll look at the possibility of sabotage in a moment, but first, let's hear what a prominent figure in AEW had to say.

Kenny Omega Fires Back

According to *Comicbook.com,* AEW wrestler (and one of the company's Executive Vice-Presidents) posted a tweet:

"If lining your pockets with blood money is okay, then what's wrong with trying to undermine a charity show for victims of gun violence? I hear that healthy competition is supposed to be a good thing and yet I can't help but feel like I'm gonna be sick." (qtd. in Casey)

Comicbook.com also noted Omega deleted it 30 minutes after posting it. He followed up with the following tweet:

"I've said my piece and it opened the door to a very toxic environment. It wasn't a message to fans, or the boys, just the decision makers. I wish everyone wrestling on any show that day all the best. That is all."
@KennyOmegamanX

Of course, Omega was undoubtedly attacking the WWE's deal with Saudi Arabia or as *Fightful.com's* Jeremy Lambert opined:

"Omega is not so subtly jabbing at WWE for running events in Saudi Arabia, where human and women's rights are suppressed. WWE is paid a hefty sum by Crown Prince Mohammad bin Salman, who was linked to the killing of journalist Jamal Khashoggi. WWE has a 10-year agreement with Salman and his Saudi Vision 2030."

Is this an example of the WWE trying to sabotage a competitor's event? Let's look briefly at some of the WWE's past tactics in sabotaging its competition's events to put things in perspective.

Stacking the Deck

During the 1980's, Vince McMahon went to great lengths to compete against his territorial rivals, luring rival promotions' top talent away and by some accounts, asking them to walk out on their bosses rather than giving them the customary notice (Rickard). However, it was later during McMahon's national expansion that he went to great lengths to sandbag his wrestling rivals, chief among them Jim Crockett Promotions.

One of the best-known incidents happened in 1987 when Crockett aired its flagship pay-per-view, *Starrcade*. Earlier that year, the WWF's *WrestleMania III* had made millions of dollars and pay-per-view providers took notice of this new cash cow. McMahon was aware that the WWF was now in the catbird seat and he told pay-per-view companies that he had a new show he wanted them to carry. Said show was *Survivor Series,* (which just happened to air on Thanksgiving, the same night as *Starrcade*). The pay-per-view company executives likely started counting all the money they'd make from two wrestling pay-per-views, but Vinnie Mac wasn't looking to help Jim Crockett Promotions. Instead, he told the pay-per-view companies that anyone who aired *Starrcade* would miss out on airing *WrestleMania IV*. Knowing who made them the most money, many pay-per-view companies aligned themselves with the WWE, effectively killing 1987's *Starrcade* as it aired on a limited number of outlets (Crockett didn't help matters either as *Starrcade* was a poorly booked show).

McMahon's hijinks continued in 1988 when Crockett aired a new pay-per-view, *The Bunkhouse Stampede,* hoping to make up for its losses with the previous year's *Starrcade.* In typical McMahon fashion, he negotiated a deal with the USA Network to air a cable special, which ultimately aired the same night as *The Bunkhouse Stampede.* That event became *The Royal Rumble* and as we know, it's been going on for the last three decades while *The Bunkhouse Stampede* is a footnote in wrestling history. Jim Crockett Promotions was sold to Ted Turner in 1988, becoming WCW.

Vince's penchant for sticking it to his competition is nothing new, but is the WWE running *EVOLVE's* anniversary show the same night on the subscription-based WWE Network a case of underhanded tactics? While *Fight for the Fallen* is a charity event, it can be argued that the tickets have been sold and the WWE's broadcast won't hurt ticket sales. Furthermore, the *EVOLVE* special is being aired on a streaming service fan have to pay for (as opposed to it airing for free).

On the other hand, consider that the AEW event is also being streamed for free on *Bleacher Report Live.* The free broadcast will likely include some sort of mention of how fans watching the event can contribute to the charity for victims of gun violence. If so, that may be why some see this as the WWE clearly undermining a charity event.

Works Cited

@BradShepard. "According to a Source in WWE..." *Twitter,* 26 June 2019, 5:29p.m., https://twitter.com/TheBradShepard/status/1143994632218599425?ref_src=twsrc%5Etfw%7Ctwcamp%5Etweetembed%7Ctwterm%5E1143994632218599425&ref_url=https%3A%2F%2Fwww.ringsidenews.com%2F2019%2F06%2F26%2Ffox-reportedly-not-impressed-with-wwe-meeting-next-week-about-changes%2F.

Casey, Connor. "Kenny Omega Calls out WWE After Booking Show Same Day as Fight For The Fallen." *ComicBook.* WWE. 26 June 2019. https://comicbook.com/wwe/2019/06/26/aew-kenny-omega-calls-out-wwe-fight-for-the-fallen-evolve-131-same-date. Accessed 26 June 2019.

Currier, Joseph. "EVOLVE 10TH ANNIVERSARY SHOW TO AIR LIVE ON WWE NETWORK." *Wrestling Observer Figure Four Online.* 26 June 2019. https://www.f4wonline.com/wwe-news/evolve-10th-anniversary-show-air-live-wwe-network-286751. Accessed 26 June 2019.

Guthrie, Marisa. "Fox and WWE Close to Massive Five-Year, $1 Billion Deal for 'SmackDown.'" *Hollywood Reporter*. TV. 21 May 2018. https://www.hollywoodreporter.com/news/fox-wwe-close-massive-five-year-1-billion-deal-smackdown-1113701. Accessed 26 June 2019.

Jenkins, H. "FOX REPORTEDLY 'NOT IMPRESSED' WITH WWE — MEETING NEXT WEEK ABOUT CHANGES." *Ringside News*. Featured News. 26 June 2019. https://www.ringsidenews.com/2019/06/26/fox-reportedly-not-impressed-with-wwe-meeting-next-week-about-changes. Accessed 26 June 2019.

Jenkins, H. "WWE NEWS FEATURED NEWS WWE NETWORK SET TO AIR EVOLVE SPECIAL OPPOSITE AEW FIGHT FOR THE FALLEN." *Ringside News*. WWE News. 26 June 2019. https://www.ringsidenews.com/2019/06/26/wwe-network-set-to-air-evolve-special-opposite-aew-fight-for-the-fallen. Accessed 26 June 2019.

Jenkins, H. "WWE'S REPORTED STRATEGY FOR DEALING WITH COMPETITION

FROM AEW IN OCTOBER." *Ringside News.* WWE News. 26 June 2019. https://www.ringsidenews.com/2019/06/26/wwes-reported-strategy-for-dealing-with-competition-from-aew-in-october. Accessed 26 June 2019.

@KennyOmegamanX. "I've said my piece…" *Twitter,* 26 June 2019, 4:34p.m., http://bit.ly/2RCtPqN.

Konuwa, Alfred. "How Billion-Dollar SmackDown Live-To-Fox Deal Could Legitimize WWE Brand Split In 2019." *Forbes.* Sports Money. https://www.forbes.com/sites/alfredkonuwa/2018/05/21/how-massive-smackdown-live-to-fox-deal-could-legitimize-wwe-brand-split-in-2019. Accessed 26 June 2019.

Lambert, Jeremy. "Kenny Omega Blasts WWE for "Lining Pockets with Blood Money And Undermining Charity Show." *Fightful.com.* WWE. 26 June 2019. https://www.fightful.com/wrestling/kenny-omega-blasts-wwe-lining-pockets-blood-money-and-undermining-charity-show. Accessed 26 June 2019.

Levine, Daniel S. "Fox Sets Premiere Dates for Fall 2019, Including WWE Smackdown Debut." *Popculture.TV*. 24 June 2019. https://popculture.com/tv-shows/2019/06/24/fox-sets-premiere-dates-fall-2019-including-wwe-smackdown-debut. Accessed 26 June 2019.

Maglio, Tony. "WWE's 'SmackDown Live' on Fox Will Remain a 2-Hour Show." *The Wrap*. TV. 13 May 2019. https://www.thewrap.com/wwe-smackdown-live-on-fox-2-hours. Accessed 26 June 2019.

Rickard, Michael. *Wrestling's Greatest Moments*. ECW Press, 2008.

Chapter Ten: Move Along, Nothing to See

Fans of Mel Brooks' classic Frankenstein spoof, "Young Frankenstein", remember the scene where Gene Wilder's Dr. Frankenstein tells Marty Feldman's hunchbacked Igor (or is it Eye-gore?) he might be able to help him with his hump, to which Igor replies "What hump?" Such is the case with these videos that the WWE would prefer you don't see. In some cases, the videos have been taken down from the WWE's content on the Peacock streaming service (in 2021, the WWE licensed the streaming rights for its WWE Network content to NBC's Peacock streaming service) but if you look deep enough, chances are you'll find them online.

Originally published 2019

Vince Using the "N" Word: Although many fans think Vince McMahon is out of touch with what's hip, the WWE's CEO clearly thinks he's cooler than Fang McFrost. Sadly, nothing could be further from the truth, as witnessed back at the 2005 *Survivor Series* where Vince McMahon approached John Cena and said, "My nig*a" as a bewildered Booker T turned to wife Sharmell and said, "Tell me he didn't just say that." McMahon's comments were both unfunny and out of line, quickly drawing criticism from fans and commentators alike. Hulk Hogan cried foul in

2015 when the WWE fired him and removed him from the WWE Hall of Fame after video footage aired of Hogan using the "n-word." Hogan pointed out Vinnie Mac's past usage of the "n-word" but the WWE countered that the 2005 segment, "was an outlandish and satirical skit involving fictional characters, similar to that of many scripted television shows and movies" ("Hulk Hogan WWE Owner is Raging Hypocrite"). McMahon's use of a racial slur came back to haunt him again in 2017 when guest LaMelo Ball appeared on *RAW* and used the same racial slur twice. The African-American basketball player's comments aired on live TV, leading to the TV issuing a statement that Ball's speech, "was not scripted nor reflects WWE's values" (qtd. in "It's Not Just LaMelo:"). The media then reminded people of McMahon's 2005 incident, giving Vince yet another reason to wish he could delete it.

The Chris Benoit Tribute: The WWE aired a Benoit tribute hours after police discovered Benoit and his family had been murdered. While there's still debate over the exact time when the WWE discovered Benoit was the killer, the WWE aired a tribute program on *RAW* featuring several of Benoit's greatest matches as well as praise from his fellow wrestlers. The terrible truth came out, forcing the WWE to backpedal on the tribute, with

Vince McMahon all but damning Benoit the next night on ECW. McMahon stated:

> "Last night on Monday Night Raw, the WWE presented a special tribute show, recognizing the career of Chris Benoit. However, now some 26 hours later, the facts of this horrific tragedy are now apparent. Therefore, other than my comments, there will be no mention of Mr. Benoit tonight. On the contrary, tonight's show will be dedicated to everyone who has been affected by this terrible incident. This evening marks the first step of the healing process. Tonight, the WWE performers will do what they do better than anyone else in the world-- entertain you." (qtd. in Clark)

The WWE would subsequently remove any mention they could of Benoit whether it was merchandise or future references to him on WWE television.

Owen Hart's Death: Owen Hart's horrific death forever changed the wrestling industry, with fans and wrestlers taking a closer look at the growing trend for more outrageous stunts in and out of the ring. Wrestling has never been innocent but some fans look to Owen's death as the moment when everything changed. Although the WWE did everything to shield fans from seeing Owen's fall and subsequent death in the ring, footage exists of the incident and was reportedly available if Martha Hart's wrongful death case against the WWF had gone to trial. Short of breaking into the WWE's tape vault, you'll never see it although ghoulish profiteers have falsely claimed to have the footage for sale.

The Curtain Call: Triple H's wish to give his fellow Kliq members Scott Hall (Razor Ramon) and Kevin Nash (Diesel)a proper send-off in Madison Square Garden nearly killed his career as the kayfabe-killing celebration outraged traditionalists backstage, leading to calls for Hunter to be fired. These defenders of old-school tradition lost it when they saw heels Diesel and Triple H hugging babyfaces Razor Ramon and Shawn Michaels in the ring as Michaels and Helmsley celebrated their friends' last days in the WWF. With Razor and Diesel leaving for WCW, McMahon couldn't punish them, but he did sanction Triple H. Arguably the worst part of this incident was that it was captured on video by a fan, who then leaked it to the then-growing Internet Wrestling Community. Fortunately for the WWF, there was no *YouTube* at the time, but the video got out and the promotion was disgusted not only at the Curtain Call, but the fact there was video proof.

Trish Barking Like a Dog: WWE Hall of Famer Trish Stratus worked at a time when female Superstars were often used as eye candy, and sometimes in degrading ways. In 2001, Vince McMahon was involved in a storyline where he'd initiated a divorce against Linda McMahon and began an affair with Trish Stratus. While fans have seen or heard about the notorious incident where Vince made Trish bark like a dog, that's only part of an angle McMahon would like the fans to forget. On 26 February 2001, Vince teamed with Trish to take on Stephanie McMahon and William Regal (Cawthon). The match was a set-up for Vince to show Stratus how little she meant to him, with Vince dragging her into the ring so Stephanie and Regal could beat her down. Stratus was then soaked with a mop that was supposed to be full of Wrestlecrap. The angle only got worse the next week when Mr. McMahon humiliated Stratus further, telling her she had to beg for his forgiveness. McMahon had Stratus disrobe down to her bra and panties before crawling on all fours while barking like a dog. While the angle was just one of many designed to show McMahon's misogynistic side, it blew up in Linda McMahon's face during her Senate campaign. With the WWE promoting its "Women's Revolution" everywhere but in Saudi Arabia, there's little doubt why it's done everything possible to hide the video.

Ric Flair Forcibly Kissing Becky Lynch:
Society changes over times as does a culture's sensibilities. Once upon a time, films and TV comedies routinely featured "funny drunks" such as Dean Martin where alcoholism was seen as the stuff of jokes. Not so much anymore as people who have battled alcoholism or dealt with loved ones battling the disease find such humor offensive. Even professional wrestling, long known for being politically incorrect has had to change with the times as seen at the 2016 *Royal Rumble* when Charlotte Flair's dad and manager Ric "Nature Boy" Flair forcibly kissed Becky Lynch in order to distract her during a match. The WWE wisely cut the segment from subsequent broadcasts as the idea of a man forcibly kissing a woman was too creepy. Of course, there are plenty of questionable segments in the past such as Flair "winning" the services of Jimmy Garvin's valet Precious that the WWE may have to address in the future, but for now, they're more concerned with rectifying oversights from when they should have known better.

The WWE's Musical Moments (Copyright violating performances by Superstars): As fans know, the days of promotions using licensed music without a band's permission are long over (which is why programs such as ECW are heavily edited on the WWE Network, replacing licensed songs such as Metallica's "Enter Sandman" with the WWE's generic music). The eagle-eyed folks in the music industry keep a close look on any use of a song, which is why until 2015, people risked being sued for public performances of the song "Happy Birthday to You" until a court settlement placed the song in the public domain, therefore making it usable for free by all (not to be confused with the WWF's old "Free for All" pay-per-view warm-up shows). However, that's the exception to the rule which is why many of the numerous impromptu musical performances by WWE Superstars can't be found on the WWE Network. Whether it's the Rock's much-acclaimed "Rock" concerts, his dueling song battles against "Stone Cold" Steve Austin, the Alliance singing Bette Midler's "Wind Beneath My Wings" to their leader "The Texas Rattlesnake" (and you probably forgot the depths the "Invasion" angle sank to), or the more recent performance of "Empire State of Mind" by the New Day, the WWE Network has cut these performances rather than risk any lawsuit (Snipes). **Triple H Makes Homophobic Comments About Kurt Angle:** Anyone who watched D-Generation X during the Attitude Era knows the edgy group crossed the line numerous times during promos with comments not safe for work and certainly to set social media on fire. After the departure of Shawn Michaels, Hunter Hearst

Helmsley managed to push the envelope further as the WWF ran with its risqué reputation during the Attitude Era. One moment the WWE would like you to forget is the night that Triple H and Mick Foley cut a promo at the expense of "Olympic Hero" Kurt Angle. The 18 September 2000 edition of *RAW* featured Triple H addressing the controversy that Kurt Angle was hitting on Hunter's then-storyline wife Stephanie McMahon. Helmsley revealed that Angle had "come out of the closet" and proceeded to offer video proof, showing Kurt Angle crying after winning his Olympic gold medal at the 1996 Olympics and hugging the referee. Mick Foley showed up to make some more comments at Angle's expense, questioning Angle's sexual orientation. While it's been suggested the WWE has deleted most of the segment due to its potentially unauthorized use of Olympic footage, the promotion is probably glad to see it gone from the official record.

Muhammad Hassan's Attack on the Undertaker: Vince McMahon is one stubborn S.O.B., something he clearly showed when he aired a disturbing segment on *SmackDown* when he clearly should not have. On 5 July 2005, the WWE taped *SmackDown!* including a segment where Muhammad Hassan battled the Undertaker. During the segment, Hassan's manager, Shawn Daivari summoned five masked men (who some claim alleged resembled terrorists) who attacked the Undertaker and carried him to the backstage area. This attack in and of itself was par for the WWE, but the events of two days later changed everything.

On 7 July 2005, London suffered a terrorist bombing just hours before *SmackDown!* was scheduled to air. Although the WWE had the option to edit out the segment, it chose to air it with the following disclaimer broadcast several times throughout the show: "In light of today's tragic events in London, parental discretion is advised in viewing tonight's episode." The segment aired in America but was edited out of segments in the United Kingdom. As might be expected, critics condemned the airing of the angle as in bad taste given the events of 7 July.

WWE spokesman Gary Davis responded: "We all feel bad about the timing of the segment," ...Gary Davis, who said the show wasn't attempting to depict a terrorist attack -- although he said he understood how some viewers might construe it as such. "People will see what happens this week (as the storyline) gets straightened out." (qtd. in "Media reacts to Muhammad Hassan")

SmackDown! executive producer Kevin Dunn also defended the segment, stating:

"We're very proud of our product…We try and be sensitive with everything we portray, but there's got to be protagonists and antagonists on our TV shows. We just happen to reflect the politics of the world sometimes — especially with these Arab-American characters." (qtd. in "Media reacts to Muhammad Hassan")

SmackDown's network home UPN disagreed and demanded the WWE get rid of the Muhammad Hassan character; a move that might not have happened had the WWE shown the right judgment.

Works Cited

Brown, Larry. "Vince McMahon's past use of N-word called into question." *Fox Sports.* 25 July 2015. https://www.foxsports.com/other/story/vince-mcmahon-s-past-use-of-n-word-called-into-question-072515. Accessed 17 Mar. 2019.

Cawthon, Graham. *The History of the WWE.* " 2001. http://www.thehistoryofwwe.com/01.htm. Accessed 17 Mar. 2019.

Clark, Ryan. "Vince McMahon Opens ECW With Benoit Message." *Wrestling Inc.* News. 26 June 2007. https://www.wrestlinginc.com/news/2007/06/vince-mcmahon-opens-ecw-with-benoit-message-498860. Accessed 17 Mar. 2019.

"11 Shocking Videos Vince McMahon Doesn't Want You to See." *Whatculture.* WWE. https://whatculture.com/wwe/11-shocking-videos-vince-mcmahon-doesnt-want-see. Accessed 16 Mar. 2019.

"Hulk Hogan WWE OWNER VINCE MCMAHON IS RAGING HYPOCRITE He Hurled the N-Word, Too." *TMZ.* TMZ Sports. 25 July. 2015. https://www.tmz.com/2015/07/25/wwe-owner-vince-mcmahon-hulk-hogan-n-word. Accessed 17 Mar. 2019.

"It's Not Just LaMelo: Video Surfaces of WWE's Vince McMahon Using Slur." *CBS KCAL 9.* News. 27 June 2017. https://losangeles.cbslocal.com/2017/06/27/lavar-ball-n-word-wwe. Accessed 17 Mar. 2019.

Konuwa, Alfred. "Since 2016 Election, The N-Word Has Been Said on WWE TV More

Times Than the Words 'Donald Trump.'"
Forbes. Sports Money. 7 July 2017.
https://www.forbes.com/sites/alfredkonuw
a/2017/07/07/since-2016-election-the-n-
word-has-been-said-on-wwe-tv-more-times-
than-the-words-donald-trump. Accessed 17
Mar. 2019.

"Media reacts to Muhammad Hassan." *WWE.com.*
http://www.wwe.com/inside/news/archive
/mediahassan. Accessed 17 Mar. 2019.

Reuters. "You can now sing 'Happy Birthday'
without being sued." *New York Post.* News. 9
Dec. 2015.
https://nypost.com/2015/12/09/you-can-
sing-happy-birthday-now-without-being-
sued. Accessed 17 Mar. 2019.

Siemon, Nick. "Too Hot For TV: 15 Wrestling
Moments That Were Cut from The
Broadcast." *The Sportster.* Wrestling. 2 Mar.
2017.
https://www.thesportster.com/wrestling/to
o-hot-for-tv-15-wrestling-moments-that-
were-cut-from-the-broadcast. Accessed 16
Mar. 2019.

Snipes, Lucas Wesley. "15 Terribly Dumb
Moments The WWE Network Erased From
History." *The Richest.* Sports. 8 Nov. 2016.
https://www.therichest.com/sports-
entertainment/15-terribly-dumb-moments-

the-wwe-network-erased-from-history Accessed 16 Mar. 2019.

Thomas, Owen. "Too Hot for Censors: 15 WWE Moments That Were Cut from The Broadcast." *The Sportster.* Wrestling. 1 Sept. 2016. https://www.thesportster.com/wrestling/too-hot-for-censors-15-wwe-moments-that-were-cut-from-the-broadcast. Accessed 16 Mar. 2019.

Wilkins, Ernest. "5 Pretty Racist Storyline Moments Still on the WWE Network." *Rolling Stone.* Sports. 24 July 2015. https://www.rollingstone.com/culture/culture-sports/5-pretty-racist-storyline-moments-still-on-the-wwe-network-48721. Accessed 17 Mar. 2019.

Chapter Eleven: Is There Systemic Racism in Wrestling?

Originally published 2019

The WWE storyline featuring Kofi Kingston's quest for the main event and Big E's recent comments have some fans wondering whether there is racism in the WWE. Let's examines the WWE's history to see if racism is at play in its corporate culture and/or policy.

In case you haven't been watching the WWE (and you certainly wouldn't be alone as WWE ratings are all over the place), New Day member Kofi Kingston has had a well-received single push on *SmackDown Live* with Kofi putting in an amazing performance at February's *Elimination Chamber* event where he came close to dethroning WWE champion Daniel Bryan in an Elimination Chamber match. Kofi was subsequently set to face Bryan at *Fastlane*—that is until Mr. McMahon yanked him out and replaced him with Kevin Owens, implying Kingston isn't a true main eventer. McMahon then told Kingston he could face Bryan at *WrestleMania XXXV* if he won a Gauntlet match last week on *SmackDown Live*, a match Kofi had won until McMahon added Bryan to the match and "The New" Daniel Bryan dispatched the beat-up Kingston.

Wrestling fans are wondering whether this program is a case of the WWE holding back a performer based on ethnicity or if it's just a storyline being used to set up an eventual match at 'Mania. Further confusing the issue are comments by Kingston's New Day teammate Big E who commented on social media:

> "We've had some time to contemplate what happened Tuesday night, and obviously Kofi's performance and the aftermath and our reaction to all of that. And a little bit of time to reflect too on - I guess kind of our careers and why we do this. You know, you think of this business to some degree being a meritocracy. If you work hard, you show up early, you stay late, you do all the right things, you jump through all the right hoops, you're respectful, you don't break the law, that you get good at your craft, that you really hone that, that you find a place with fans, you separate yourself, you find a niche, you separate yourself from a character perspective, from an in-ring perspective. You do everything, you check all the boxes, you show up

in shape - you do everything that's asked of you in this business - that if you do all those things you have a good chance of making it to the top. But now we understand the game. We see what the game is - that people like us will only get so far. That you can climb the mountain. They'll let you climb the mountain, but as far as getting to the peak and staying at the peak - it's not a thing that people like us, historically and moving forward clearly, can only get so far." (qtd. in Rueter)

WWE Superstars have been accused of making racists remarks and in some cases, they've even been caught making racist remarks, but does this reflect the WWE's corporate policy? When Hulk Hogan's racist remarks came to light, the WWE fired him immediately and removed him from their Hall of Fame. This apparent zero tolerance policy suggests a strong stance against racism, but what of things behind the scenes at Titan Tower?

Claims have been made that the WWE's management is racist. Consider the remarks of former WWE Superstar, Gail Kim Irvine who commented on Hulk Hogan's reinstatement, "Plus they're racist anyway. They don't care if anyone is racist Because they have the same thoughts" (qtd. in Satin).

Kim would issue a clarification, stating:

> "I think due to the fact that sometimes terms like racism are thrown around easily, especially in today's climate. Racism is a serious thing and I realized that saying "they", that I was putting a blanket over everyone who works in the company. This is not true. The culture or environment of a company starts from the top. The leadership. The leadership of a company sends a message to its employees of what is tolerated and what is not...As an ethnic female in wrestling, there will be people reading my words and I want to set an example. I did experience racism. I never even understood the term 'gook' until I worked for the company or heard the usage of so many ugly racial slurs. I think it's important to educate, listen and talk about these issues. I want to be very clear on where I stand. I want racial and gender equality. I hope that we can make strides to talk about and create change for the good of our industry and others." (qtd. in Satin)

As we'll show later, Kim's concerns about WWE management seem to have merit.

Wrestling itself has a history of insensitive promoting tactics that relied on exploiting stereotypes. Professional wrestling, like other forms of American entertainment was not afraid to rely on stereotypes whether it was African-American wrestlers being depicted as having naturally hard heads, their playing hustlers and pimps such as Cryme Tyme and the Godfather, "sneaky" Asian wrestlers who speak broken English, or Latino wrestlers with exaggerated accents who portray thugs and/or have fiery tempers. Stereotypes have not been limited to persons of color as seen with formulaic characters including dumb hillbillies, evil Russians, and money-hungry femme fatales. Fans can look back to undeniably racially insensitive and racist angles such as One-Man Gang's embracing his non-existent African heritage by becoming "Akeem the African Dream," "Rowdy" Roddy Piper painting himself half-black before wrestling African-American wrestler "Bad" News Brown for their *WrestleMania VI* bout (Piper played a babyface at the time), and endless ethnic stereotypes such as the aforementioned Cryme Tyme, the Mexicools and Los Matadores.

Consider Triple H, who now works behind the scenes in the WWE cut the following promo on Booker T when the five-time WCW champion challenged him for the World Heavyweight Championship at *WrestleMania XIX:*

> "I think you're a little bit confused about your role in life here. You're going to get to go to WrestleMania, but the fact is, Booker ... somebody like you doesn't get to be a world champion. People like you don't deserve it. That's reserved for people like me. That's where the confusion is. You're not here to be a competitor. You're here to be an entertainer. That's what you do. You entertain people. Hell, you entertain me all the time. Go ahead, do a little dance for me. Go ahead. Give me one of those Spinaroonies. Entertain me. That's your job. Don't be embarrassed. You're here to make people like me laugh. With your nappy hair and your 'suckas.' Hell, I was laughing all week long after you won that battle royal." (qtd. in Dennis)

The interview was troubling but all the more troubling when Helmsley pinned Booker T cleanly at 'Mania with Booker T getting no payback for Helmsley's remarks.

However, some wrestlers who have portrayed roles seen by others as demeaning, have defended their roles. For example, "Cryme Tyme's" Jayson "JTG" Paul wrote in 2018:

> "No, I don't feel Cryme Tyme's image and persona was racist. Absolutely not! Shad and I were a tag team down in Ohio Valley Wrestling (OVW) in Louisville, KY. It was actually us who came up with the characters and our look, as it was an extension of our personalities with the volume turned all the way up. We were authentic and that's the reason we were so over with the crowd. Shad and I both are from Brooklyn, NY. We were born and raised there. We both grew up in a low income, single-parent household and had similar experiences being raised in the 'hood. Even though I didn't meet shad until I was 18-years-old, we made a great team as soon as we paired because of the chemistry we had outside of the ring. Shad and I had shot a few comedic training videos down in OVW, exactly like the ones they showed prior to our debut for RAW. I was told that the first time WWE Chairman Vince McMahon saw

Shad and me together, we made him laugh. He asked if I was already under contract — and I wasn't. Vince then wanted to hire me on the spot! The man never even saw me wrestle!"
(Paul)

The question of racism in wrestling is more than hearsay. WWE's now defunct rival World Championship Wrestling was sued by a number of individuals who claimed unequal treatment by WCW including a pay disparity between white and non-white wrestlers, fewer merchandising opportunities for minority wrestlers, and constant negative portrayal of minority wrestlers in storylines. There were also allegations of a racial discrimination backstage and a hostile workplace environment for minority employees. The lawsuit was eventually settled out of court.

The case did not involve the WWE but it raises the questions, are there similar situations in the WWE today? If so, the WWE faces a potentially devastating lawsuit both in terms of damages and the company's public image. As often happens with issues involving racial discrimination, there is no "smoking gun" piece of evidence to prove those in power at the WWE are racist or that racism affects the promotion and other treatment of wrestlers from minority groups.

Let's review the WWE's history and allegations of racial discrimination backstage and/or a hostile work environment.

The Lack of African-American world champions: Some analysts point to the WWE Championship and its World Heavyweight Championship, noting the lack of champions from minority backgrounds, particularly black wrestlers. Mark Henry, the Rock, and Booker T are the only black wrestlers to have held either belt (although it should be noted that other minority wrestlers such as Rey Mysterio, Alberto Del Rio, and Eddie Guerrero held world championships). The problem hasn't gone unnoticed. For example, *Forbes* writer Alfred Konuwa recently penned a column "The 5 Most Embarrassing Facts About WWE And Its Handling of Black Superstars," discussing how an African-American wrestler hasn't main evented *WrestleMania* since Lawrence Taylor at *WrestleMania X* (although Konuwa is splitting hairs with the Rock, who is both African-American and Samoan), that no black wrestler has ever won a Money in the Bank Ladder Match, and other alarming facts.

Michael Hayes/Mark Henry Incident: Evidence of a hostile work environment can lead to legal repercussions. Consider the case of Michael Hayes, who reportedly used the "n-word" to Mark Henry. In 2008, *Pro Wrestling Net* reported:

"Hayes and MVP had been using the word while joking around together earlier in the night. It was a party setting and Hayes had been drinking when he approached Henry. A pair of sources confirmed that Hayes told Henry, "I'm more of a n----- that you are." One of the sources claims that it was a play on something MVP jokingly said about Hayes earlier in the night because of the white suit that he wore to the WWE Hall of Fame ceremony. Hayes then headbutted Henry in what one source described as a playful manner. Henry and Hayes exchanged words, and the former reported the issue to WWE officials." (Powell, "Dot Net Exclusive).

Hayes was suspended for 60 days without pay after Henry filed a complaint. Hayes currently works behind the scenes for the WWE. In 2008, Booker T discussed the incident during a conference call for TNA Wrestling, ""I don't look at Michael as a racist myself. I've heard him use the N-word before... He's one of the people who can use the word around me because I know there's no malice behind it." (qtd. in "Booker T discusses"). If Hayes has changed his ways, the WWE can point out that it gave him a second chance, but if things turn out differently, the WWE could face legal sanctions should one or more wrestlers prove discrimination and/or a hostile work environment.

Alberto Del Rio Incident: Despite Mexican-American grappler José Alberto Rodríguez enjoying a solid push in the WWE, he reportedly had to deal with racism backstage on more than one occasion. In 2014, Rodriguez was released from the WWE after slapping social media manager Cody Barbierri after Barbierri reportedly insulted Rodriguez' heritage. In 2014, Rodriguez discussed the incident on Televisa's *Primero Noticias* morning show, mentioning that it was not the first time the WWE's Barbierri made a racist remark:

> "The interviewer asks if he's had any incidents with this employee before and Alberto says yes. He said that "a while back" there was a time the WWE employee was pretending to read something on his laptop and said, "It says on here Alberto is a 'tal por cual' "(Mexican slang for a slut) and that he tried to play it off like it was a joke and shake Alberto's hand. Alberto refused and told the employee to get away from him. He said this incident

occurred 7 or 8 months prior to the slap. So when this incident occurred recently, Alberto demanded an apology, but that the WWE employee walked right up to Alberto's face, smirked at him and said nothing. That's when Alberto smacked him." (qtd. in Stroud).

Barbierri left the WWE several months after the incident and Rodriguez eventually returned to the WWE for a second but less successful run.

The WWE Chairman Himself—Out of Touch or Racist? Wrestling fans often point to 73-year-old McMahon as being out of touch when it comes to the wrestling product. Is he also out of touch with societal norms when it comes to ethnicity and gender? In the 2008 book *Ring of Hell: The Story of Chris Benoit and the Fall of the Pro Wrestling Industry:* WWE writer Dan Madigan discussed an incident involving Vince and Puerto Rican wrestler Carlito Colon:

"I remember when I was working with Carlito [Puerto Rican wrestler Carlos Colon] when he just started. Vince wanted to talk to him to get to know him, and I was asked to attend the meeting to help work out a character. So we're there, Carlito's talking to him, just a normal conversation; Carlito comes from a normal background, has money. He speaks well. Vince interrupts Carlito mid-sentence and says to him, 'Hey, can you spic it up some? Y'know spic it up when you talk?' I look at Vince, this billionaire who just asked some Puerto Rican employee to 'spic it up' right to his face, and I just look at Carlito and say, 'Yeah, spic it up' like it was a joke," says Madigan, laughing. "Vince's image of a Puerto Rican was a Puerto Rican pimp. How out of touch do you have to be to not realize you could get in trouble for that?" (qtd. in Clark, "Big RAW Spoiler")

That's not the only allegation made concerning McMahon's questionable opinions and conduct. In a 2015 podcast, Jim Ross recalled his discussion with McMahon about bringing in Gail Kim into the WWE, "I remember Vince said, 'You want to hire this Asian girl, right? I don't know, I just don't know.' And I said, 'Well Vince, you know, there's a lot of guys that like Asian women. There's Asian porn sites.'" (Clark). Ross recalls Vince was surprised at the revelation. After Ross' podcast, Gail Kim tweeted, "Nothing I'm really surprised at concerning @VinceMcMahon yes it's in poor taste but it's his character" (qtd. in Clark "Vince McMahon Reportedly").

Fans can only look at these and other allegations before deciding how to view the WWE's past, but it is too early to tell if the Kofi Kingston storyline represents a racist policy. Although the WWE has a questionable history in terms of racism, the current storyline involving Kofi Kingston seems to be a case of the WWE playing up an underdog story while incorporating elements of individuals dealing with racial discrimination. Given the WWE's history, the company is treading on dangerous ground and would be wise in how they frame Kofi's narrative. The WWE's track record with handling sensitive issues such as discrimination speaks for itself whether it's Booker T's quest to defeat Triple H for the World Heavyweight Championship or their treatment of wrestler Muhammad Hassan, whose original gimmick was that of an Arab-American angered by negative depictions of all Arab-Americans as villains, but who quickly degenerated into a stereotypical villain himself.

2019 would be a huge year for Kofi Kingston as he went on to win the WWE Championship at the WWE's flagship show WrestleMania and hold the title for six months, a testament to the WWE's faith in him. Kingston eventually dropped the title but it was controversial as he lost it to the WWE's resident monster, Brock Lesnar in nine seconds. This is known as a squash match (a wrestling match where a wrestler gets no offense in and is summarily destroyed). Some critics saw this as the WWE downplaying Kingston's reign as champion while others pointed out that Lesnar has destroyed other opponents in squash matches.

Kofi Kingston would be one of several African-American world champions in the WWE since 2019 including his New Day teammate "Big E" and Bobby Lashley, who held the WWE Championship twice.

Works Cited

Beary, Dion. "Pro Wrestling Is Fake, but Its Race Problem Isn't." *The Atlantic.* Culture. 10 July 2014. https://www.theatlantic.com/entertainment/archive/2014/07/the-not-so-fictional-bias-in-the-wwe-world-championship/374042. Accessed 23 Mar. 2019.

"Booker T discusses Michael Hayes and racism in WWE, Bobby Lashley's future, the new heel faction in TNA, Slammiversary's King of the Mountain match." *Prowrestlingnet.* News. 3 June 2008. https://prowrestling.net/artman/publish/TNA/article1001638.shtml. Accessed 23 Mar. 2019.

Clark, Ryan. "Big RAW Spoiler, Vince's Racist Remarks Towards Carlito?" *WrestleZone.*

Home. 23 June 2008.
https://www.mandatory.com/wrestlezone/news/204941-big-raw-spoiler-vinces-racist-remarks-torward-carlito#jzsOk67Wyr7fpPvo.99. Accessed 23 Mar. 2019.

Clark, Ryan. "Vince McMahon Reportedly Hesitated on Hiring Gail Kim Because She Was Asian-American, JR Reacts." *EWWrestling News.* News. 11 July 2015. https://www.ewrestlingnews.com/articles/vince-mcmahon-reportedly-hesitated-on-hiring-gail-kim-because-she-was-asian-american-jr-reacts. Accessed 23 Mar. 2019.

Dennis Jr., David. "Triple H Beating Booker T at WrestleMania 19 Is Still Unforgivable 15 Years Later." *Uproxx.* With Spandex. 3 Apr. 2018. https://uproxx.com/prowrestling/triple-h-booker-t-wrestlemania-19-anniversary. Accessed 23 Mar. 2019.

"Dot Net Exclusive: WWE Smackdown lead writer Michael Hayes serving a 60-day suspension for using a racial slur." *Prowrestling.net.* News. 23 Apr. 2008. https://prowrestling.net/artman/publish/WWE/article1001127.shtml. Accessed 23 Mar. 2019.

Harris, Keith. "Racial whistleblower Mark Henry is

tormented again by WWE management."
Cageside Seats. WWE. 3 June 2011.
https://www.cagesideseats.com/2011/6/3/2203867/racial-whistleblower-mark-henry-is-tormented-again-by-wwe-management.
Accessed 23 Mar. 2019.

Konuwa, Alfred. "The 5 Most Embarrassing Facts About WWE And Its Handling of Black Superstars." *Forbes*. Sports Money. 6 Feb. 2019.
https://www.forbes.com/sites/alfredkonuwa/2019/02/06/the-5-most-embarrassing-statistics-about-black-wwe-superstars.
Accessed 23 Mar. 2019.

Konuwa, Alfred. "WWE Raw Results: Hulk Hogan And the Winners and Losers of The First Raw Of 2019." *Forbes*. Sports Money. 8 Jan. 2019.
https://www.forbes.com/sites/alfredkonuwa/2019/01/08/wwe-raw-results-hulk-hogan-and-the-winners-and-losers-of-the-first-raw-of-2019. Accessed 23 Mar. 2019.

Paglino, Nick. "Alberto Del Rio Reveals More Details Behind Backstage WWE Incident, Says Another Incident Took Place with the Same WWE Employee 8 Months Ago." *Wrestlezone*. Wrestling News. 18 Aug. 2014.
https://www.mandatory.com/wrestlezone/news/503655-alberto-del-rio-reveals-release-

details#e4iPyQgTB4hk6Psa.99. Accessed 23 Mar. 2019.

Paul, Jayson. "JTG: Was Vince McMahon Showing Racial Stereotypes by Creating Cryme Tyme?" *The Sports Daily*. Floor Seat. 23 Aug. 2018. https://thesportsdaily.com/2018/08/23/was-vince-mcmahon-showing-racial-stereotypes-by-creating-cryme-tyme-tfs11. Accessed 23 Mar. 2019.

Rueter, Sean. "Big E: 'People like us can only get so far' in WWE." *Cageside Seats*. WWE. 20 Mar. 2019. https://www.cagesideseats.com/wwe/2019/3/20/18274358/big-e-twitter-promo-video-addresses-racial-aspect-kofi-kingston-vince-mcmahon-wrestlemania-story. Accessed 23 Mar. 2019.

Satin, Ryan. "Gail Kim Clarifies WWE Racism Allegations, 'It Comes from The Top.'" *Pro Wrestling Sheet*. Home. 6 Nov. 2018. http://www.prowrestlingsheet.com/gail-kim-wwe-racism/#.XJZpw5hKhPY. Accessed 23 Mar. 2019.

Stroud, Brandon. "The WWE Employee Who Made A Racist Joke and Got Alberto Del Rio Fired Has Left the Company." *Uproxx*. With Spandex. 24 Oct. 2014. https://uproxx.com/prowrestling/the-wwe-employee-who-made-a-racist-joke-and-got-alberto-del-rio-fired-has-left-the-company. Accessed 23 Mar. 2019.

Wong, Kevin. "12 Other Pro Wrestling Personalities Who Reportedly Said Horrifically Racist Things." *Complex*. 27 July 2015. https://www.complex.com/sports/2015/07/wwe-racism. Accessed 23 Mar. 2019.

Works Referenced

Clark, Tom. "WWE: Race and the WWE Championship." *Bleacher Report*. WWE. 27 May 2011. https://bleacherreport.com/articles/714642-wwe-race-and-the-wwe-championship. Accessed 23 Mar. 2019.

Powell, Jason. "TMZ questions whether the Michael Hayes incident led to Mark Henry's ECW Title win." *Prowrestlingnet*. WWE News. 30 June 2008. https://prowrestling.net/artman/publish/WWE/article1001963.shtml. Accessed 23 Mar. 2019.

Price, Mark. "Wrestling star Charlotte Flair hurled racist remarks at cops in Chapel Hill, lawsuit says." *Charlotte Observer*. Local. 22 Oct. 2018. https://www.charlotteobserver.com/news/l

ocal/article220428260.html. Accessed 22 Mar. 2019.

Wilkins, Ernest. "5 Pretty Racist Storyline Moments Still on the WWE Network." *Rolling Stone.* Sports. 24 July 2015. https://www.rollingstone.com/culture/culture-sports/5-pretty-racist-storyline-moments-still-on-the-wwe-network-48721. Accessed 23 Mar. 2019.

The WWE has found itself accused of some questionable promotional tactics but its 2018 decision to partner with the Saudi Arabian government is one of its most controversial in recent memory.

Chapter Twelve: Financial Opportunity or Blood Money?

Originally published 2019

In 2018 the WWE announced it had signed a 10-year deal with Saudi Arabia to run WWE live events in the Middle Eastern country. The events are rumored to bring the WWE anywhere from $45 to $70 million per year (Giri). In 2018, the WWE ran two events, *The Greatest Royal Rumble* and *Crown Jewel,* which featured many WWE top stars. This continued in 2019 with the WWE running *Super Show-Down* and its second *Crown Jewel* event scheduled for 31 October. However, the shows were not without controversy, and several WWE Superstars refused to participate in the event, citing the many claims of human rights abuse leveled at the Saudi government. While the WWE saw this as an opportunity to help Saudi Arabia's harsh treatment of women and the LGBT community, others see it as nothing less than a cold-hearted cash grab.

What Makes Saudi Arabia Different?

The WWE is a company that routinely tours around the globe, yet what is it about Saudi Arabia that has generated so much backlash? The answer is that Saudi Arabia has come under scrutiny for its human rights abuses and a government accused of repressing the rights of women and the LGBT community. There have been many complaints made against the Saudi government, too many to discuss in detail in this video. However, let's address some of the more serious allegations.

In 2019, the group Human Rights Watch summarized many of the complaints made against the Saudi government in 2018:

> Saudi authorities stepped up their arbitrary arrests, trials, and convictions of peaceful dissidents and activists in 2018, including a large-scale coordinated crackdown against the women's rights movement beginning in May. In June, Saudi Arabia ended the long-standing ban on women driving, but authorities continued to discriminate against women and religious minorities. Through 2018, the Saudi-led coalition continued a military campaign against the Houthi rebel group in Yemen that has included scores of unlawful airstrikes that have

killed and wounded thousands of
civilians. ("Saudi Arabia. Events")

Repressing Women

While there have been reforms made in
Saudi Arabia, women are still treated much
differently from men, whether it is gender
segregation, limited employment opportunities, or
seemingly trivial activities. For example, according
to a 3 September 2019 news article, women are
still prohibited from: 1) wearing clothes or make-
up that" show off their beauty,"; interacting with
men to whom they aren't related; 3) competing
free in sports; and 4) trying on clothes when they
go shopping (Powe).

One of the prime examples of the Saudi
government treating women differently is its ban
on women performing at WWE events. The
WWE has repeatedly stated it hopes to change this
at some point, but so far it hasn't happened.
However, the Saudi government has relaxed some
of its harsher policies towards women as we'll
address shortly.

Persecuting the LGBTQ Community

Although Saudi Arabia is by no means
alone in its nontolerance of gay and transgender
persons. According to a report by human-rights
group Amnesty International:

"Same-sex sexual activity is a crime in
70 countries, and can get you a death

sentence in nine countries, including Iran, Saudi Arabia, Sudan and Yemen. And even where these restrictive laws are not actually enforced, their very existence reinforces prejudice against LGBTI people, leaving them feeling like they have no protection against harassment, blackmail and violence.

A Harsh Criminal Justice System

The Saudi Arabian criminal justice has been criticized for its harshness as noted in a 2019 report by Human Rights Watch:

Saudi Arabia applies Sharia (Islamic law) as its national law. There is no formal penal code, but the government has passed some laws and regulations that subject certain broadly-defined offenses to criminal penalties. In the absence of a written penal code or narrowly-worded regulations, however, judges and prosecutors can convict people on a wide range of offenses under broad, catch-all charges such as "breaking allegiance with the ruler" or "trying to distort the reputation of the kingdom." Detainees, including children, commonly face systematic violations of due process and fair trial rights, including arbitrary arrest. Judges routinely sentence defendants to floggings of hundreds of lashes. Children can be tried for capital crimes and sentenced as adults if they show physical signs of puberty. ("Saudi Arabia Events")

Saudi Arabia's Involvement in the War in Yemen

Since 2015, Saudi Arabia has led a coalition to restore the former Yemeni government. However, Saudi Arabia has come under pressure for allegedly targeting civilians and engaging in activities possibly classifiable as war crimes (although opposition forces have been accused of similar practices).

The Murder of Journalist Jamal Khashoggi

On 2 October 2018, Saudi journalist entered the Saudi consulate in Istanbul, Turkey. However, Khashoggi, a critic of the Saudi government's oppressive policies, never left the consulate. Saudi officials initially claimed he had left the building, but Turkish officials and the CIA argued that he'd been murdered in the consulate by Saudi agents. Ultimately, evidence surfaced proving Khashoggi had been strangled there and dismembered with a bone saw. Saudi Crown Prince Mohammed bin Salman denied knowledge of the assassination before it happened, but eventually acknowledged that it happened "on his watch."

Saudi Arabia Defends Itself

The Saudi government has defended its actions and refuted many of the accusations made against it. Concerning the war in Yemen, the Saudi United Nations mission stated:

> "We were alarmed and outraged at Amnesty International and Human Rights Watch's statement accusing Saudi Arabia of unlawful attacks in Yemen. Saudi Arabia and the coalition have complied with international law at every stage in the campaign to restore Yemen's legitimate government."
> ("Saudi Arabia outraged")

The Saudis also rebuffed accusations that it targeted civilians (including children):

> "We have created an independent team of experts tasked with assessing such cases and developing enhanced targeting mechanisms to ensure the safety and protection of civilians. Attempts at delegitimizing Saudi Arabia's efforts to restore stability and find a sustainable political solution by these organizations run counter to their very mission and risks peace and

security in Yemen and the world."
("Saudi Arabia outraged")

It's important to mention the Saudi government has implemented reforms, such as allowing women to drive, allowing women to serve in the military, and discontinuing the former policy that put women under the guardianship of men (the law now states women over 21 are free from guardianship. However, the Saudi government continues to crack down on political dissent, with accusations made that it censors free speech and represses any opposition voices.

Blood Money

Critics have accused the WWE of taking "blood money" from the Saudi government. Blood money is also associated with "money gained at the expense/suffering of others" ("blood money" Idioms). This concept ties in with "blood diamonds," (aka conflict diamonds or war diamonds)—diamonds mined in a war zone and sold to finance an insurgency, an invading army's war efforts, or a warlord's activity" ("Blood diamond"). In this case, the WWE is being paid to provide a commodity to legitimize the government of Saudi Arabia. Not everyone agrees with his analogy, but as always, I'll present the evidence and leave the judgment to you, the reader.

Sports-washing and Soft Power

The main argument against the WWE running a show in Saudi Arabia is that its presence there legitimizes the Saudi Arabian government, despite the many allegations of human rights leveled against it. The WWE is by no means the only entertainment agency which has succumbed to the practice known as sports-washing.

> The term sports-washing is:
>> derived from whitewashing - a deliberate attempt to conceal unpleasant or incriminating facts. By definition, this means co-opting the backing, even the gratitude, of one group of people while riding roughshod over another. Divide, conquer, bask in the glow. Individuals and corporations have their own versions, bankrolling the feelgood factor of sport in the expectation that it will rub off on them. (Slattery)

In an article on sports-washing, the Asia and Pacific Policy Society discusses the term at length:

>> Although the term sport-washing has strongly established itself in the mainstream global vernacular this year, it is not entirely clear what it is… In one definition, sport-washing is identified as being employed by authoritarian regimes that use mega-

161

> sports events to reboot their reputations and distract audiences from their horrific human-rights records. In another definition, sporting events are used to sideline critical views of a government and serve to launder its image and reputation." (Chadwick)

As noted in the article about sports-washing:

> such definitions are both presumptuous and troubling. In particular, they both imply that people readily (and instantaneously) forget about a nation's misdemeanours and underpinning ideology simply because, for example, a group of cyclists spend little more than ten hours riding around the country. (Chadwick)

Examples of sports-washing include Israel hosting the Giro D'Italia cycling event and Russia hosting the football World Cup in 2018. There were calls for boycotts of the Giro D'Italia due to Israel's alleged human rights' abuses (Abraham) but the event went on as planned. Hosting the World Cup was seen as a way for Russia to deflect its image as a repressive and authoritarian government.

Sports-washing is often considered a form of soft power:

a term coined by the US political scientist Joseph Nye, broadly defined as a way of reaching objectives through the power of attraction rather than military and economic force. Sources of soft power can be movies, music, world-renowned universities and, of course, sports. (Jiménez-Martínez and Skey).

Likewise, the WWE has been criticized for its arrangement with the Saudi government, with critics arguing it knowingly legitimizes a government with well-documented human rights violation.

WWE Superstars Refuse to Work

Some WWE Superstars have refused to participate in the WWE's Saudi events, including Daniel Bryan, John Cena, and Kevin Owens. Owens is rumored to have refused to work the event because Saudi officials asked that Sami Zayn not participate (Zayn, a Canadian citizen is of Syrian descent and Saudi Arabia has an uneasy relationship with Syria). Aleister Black has not worked the events either, although it's unclear if it's by choice or due to rumors his tattoos offend Saudi officials' religious sensibilities.

Many Superstars worked the Saudi events and defended their decision. Randy Orton told *TMZ* about why he chose to go:

> "I think we should go. I think the only way to help with change over there is to go and not cancel the trip. Our girls performed in Abu Dhabi not too long ago and I think we'll be there eventually with Saudi and Crown Jewel. That's the goal, to make things better everywhere, and I think us not going, doesn't help. Going helps… I've got 5 kids, I gotta go make that dollar. If they want me in Saudi, I'm going to Saudi." (Konuwa)

Interestingly, there were defenses made by female Superstars, despite Saudi Arabia prohibiting women from competing in the WWE events held there. Natalya spoke with *The Tampa Bay Times* about the situation: "You're not going to change a culture overnight. I think WWE is taking such positive steps in doing positive things over in Saudi Arabia. One day, I believe that we will be over there" (qtd. in Konuwa). Ronda Rousey likened the event to her time in the Olympics where athletes from a variety of nations competed, ignoring politics. She went on to tell *TMZ Sports:*

> "I think pulling out of Crown Jewel would be the wrong move because this is an opportunity to share our cultures and find what we have in common. Especially in times of adversity

between two countries that's the absolute wrong time to be able to pull away. That's the time to find out what we have in common and be able to understand each other more. It seems almost frivolous—these WWE events and these big world issues, but in a world where we're always looking at it like 'us' and 'them,' I think those big events like Crown Jewel that bring everyone together just makes us realize it's 'us' all around. "I think having these events and sharing our culture in Saudi Arabia is the first step for us to really be able to understand each other and find that common ground. I mean, this is a great opportunity for a bunch of kids in Saudi Arabia [who love] American culture—WWE is part of American culture [and] they are inviting [it] in and embracing it...I think that should be the goal. An 'eye for and eye' leaves the whole world blind." (qtd. in Konuwa)

The WWE's Response

The WWE's chief argument for running the event (besides the boatload of cash it brings in every year) is that it is a way to effect changes in the Saudi government's treatment of women. The

WWE's Triple H defended the company when it ran its first Saudi show, *The Greatest Royal Rumble:*

"I understand that people are questioning it, but you have to understand that every culture is different and just because you don't agree with a certain aspect of it, it doesn't mean it's not a relevant culture. "You can't dictate to a country or a religion about how they handle things but, having said that, WWE is at the forefront of a women's evolution in the world and what you can't do is affect change anywhere by staying away from it. "While, right now, women are not competing in the event, we have had discussions about that and we believe and hope that, in the next few years they will be. That is a significant cultural shift in Saudi Arabia. The country is in the middle of a shift in how it is dealing with that – the position is changing, and rights are changing, as are the way women are handled and treated in society. We think that's a great thing and we're excited to be at the forefront of that change." (Paddock)

When journalist Jamal Khashoggi was murdered in Saudi Arabia's consulate in Istanbul, Turkey, the WWE was urged to pull out of *Crown Jewel*. The WWE issued the following statement:

> "WWE has operated in the Middle East for nearly 20 years and has developed a sizeable and dedicated fan base," the company said. "Considering the heinous crime committed at the Saudi consulate in Istanbul, the company faced a very difficult decision as it relates to its event scheduled for November 2 in Riyadh." (qtd. in Osborne)

The WWE's Stephanie McMahon discussed the WWE's choice:

> "Moving forward with Crown Jewel in Saudi Arabia was an incredibly tough decision, given that heinous act. But, at the end of the day, it is a business decision and, like a lot of other American companies, we decided that we're going to move forward with the event and deliver Crown Jewel for all of our fans in Saudi Arabia and around the world." (qtd. in Javed)

The WWE's decision to go through was criticized by many, with ESPN's Dan LeBatard's commenting:

"Did you see that WWE is still going to Saudi Arabia? What a bad decision that is. But, it's the sewer and the sewer is going to behave like the sewer. There's a lot of money in Saudi Arabia, so much money, so wrestling is going back to Saudi Arabia as we wonder whether Saudi Arabia kills journalists with bone saws. We're usually not quite that overt like, 'Yeah, we'll take your money, your blood money, no matter what.'" (qtd. in Javed)

The Future

The WWE shows no sign of letting up in running shows in Saudi Arabia and seems to have doubled down for this year's *Crown Jewel,* airing two marquee matches (Cain Velasquez vs. Brock Lesnar and Tyson Fury vs. Braun Strowman) with reports of Fury receiving around $15 million for his appearance. While WWE Superstars may refuse to participate in the event, only a handful of performers have abstained from participating and it's arguable there is considerable pressure to perform.

As for the WWE itself, the promotion ran an event after the murder of a journalist at a Saudi embassy. The WWE ignored the firestorm of controversy surrounding the crime, so it's doubtful anything short of Stephanie McMahon disappearing in Saudi Arabia would lead to any withdrawal from the agreement.

The WWE's arrangement with Saudi Arabia will continue to generate controversy, but it also generates a lot of cash into the WWE's coffers so it is unlikely to go away soon.

In 2019, the first women's professional wrestling match was held in Saudi Arabia. 2019's **Crown Jewel** *show featured Natalya vs. Lacey Evans. Both women wore much more modest ring gear than they would in most of the countries they tour in. Since this event, the WWE has held women's matches in Saudi Arabia.*

On a less stellar note, a number of WWE wrestlers and employees experienced what the WWE called travel delays after its 2019 **Crown Jewel** *event. However, there were allegations that the Saudi Arabian government detained the WWE personnel after a dispute over payments owed to the WWE.*

Works Cited

Abraham, Richard. "Giro d'Italia's start in Israel provokes accusations of 'sport-washing'" *The Guardian.* The Observer. 24 Sept. 2017. https://www.theguardian.com/sport/2017/sep/24/israel-giro-ditalia-race-conflict-2018-start-cycling. Accessed 23 Oct. 2019.

"Amnesty turns the heat up on 'sportswashing' Manchester City owners." *The Guardian.* 10

Nov. 2018.
https://www.theguardian.com/football/201
8/nov/10/manchester-city-amnesty-
international-football-leaks. Accessed 22
Oct. 2019.

"Blood money." *Merriam Webster.* Dictionary.
https://www.merriam-
webster.com/dictionary/blood%20money.
Accessed 23 Oct. 2019.

"Blood money." *The Free Dictionary.* Idioms.
https://idioms.thefreedictionary.com/blood
+money. Accessed 23 Oct. 2019.

Chadwick, Simon. "Sport-washing, soft power and
scrubbing the stains." *Policy Forum.* 24 Aug.
2018. https://www.policyforum.net/sport-
washing-soft-power-and-scrubbing-the-
stains. Accessed 23 Oct. 2019.

Chiari, Mike. "WWE 'Monitoring the Situation' in
Saudi Arabia Ahead of Crown Jewel Event."
Bleacher Report. WWE. 12 Oct. 2018.
https://bleacherreport.com/articles/280046
9-wwe-monitoring-the-situation-in-saudi-
arabia-ahead-of-crown-jewel-event. Accessed
22 Oct. 2019.

Giri, Raj. "How Much WWE May Have Made
with Saudi Arabia Deal In 2018." *Wrestling
Inc.*
7 Feb. 2019.
https://www.wrestlinginc.com/news/2019/

02/how-much-wwe-may-have-made-with-saudi-arabia-deal-in-2019-650684. Accessed 23 Oct. 2019.

"Hold Saudi Arabia Accountable for Rights Violations." *Scholars at Risk Network.* 26 June 2019. https://www.scholarsatrisk.org/2019/06/hold-saudi-arabia-accountable-for-rights-violations. Accessed 23 Oct. 2019.

Javed. Saman. "WWE defends 'incredibly tough decision' to go to Saudi Arabia." *Independent.* News. 28 Oct. 2018. https://www.independent.co.uk/news/world/americas/wwe-wrestling-us-riyadh-saudi-arabia-jamal-khashoggi-a8605621.html. Accessed 23 Oct. 2019.

Jiménez-Martínez, César and Michael Skey. "How repressive states and governments use 'sportswashing' to remove stains on their reputation." *The Conversation.* Politics and Society. 25 July 2018. https://theconversation.com/how-repressive-states-and-governments-use-sportswashing-to-remove-stains-on-their-reputation-100395. Accessed 23 Oct. 2019.

Konuwa, Alfred. "'I've Got 5 Kids, I Gotta Go Make That Dollar': WWE Superstars Defend Crown Jewel in Saudi Arabia." *Forbes.* Sports Money.

https://www.forbes.com/sites/alfredkonuwa/2018/11/01/ive-got-5-kids-i-gotta-go-make-that-dollar-wwe-superstars-defend-crown-jewel-in-saudi-arabia. Accessed 23 Oct. 2019.

"LGBTI RIGHTS." *Amnesty International.* News. https://www.amnesty.org/en/what-we-do/discrimination/lgbt-rights. Accessed 23 Oct. 2019.

Osborne, Samuel. "Khashoggi news: Turkish president Erdogan urges Saudi Arabia to disclose who gave order to murder journalist." *Independent.* News. 26 Oct. 2018. https://www.independent.co.uk/news/world/middle-east/khashoggi-latest-update-saudi-arabia-extrajudicial-killing-bin-salman-mbs-recording-timeline-a8602191.html. Accessed 23 Oct. 2019.

Paddock, Matty. "WWE Greatest Royal Rumble: Triple H defends hosting event in Saudi Arabia without women wrestlers." *Independent.* Indy/Life. 26 Apr. 2018. https://www.independent.co.uk/sport/general/wwe-mma-wrestling/wwe-greatest-royal-rumble-saudi-arabia-triple-h-interview-defends-no-women-wrestlers-a8319446.html. Accessed 23 Oct. 2019.

Porter, Conor. "Details of WWE's 10-year deal with Saudi Arabia revealed." *Givemesport.*

News. 29 July 2018.
https://www.givemesport.com/1362981-details-of-wwes-10year-deal-with-saudi-arabia-revealed. Accessed 23 Oct. 2019.

Powe, Gabriel. "Things that women in Saudi Arabia still can't do." *The Week*. Middle East. 3 Sept. 2019. https://www.theweek.co.uk/60339/things-women-cant-do-in-saudi-arabia. Accessed 22 Oct. 2019.

"Saudi Arabia Events of 2018." *Human Rights Watch*. World Report 2019. https://www.hrw.org/world-report/2019/country-chapters/saudi-arabia. Accessed 23 Oct. 2019.

"Saudi Arabia Human Rights." *Amnesty International*. Saudi Arabia. https://www.amnestyusa.org/countries/saudi-arabia. Accessed 23 Oct. 2019.

"Saudi Arabia outraged by Amnesty International and Human Rights Watch's criticism." *YaLibnan.com*. Featured News. 1 July 2016. http://yalibnan.com/2016/07/01/saudi-arabia-outraged-by-amnesty-international-and-human-rights-watchs-criticism. Accessed 23 Oct. 2019.

"Saudi bout will 'grow boxing.'" *The Straits Times*. Sport. 14 Aug. 2019.

https://www.straitstimes.com/sport/saudi-bout-will-grow-boxing. Accessed 22 Oct. 2019.

Slattery, Laura. "'Sportswashing' is the grim game of our times." *Irish Times*. 30 Oct. 2018. https://www.irishtimes.com/business/media-and-marketing/sportswashing-is-the-grim-game-of-our-times-1.3679671. Accessed 23 Oct. 2019.

Wikipedia contributors. "Blood diamond."

Wikipedia, The Free Encyclopedia. Wikipedia, The Free Encyclopedia, 22 Oct. 2019. https://en.wikipedia.org/wiki/Blood_diamond. Accessed 23 Oct. 2019.

While the question of whether professional wrestling is a sport continues to rage, there's little doubt its stars are athletes. As such are they entitled to the same protections as NFL players who sued the NFL for the harm caused by concussions? The WWE was forced to address this when a group of former wrestlers participated in a class-action lawsuit against the company based on alleged harm caused by their time in the ring.

Chapter Thirteen: The WWE Concussion Lawsuit

Originally published 2017

Over the last decade there has been litigation against sports leagues alleging that they knew the dangerous effects of concussions on players but failed to inform them. Such was the case with the WWE when a group of former wrestlers sued the WWE in a class-action lawsuit based on concussions. However, who are the players, what is the basis, for their claims, and what does the lawsuit look like? What ended up happening to the case and is the WWE free and clear of any further lawsuits? Keep in mind that the lawsuit is a complicated case so this is an overview rather than a detailed summary.

The Players

The lawsuit included 53 wrestlers pursuing a class-action lawsuit against the WWE. This includes Superstars who worked in the WWWF, the WWF, and the WWE. Some of these wrestlers had short runs in the WWE while others had extended stays. Since some of these wrestlers have passed away, the case may be in the wrestler's estate, waiting to be divided should the plaintiffs prevail either at trial or via settlement. The Kyros Law Firm represents the wrestlers with managing partner Konstantine Kyros working in the six-member legal team. This is not the first time the Kyros Law Firm has represented wrestlers suing the WWE.

World Wrestling Entertainment has been named as the defendant. The WWE responded to the lawsuit with a statement that read:

> This is another ridiculous attempt by the same attorney who has previously filed class-action lawsuits against WWE, both of which have been dismissed...A federal judge has already found that this lawyer made patently false allegations about WWE, and this is more of the same. We're confident this lawsuit will suffer the same fate as his prior attempts and be dismissed (Hohler "WWE wins important rulings in concussion lawsuits").

The Kyros Firm responded, ""It has been the studied practice of WWE through its counsel to denigrate the motives and integrity of anyone who is courageous enough to protest WWE's self-serving choice to ignore the human toll and health crisis that its policies, fraud, and mistreatment of its workers have created" (Hohler "WWE wins important rulings in concussion lawsuits").

The Claims

The authors investigated the plaintiffs' claims, relying on the Kyros Law Firm's blog concerning the lawsuit. The lawsuit contains five main arguments why the WWE should be held responsible for the concussions and CTE suffered by wrestlers. First, the plaintiffs argue there is a history of medical neglect and indifference by the WWE. Second, plaintiffs refer to the long and grueling schedule they worked where there is no off-season and few days to rest. Third, the plaintiffs argue said medical neglect and dangerous work schedule led to injuries, drug addiction, and even death for wrestlers. Fourth, plaintiffs point out that long-term head injuries take a toll. Fifth, the plaintiffs argue the WWE knew about the CTE crisis and did not take any steps to deal with it until 2007. Furthermore, they argue the WWE has not helped retired wrestlers who may have concussions and/or CTE. Central to this lawsuit is the idea the WWE intentionally mislabeled wrestlers as independent contractors rather than employers so they could shift liability for injuries. Part of the plaintiffs' complaint alleges, "WWE control[s] Plaintiffs' personal lives just as strictly as their professional careers. The WWE regulated what the Plaintiffs could wear in public, how they traveled, where they trained, how they trained, where, when, and how they performed, and what medical treatment they received, if any" ("WWE Misclassification Lawsuit Claims Performers' Status as Independent Contractors Caused Long-Term Brain Injuries").

This Kyros website log contains two important statements regarding the foundation of the lawsuit. The first is the argument the WWE's policies and practices exploited wrestlers:

> … an extensive investigation into the policies and practices of the WWE which has revealed a systematic exploitative business practice which use unconscionable booking contracts to deceive the wrestlers about their legal rights- which deprived them of the legal protections that are given to US workers under federal labor and employment laws. Without these protections which were enacted to protect workers health and safety, the wrestler after retirement is now in a

health crisis with many disabled because of their wrestling careers. Also note that the wrestlers are, per the plaintiffs' allegations, misclassified as independent contractors, deprived of statutory rights and OSHA regulation further eroding a defense by WWE as compared to other contact sports in which there is an employment relationship, unionization, regulation and public oversight of the activities that may result in injury. A quick review of the plaintiffs' factual allegations in the complaint reveals where they are now (broken in body and mind, many now disabled) graphically showing the outcome of the unregulated regime that WWE has maintained over these athletes" ("WWE Concussion Lawsuit Claims Center").

The second argument concerns the head injuries suffered by wrestlers:

The plaintiffs allege head injuries in two forms: 1) Open and obvious concussions that WWE failed to adequately treat and diagnose as well as 2) long term effects and risks of repeated head trauma that can cause an occupational disease like CTE that a wrestler would not know about unless educated by a doctor or WWE. Thus, the wrestling match in ring activity itself (the routine, ordinary bumps and maneuvers) as well as the so called "accidental" incidents that often result in concussion cause latent, unseen and long-term harm that results in damages to the plaintiffs. That physical activity itself which during its routine performance is causing unseen harm for which there is a duty to warn, the same is true in other contact sports Such as the NFL, and NHL in which routine head trauma also appears to result in CTE and latent occupational neurological disease ("WWE Concussion Lawsuit Claims Center").

There is also plaintiffs' claim the WWE assumed liability for ECW and WCW when it acquired the companies in 2001. As we discussed in the chapter on the WCW racism lawsuit, a company normally does not acquire another company's liabilities when it purchases it. However, plaintiffs argue the WWE accepted the liabilities because it met the conditions that "...the transaction may be viewed as a de facto merger or consolidation...and...the successor is the mere continuation of the predecessor" ("WWE's Liability extends to all ECW and WCW Matches"). Given the firm that pursued the WCW case to a successful settlement did not pursue the WWE for damages concerning WCW, it can be argued Kyros' case for the WWE being liable for ECW and WCW's actions is weak here.

The Defense

The WWE has several defenses concerning the lawsuit. One is there was an assumption of risk by the wrestlers, i.e., they knew the job involved a worked environment, but there were still assumed risks of injury. A second is WWE Superstars are independent contractors rather than employees, and responsible for their own medical care. A third defense is that 19 of the individuals named in the lawsuit waived their right to suing the WWE when they signed earlier agreements (Nath). This includes stars such as Bill Eadie (aka Demolition Ax) who the WWE claims signed an earlier agreement concerning his use of the Demolition Ax character which also saw him sign away his right to sue concerning anything related to his WWE career. Another example is, "Henry Godwin (Mark Canterbury), who signed on June 15th of this year 'from any and all personal injury claims, now known or later discovered, arising out of or related to [his] past affiliation with, or performances rendered to, WWE' (Bixenspan).

Keep in mind in some cases, a plaintiff cannot sign away rights to pursue a lawsuit, but that is something the court will have to determine.

What is CTE?

Chronic traumatic encephalopathy (CTE) was named by Dr. Bennet Omalu, a physician, forensic pathologist, and neuropathologist. Dr. Omalu noticed abnormalities in the brains of football players after conducting autopsies on them, which led to further exploration of the brain damage caused by repeated blows to the head. Dr. Omalu called this condition chronic traumatic encephalopathy (CTE) and warned the NFL about it. The NFL's response was slow but a lawsuit settlement in August of 2013 ("Concussions in American Football") suggests the NFL realized the dangers of CTE (if not, then the dangers of CTE litigation).

The role of concussions in affecting people's long-term health has been brought to the public's attention, largely due to the NFL's legal settlement with former players who claimed concussions impacted their health and the NFL did not take the proper steps to protect them.

The effects of even a mild concussion can be powerful. According to the U.S. National Institute of Health, a study found:

Comparing 50 concussion patients with the same number of healthy people, researchers found that the brains of those suffering concussions showed abnormalities four months later. This happened despite the fact that their symptoms had already eased to some degree (Salamon). In some cases, people who are concussed suffer from post-concussion syndrome. The treatment for post-concussion syndrome is rest and avoiding stress. Since professional wrestlers often work hurt, it's easy to see how a concussed wrestler may suffer for a long time (qtd. in Salamon).

Given the proliferation of unprotected chair shots and other impactful moves that can be go wrong, some suggest there is evidence to support the dangerous work environment of wrestlers. However, according to a 2016 article, scientists have not linked CTE with the activities performed by professional wrestlers, unlike research connecting CTE with NFL players (Hohler "Ex-wrestlers say one of their own sells them short").

Wrestlers' Thoughts

What do wrestlers and retired wrestlers think of the lawsuit? There are a number of opinions but each of them summarizes the perceived merit or perceived lack of merit concerning the claims.

Wrestler "Jumping" Jim Brunzell of the Killer Bees is a plaintiff in the case and recalls having to work a match the night after he was accidentally knocked out in the ring. Brunzell said in a 2016 interview:

> So, I can't remember who the agent was who said, 'He has to work tonight, because we have no substitute.' We went over and I was working with Hercules, Ray Fernandez, and the doctor told him, 'The only way that I will let Jim wrestle tonight is if you don't hit him in the head, slam him, or - in any way - kick him in the head.' We agreed and had a pretty decent match, and he got disqualified. But, the reason why I did that, was because there [was] no thought in head injuries during that early time of the [WWE]. And what this lawsuit is trying to get is money from the WWE to put it in a pool to compensate for these guys that might have early dementia, and it's the same lawsuit that got the four billion dollars from the NFL ("Former WWE Tag Team Star 'Jumping' Jim Brunzell Explains Current WWE Lawsuit, Says Vince McMahon 'Does Not Like Him. Hulk Hogan Returning'").

Against

Retired wrestler Lance Storm is against the lawsuit. In a 2016 interview with *The Calgary Eyeopener*, Storm noted, ""At the end of the day, pro wrestling is designed to be a non-contact sport in a way...It's not a true competitive sport, it's a performance art and when you do the job properly, you don't actually hit people very hard" (Dormer). The 25-year veteran wrestler claims he never was diagnosed with a concussion but he is working with the Concussion Legacy Foundation, participating in an annual evaluation to help study the impact of concussions. Storm also has made plans to donate his brain and brain stem to the Foundation. Storm believes drugs and alcohol may play a role in CTE:

> There's a lot of drugs and alcohol involved in sport and we don't know what role that plays in addition to concussions…They've got football players, they've got basketball players, they've got wrestlers. I was someone that never drank and never did drugs of any kind, so when they're doing this study, if my results are different than other athletes that suffered the similar physical symptoms, then perhaps the results could be compounded or due more to the drugs and alcohol and

lifestyle of professional athletes (Dormer).

Wrestler Dan Spivey has his own thoughts on the lifestyle of WWF Superstars during the 1980's:

> I got into wrestling because I loved it. I wanted more than anything to be a WWF/WWE Superstar. Did I get injured? Yes. 6 hip replacements, neck fusion, knee replacement, plus a few other minor injuries, but I was never forced to work hurt and these never stopped me from living my dream. Did I work 7 days a week? Yes, because in the 80s thats what you did to be the best at what you loved. Because of the WWF/WWE I traveled the world, I became a household name, and loved it! Did I have an addiction to drugs and alcohol? Yes, but not because of wrestling, but because of me. I can tell you, 6 years later I am clean and sober...because of the WWE. The WWE has a program in place where former WWF/WWE Superstars can go to a rehab facility, all expenses paid, no questions asked, which I was able to take advantage of. The WWE has had

this program in place since 2007 (Pena).

The Wild Card

One of the most interesting aspects of the case is Chris Nowinski's Concussion Legacy Foundation, a non-profit organization which studies CTE. Some believe the WWE will rely on Nowinski's Foundation to support their defense. A possible problem is the WWE has pledged $2.7 million dollars to the Foundation and Triple H is a member of their board of directors. In a 2016 interview, Marc Pollick of the Giving Back Fund, a nonprofit which manages charities for athletes, entertainers, and corporations commented, "It certainly seems like a situation where you're asking the foxes to help guard the chicken coop...If you're partnering with a company that is facing those kinds of [concussion lawsuits], where's the firewall?" (Hohler, "Ex-wrestlers say one of their own sells them short"). WWE attorney Jerry McDevitt was quoted in a 2016 article, "'We don't in any way try to control their affairs,' McDevitt said of Nowinski, his foundation, and its related organizations" (Hohler).

Attempting a Settlement

The judge ordered both parties to settle the case, looking to avoid a trial. The Kyros Law Firm stated on its August 30,2017 blog, "What types of relief do wrestlers want? This is a very basic summary. Ideas for resolving the case include:

1. Full Health insurance coverage for all Plaintiffs and their families who do not have it or cannot afford it/supplemental polices for people on Medicare/Medicaid;

2. Lump sum disability and/or disability payouts based on medical diagnosis- in part based on total number of WWE/ECW/WCW matches/offset by SSDI/SSI;

3. WWE should pay for medical monitoring for CTE for all Plaintiffs;

4. Additional payouts for diagnosed neurological conditions for Plaintiffs with qualifying diagnoses (real issues discovered by a doctor);

5. WWE should Pay for comprehensive Mortality/Death Rate in Wrestling Study with view to helping lower it;

6.Program to build and improve outreach to wrestlers in need (expand drug and alcohol program and tie it to overall medical care);

7. Fair royalty payments and a full accounting to all plaintiffs;

8. WWE should Correctly classify wrestlers as employees;

9.WWE should Finance wrestler-specific CTE research (unlike just giving millions to other sports/military CTE studies); and

10. WWE should give lump sum payments to Plaintiffs with CTE diagnoses after death

The WWE has denied a link between CTE and wrestlers so would they settle?

Possible Outcomes

While the case was in the settlement phase, there was the possibility the WWE might concede and make a payment rather than taking the case to trial and risking an even larger judgment should the plaintiffs prevail. Anyone familiar with Vince McMahon's refusal to give in during his steroid trial, and his hard-fought battle against WCW knew there was little chance of a settlement. McMahon did not give in and the case proceeded further.

On September 20, 2018, the court reached a decision. According to *NBC News:*

> U.S. District Judge Vanessa Bryant in Hartford threw out the lawsuit Monday, saying many of the claims were frivolous or filed after the statute of limitations expired. Stamford-based

WWE denied the lawsuit's allegations. Bryant also criticized the wrestlers' lawyer, Konstantine Kyros, based in Hingham, Massachusetts, for repeatedly failing to comply with court rules and orders and ordered him to pay WWE's legal fees, which could total hundreds of thousands of dollars. ("Former WWE stars' concussion lawsuit")

The plaintiffs' attorney vowed to file an appeal and on July 9, 2019, the Kyros WWE Concussion Lawsuit blog announced:

The WWE wrestlers suing WWE for CTE, employment misclassification, wrongful death and concealment of the risks of head injuries filed their final appeal in the Second Circuit Court of Appeals in New York on July 8, 2019. The Appeal was filed by Kyros Law Offices. We are grateful to everyone for your support for wrestlers' rights and our efforts to help these women and men who have given their lives to entertainment and professional wrestling. The Appeal consolidates five appeals (and two motions for sanctions) for over 60 wrestlers and their families. ("Wrestlers' Last Stand")

Regardless of how the lawsuit turns out, it raises important issues about wrestlers' safety and the shadowy border wrestlers walk between being independent contractors and employees. The WWE has taken steps to deal with concussion issues, substance abuse issues, and the use performance enhancing drugs. While it can be argued these are self-serving and not flawless (particularly its Wellness Policy concerning the use of performance enhancing drugs), it can also be argued the WWE deserves credit for this, particularly its open invitation for any former employee to avail themselves of substance abuse rehabilitation treatment.

Given the NFL's recent settlement concerning concussions, the WWE faces possible liability if the case were to be continued via a successful appeal. If the appellate court denies the plaintiffs' appeal, the case will go away and the WWE will have dodged a bullet.

In 2020, the United States Court of Appeals for the Second Circuit dismissed the lawsuits. An appeal was filed to the Supreme Court of the United States, but the court declined to hear the case, effectively ending it.

Works Cited

Bieler, Des. "Dozens of wrestlers sue WWE over

CTE, effects of traumatic brain injuries." *Chicago Tribune.* 19 July 2016. http://www.chicagotribune.com/sports/breaking/ct-wwe-cte-lawsuit-20160719-story.html. Accessed 1 Sept. 2017.

Bixenspan, David. "WWE Claims 19 of 50+ Wrestlers in Concussion Lawsuit Signed Away Right to Sue." *SE Scoops.* 17 Oct. 2016. http://www.sescoops.com/wwe-claims-19-of-50-wrestlers-in-concussion-lawsuit-signed-away-right-to-sue. Accessed 3 Sept. 2017.

Clark, Ryan. "Judge Orders Settlement Discussions in WWE Concussion Lawsuit – Details." *EyeWrestlingNews.* News. 18 May 2017. https://www.ewrestlingnews.com/news/judge-orders-settlement-discussions-wwe-concussion-lawsuit-details. Accessed 4 Sept. 2017.

Diamond, Jason. "WWE Concussion Lawsuit: Everything We Know So Far." *Rolling Stone.* 19 July 2016. http://www.rollingstone.com/sports/news/everything-we-know-so-far-about-the-wwe-concussion-lawsuit-w429830. Accessed 1 Sept. 2017.

Dormer, Dave. "Concussion lawsuit should be

slammed, says former professional wrestler." *CBC News.* Calgary. 26 July 2016. http://www.cbc.ca/news/canada/calgary/lance-storm-concussion-study-1.3695654. Accessed 2 Sept. 2017.

"Former WWE stars' concussion lawsuit tossed by judge." *NBC News.* Sports. 20 Sept. 2018. https://www.nbcnews.com/news/sports/former-wwe-stars-concussion-lawsuit-tossed-judge-n911321. Accessed 22 July 2019.

"Former WWE Tag Team Star 'Jumping' Jim Brunzell Explains Current WWE Lawsuit, Says Vince McMahon 'Does Not Like Him. Hulk Hogan Returning." *Rainy Corps.* 23 Sept. 2016. https://rainycorps8076.jimdo.com/2016/09/23/former-wwe-tag-team-star-jumping-jim-brunzell-explains-current-wwe-lawsuit-says-vince-mcmahon-does. Accessed 2 Sept. 2017.

Giri, Raj. "Full List Of 51 Plaintiffs Involved in WWE Lawsuit." *Wrestling Inc.* 18 July 2016. http://www.wrestlinginc.com/wi/news/2016/0719/614697/full-list-of-51-plaintiffs-involved-in-wwe-lawsuit. Accessed 1 Sept. 2017.

Harris, Keith. "WWE wins important rulings in concussion lawsuits." Cageside Seats. WWE. 28 Mar. 2016.

https://www.cagesideseats.com/wwe/2016/3/28/11319008/wwe-wins-important-rulings-in-concussion-lawsuits. Accessed 2 Sept. 2017.

Hohler, Bob. "Ex-wrestlers file suit against WWE for concealing concussion dangers." *Boston Globe.* Sports. 18 July 2016. https://www.bostonglobe.com/sports/2016/07/18/wrestlers-file-suit-against-wwe-for-concealing-concussion-dangers/iMyGbjD8ZtY58DhS8OXdaK/story.html. Accessed 1 Sept. 2017.

Hohler, Bob. "Ex-wrestlers say one of their own sells them short: See conflict in WWE's $2.7m gift to concussion nonprofit." *Boston Globe.* 2 June 2016. http://edition.pagesuite.com/popovers/article_popover.aspx?guid=4c2da0c2-b291-47cf-8335-fab39edc90ac. Accessed 1 Sept. 2017.

Kettle, Harry. "WWE News: Ongoing concussion lawsuit takes another big twist." *Sportskeeda.* WWE. 18 May 2017. https://www.sportskeeda.com/wwe/wwe-news-judge-orders-settlement-discussions-in-concussion-lawsuit. Accessed 1 Sept. 2017.

"Kyros Law." *Home.* https://www.kyroslawoffices.com. Accessed 1 Sept. 2017.

Kounang, Nadia. "More than 50 wrestlers sue

WWE over brain damage." *CNN*. 20 July 2016.
http://www.cnn.com/2016/07/19/health/wwe-brain-injury-lawsuit/index.html. Accessed 2 Sept. 2017.

Nathan, Alec. "NFL to End Partnership with National Institutes of Health on Concussion Study." *Bleacher Report*. NFL. 28 July 2017. http://bleacherreport.com/articles/2724307-nfl-to-end-partnership-with-national-institute-of-health-on-concussion-study. Accessed 3 Sept. 2017.

Nath, Rohit. "WWE News: WWE claims that over 19 of 50 wrestlers in the concussion lawsuit signed away their right to sue." *Sportskeeda*. WWE. 18 Oct. 2016. https://www.sportskeeda.com/wwe/wwe-news-wwe-claims-that-over-19-of-50-wrestlers-in-the-concussion-lawsuit-signed-away-their-right-to-sue. Accessed 3 Sept. 2017.

Pena, Daniel. "Dan Spivey Weighs in On Health-Related Lawsuits Against WWE, Praises Rehab Assistance Program." *Wrestling Inc*. 3 July 2015. http://www.wrestlinginc.com/wi/news/2015/0703/597922/dan-spivey-weighs-in-on-health-related-lawsuits-against-wwe. Accessed 3 Sept. 2017.

Salamon, Maureen. "Concussion's Damage to Brain May Linger." *Health Day News*. 20 Nov. 2013. Web. 01 Sep. 2016.

Wikipedia contributors. "Concussions in American football." Wikipedia, The Free Encyclopedia. Wikipedia, The Free Encyclopedia, 31 Jul. 2016. Web. 2 Sep. 2016.

"Wrestlers' Last Stand: Full Appeal Brief Filed July 8, 2019." *WWE Concussion Lawsuit*. Blog. 9 July 2019. https://wweconcussionlawsuitnews.com/wrestlers-last-stand-full-appeal-brief-filed-july-8-2019. Accessed 22 July 2019.

"WWE attorney Jerry McDevitt on Vince McMahon, WWE Network royalties, World Wrestling Federation being rebranded as World Wrestling Entertainment." *Pro Wrestling Net*. 26 Apr. 2016. http://prowrestling.net/site/2016/04/26/wwe-attorney-jerry-mcdevitt-on-vince-mcmahon-wwe-network-royalties-world-wrestling-federation-being-rebranded-as-world-wrestling-entertainment. Accessed 1 Sept. 2017.

"WWE Concussion Lawsuit Claims Center." http://www.wweconcussionlawsuit.com. Accessed 1 Sept. 2017.

"WWE's Liability extends to all ECW and WCW

Matches." *WWE Concussion Lawsuit.* WWE Concussion Lawsuit Blog. 31 Jan. 2017. http://wweconcussionlawsuitnews.com/wwe-wrestlers-misclassified-as-independent-contractors. Accessed 4 Sept 2017.

"WWE Misclassification Lawsuit Claims Performers' Status as Independent Contractors Caused Long-Term Brain Injuries." *Bradley.* Labor and Employment Newsletter. 27 Aug. 2016. https://www.bradley.com/insights/publications/2016/08/wwe-misclassification-lawsuit-claims-performers. Accessed 4 Sept. 2017.

198

Part Four: Turning a Blind Eye

There's no avoiding wrestling's unsavory past and wrestling is by no means the only entertainment medium with a slimy underbelly. Wrestling's perception as a glorified freak show often gives it a pass when it comes to the media's coverage of its bad players and as we'll see, the WWE doesn't seem eager to expose these bad players. Some fans and critics have argued that when the WWE does acknowledge their wrestlers' misdeeds, it's only because the media coverage leaves them no other options. Some fans and critics also argue that even when the WWE takes disciplinary action, the wrestler is quickly brought back into the company's good graces.

Murder was the case—or was it? The 1983 death of wrestler Jimmy Snuka's girlfriend Nancy Argentino caught little attention when it happened, a reminder of how anything involving wrestling is often ignored by the media. However, the quest for justice would not be denied, leading to questions about what happened when Nancy Argentino died and a fight decades later to reopen the case.

Chapter Fourteen: Did Jimmy Snuka Get Away with Murder?

Originally published 2017

During the early 1980's, "Superfly" Jimmy Snuka was one of the WWF's top babyfaces but he was plagued by personal demons that ended what could have been a main event career. However, did Snuka's personal demons also end his girlfriend's life and if so, did "The Superfly" elude justice, perhaps even with the help of Vince McMahon?

A Death Shrouded in Mystery

On the night of 10 May 1983 shortly before midnight, an ambulance crew responded to a call from Jimmy Snuka concerning his girlfriend Nancy Argentino. Ms. Argentino was taken to the hospital where she died shortly thereafter at 2am. The case would be recommended as a homicide but after an investigation, no charges were filed. In 1985, the family received a default judgment

(Snuka failed to appear in court) in federal court but was unable to collect as Snuka claimed he was insolvent. On 1 Sept. 2015, 32 years after Ms. Argentino's death, the Lehigh County prosecutor charged Snuka with third-degree murder and involuntary manslaughter. On 1 June 2016 Judge Kelly Banach ruled Snuka was unfit to stand trial due to Snuka's dementia. Snuka died on 15 January 2017 leaving more unanswered questions. What happened to Nancy Argentino and did Jimmy Snuka get away with murder?

A Superstar Flying High in More Ways Than One

Jimmy Snuka (real name James Wiley Smith Reiher) entered the WWF as a heel in 1982, quickly working his way into a main event program with WWF Champion Bob Backlund. The Snuka-Backlund series at Madison Square Garden became legendary when Snuka dived off of a steel cage during his 28 June 1982 match against the WWF Champion. By this time, Snuka was being cheered and before long, the WWF turned him babyface. A year later, Snuka was arguably the company's top babyface, embroiled in a feud with Intercontinental Champion "The Magnificent" Muraco. The sky seemed the limit but Snuka's demons were dragging him down. The legendary Buddy Rogers (The first man to win both the NWA and WWWF Championship) served as

Snuka's storyline manager and behind the scenes, helped get Snuka to important matches. Why would a grown man need someone to get him to his matches is a question to consider when analyzing this story. According to Irv Muchnick's book, *Justice Denied,* Rogers stopped driving with Snuka because of "The Superfly's" blatant cocaine use during their travels.

Rogers, who had managed Snuka years earlier in Jim Crockett Promotions is quoted in *Justice Denied* as saying:

> "Jimmy could be a sweet person, but on that stuff he was totally uncontrollable." said Rogers, who was also Snuka's neighbor on Coles Mill Road in Haddonfield, New Jersey. Snuka's wife, with whom he had four children, befriended Rogers' wife. "Jimmy used to beat the shit out of that woman." Rogers said. "She would show up at our house, bruised and battered. But she couldn't leave him-he had her hooked on the same junk he was using."

A criminal complaint mentioned in a 2015 *Daily Beast* story discusses how, "In October 1983, Debbie Rogers, the wife of Snuka's manager, Buddy, took photos and notes of 'injuries to Sharon as a result of her beating by Snuka and her hospitalization.'" If so, these photos might have been entered into evidence if Snuka had been charged with Argentino's death.

Nancy Argentino

One of three sisters Nancy Argentino came from an Italian-American home in Brooklyn, attending Catholic school through eighth grade. In an 18 June 2013 article, her older sister Lorraine fondly remembered her, "I always admired her because she had a fun spirit… She didn't have any trouble relating to people. People were drawn to her. She was just fun to be around" ("Jimmy 'Superfly' Snuka and the Mysterious Death of Nancy Argentino"). Nancy worked in a dentist's office, and her employer encouraged her to pursue nursing so Ms. Argentino enrolled at a local community college. However, the allure of the squared circle would put her plans on hold when she took time off to travel with Jimmy Snuka.

How did Nancy Argentino get involved with Snuka? According to *Justice Denied,* Nancy Argentino's childhood friend Ellen was married to wrestler Johnny Rodz and this relationship led to Ms. Argentino's interest in wrestling. At one point, Ms. Argentino dated Hulk Hogan, but reportedly ended their relationship when she learned Hogan had other girlfriends. Wrestler Johnny Rodz is rumored to have introduced Nancy to Snuka. Conflicting reports exist whether Argentino knew

Snuka was married. One story is Snuka had an "open marriage" while another is Argentino was unaware of Snuka's marriage.

Snuka, who was 16 years older than Argentino wrote in his autobiography, "We slept together each time, but we also hung out…She was a very nice girl and we got along right away." According to a 1983 conversation with police, Caroline Argentino, Nancy's mother, told them Snuka gave Nancy money to buy for things such as furs and dresses, as long as she could account for the money.

Argentino discovered traveling with Snuka could be dangerous. On 18 January 1983, police reportedly found Snuka dragging Argentino by the hair through a motel in Salina, New York. Snuka engaged in a no-holds barred brawl with an assortment of cops and K-9 dogs before being subdued. Snuka, "was charged with second- and third-degree assault, resisting arrest and obstruction of governmental administration but accepted a plea deal that dropped all of those charges in exchange for pleading guilty to harassment in April 1983" ("Jimmy 'Superfly' Snuka and the mysterious death of Nancy Argentino"). A police report listed Argentino as having suffered, "a bruised right thumb, a contusion to the neck, possible fractured ribs and injury to the lower back," but Argentino later swore in a deposition that Snuka never touched her. In his autobiography, Snuka claims the situation was a misunderstanding but another story is he became enraged when he couldn't find his drugs.

Nancy's younger sister recalls a troubling incident in which Nancy returned home with Snuka to pick up clothes. Snuka was talking with Nancy's younger sister while Nancy was getting her clothes, when "The Superfly" pulled out some cocaine and began snorting it. An angry Nancy admonished Snuka for doing the drugs in front of her sister and the two began arguing. Later that day, Snuka and Nancy began arguing again and according to *Justice Denied,* Snuka looked at Nancy's sister and said, "I could kick you and put hands around your throat and nobody would know."

Over time, Nancy's mother reportedly grew concerned and hoped she would return home. On or around May 9, 1983, Nancy called her mother to let her know she was coming home the next day. Tragically, things turned out much different than Nancy's mother envisioned.

10 May 1983

On or around 10 May 1983, Nancy Argentino suffered a head injury. As we shall soon see, the details of how and why differ, depending on which of Jimmy Snuka's many alibis you believe (if any). According to Snuka, "When they arrived at the George Washington Motor Lodge, about 45 minutes later, Nancy said her head hurt and she wanted to lie down. They went to sleep for a few hours. Snuka left for the fairgrounds around 1 p.m. and Nancy was breathing normally, he told police. He kissed her and said, "I'll be right back as soon as I get done" ("Jimmy 'Superfly' Snuka and the Mysterious Death of Nancy Argentino").

On 10 May 1983, Snuka returned to his and Nancy's motel following a TV taping in Allentown Fairground. Snuka reportedly found Nancy Argentino gasping for air. According to his 1983 police interview, "I thought, my God, I better try to call a doctor right away. Right away, I just went out of my mind. I didn't know what to do with her, I just called the front desk. I told them my girl is having a hard time breathing, just seems like she can't even breathe at all, whatever you do, please hurry up" ("Jimmy 'Superfly' Snuka and the mysterious death of Nancy Argentino"). Paramedics were summoned and Ms. Argentino was taken to Lehigh Valley Hospital where she died around 2am.

The Investigation

In an interview with police inside the morgue, Deputy Coroner Wayne Snyder said Nancy's body had "several black and blue marks." He suggested police interview Snuka and compare his verbal statement with the professional results of an autopsy. In an interview with Irv Muchnick for his book *Justice Denied,* Snyder recalls, "Upon viewing the body and speaking to the pathologist, I immediately suspected foul play and so notified the district attorney."

According to police records, Vince McMahon and his company cooperated with the investigation. On 1 June 1983, Snuka and McMahon met with District Attorney Platt, Assistant District Attorney Robert Steinberg, Mihalakis, the medical examiner, and Whitehall Police Detectives Gerry Procanyn, Al Fritzinger and Vincent Geiger. According to Irv Muchnick, no charges were filed in the case, no coroner's inquest was held, and no evidence was presented to a grand jury (at the time in 1983).

Whitehall's former police chief defended Platt's actions at the time, ""Bill was one of the most professional, intelligent and concerned prosecutors that I've ever run into…He was certainly not the kind of guy who was going to shy away from anything if he thought it wasn't right" ("Jimmy 'Superfly' Snuka and the mysterious death of Nancy Argentino").

The Argentino family obtained two private investigations into the case. The first was conducted by Richard Cushing, a New York attorney who spoke to officials and sought access to records. Cushing told Irv Muchnick,

> "It was a very peculiar situation. I came away feeling Snuka should have been indicted. The police and the D.A. felt otherwise. The D.A. seemed like a nice enough person who wanted to do nothing. There was fear, I think on two counts: fear of the amount of money the World Wrestling had, and physical fear of the size of these people" (*Justice Denied*).

Cushing eventually declined to take the case but Nancy's father's employer hired a law firm to take the case, leading to the family's default judgment against Snuka.

A Number of Alibis

Arguably the biggest reason the case is shrouded in mystery is Snuka's plethora of explanations as to what happened. Snuka reportedly, "told at least five different people he pushed Nancy, and she fell and hit her head. He later said they misunderstood him" ("Jimmy 'Superfly' Snuka and the mysterious death of Nancy Argentino").

The article "Jimmy 'Superfly' Snuka and the mysterious death of Nancy Argentino" lists the various stories made to police by Snuka and other witnesses:

1. Snuka told the responding officer he and Nancy "were fooling around" outside the hotel room door when he pushed her and she fell, striking her head.
2. Two emergency room employees, Carol McBride and Susan St. Clair, told police Snuka stated he and Nancy got into an argument and "he pushed her and she fell back and hit her head."
3. Emergency room doctor John Fassl told police Snuka said he and Nancy were fooling around and she "was pushed and fell backwards and struck her head." At some point after the fall, they were fooling around again, with Snuka giving Nancy "light slaps to the face," Fassl told police. He also said Snuka seemed genuinely concerned for Nancy's condition.
4. Hospital chaplain Barbara Smith helped Snuka call the Argentino family after Nancy was pronounced dead. She told police that Snuka told her he and Nancy had stopped on the way to Allentown to go to the bathroom and were clowning

around when he shoved her with "his forearm and she fell backward on her back and hit her head on the concrete."

Which if any, of these stories is true? And if any of them are true, why didn't Snuka get help for Nancy Argentino right away? According to Irv Muchnick's *Wrestling Babylon,* forensic pathologist Dr. Isadore Mihalakis confronted Snuka about his failure to get medical care right away.

The Aftermath

The case refused to go away though. Journalist Irv Muchnick continued writing about the case, pointing out the discrepancies in Snuka's stories. Then in 2013, an article in *The Morning Call* brought renewed interest to the case. On June 28, 2013, Lehigh County District Attorney Jim Martin announced that the still-open case would be reviewed by his staff. On September 1, 2015, 32 years after the incident, Snuka was arrested and charged with third-degree murder and involuntary manslaughter for Argentino's death. Snuka's attorney waived a preliminary hearing in order to get grand jury evidence. However, that became moot when Snuka's attorney argued he had dementia and was incompetent to stand trial and a judge agreed on 1 June 2016. On 15 January 2017, Snuka passed away from a terminal illness.

The information presented to you is all that is known about the case, leaving some to believe Jimmy Snuka got away with killing Nancy Argentino (intentional or not) while others believing her death was a tragic accident. With Jimmy Snuka dead, there seems no hope of justice except in the afterlife.

Works Cited

Amerman, Kevin and Adam Clark. "DA taking 'fresh look' at death of 'Superfly' Snuka mistress." *The Morning Call.* 28 June 2013. http://articles.mcall.com/2013-06-28/news/mc-allentown-jimmy-snuka-grand-jury-20130628_1_nancy-argentino-argentino-family-motel-room. Accessed 19 Apr. 2017.

Amerman, Kevin and Adam Clark. "Jimmy 'Superfly' Snuka and the Mysterious Death of Nancy Argentino." *The Morning Call.* 18 June 2013. http://articles.mcall.com/2013-06-18/news/mc-jimmy-snuka-cold-case-20130608_1_snuka-hotel-room-don-muraco. Accessed 24 Apr. 2017.

"Jimmy (Superfly) Snuka's lawyer argues all those years getting bashed in the ring make him unfit to stand trial for girlfriend's 1983 murder." *The Daily News.* http://www.nydailynews.com/new-york/jimmy-superfly-snuka-unfit-murder-trial-lawyer-article-1.2346455. Accessed 24 Apr. 2017.

"Judge: Former pro wrestler "Superfly" Snuka incompetent to stand trial." *CBS News*. 1 June 2016. http://www.cbsnews.com/news/judge-former-pro-wrestler-jimmy-superfly-snuka-incompetent-to-stand-trial. Accessed 19 Apr. 2017.

Muchnick, Irv. *Justice Denied: The Untold Story of Nancy Argentino's Death in Jimmy "Superfly" Snuka's Motel Room.* Amazon Digital Services LLC, 2013.

---. *Wrestling Babylon: Piledriving Tales of Drugs, Sex, Death, and Scandal.* ECW Press, 2007.

Nestel, M.I. "Family Begged Girl to Dump 'Superfly' Snuka Before She Died." *The Daily Beast*. 2 Sept. 2015. http://www.thedailybeast.com/articles/2015/09/02/family-begged-girl-to-ditch-brutal-jimmy-superfly-snuka.html. Accessed 24 Apr. 2017.

"13 Things You Need to Know About Jimmy Snuka Murder Case." *Whatculture*. http://whatculture.com/wwe/13-things-you-need-to-know-about-jimmy-snuka-murder-case. Accessed 24 Apr. 2017.

Hulk Hogan was the cornerstone of the WWF in the 1980s as Vince McMahon used Hogan to build his regional promotion into a national one. However, Hogan's status as "The Babe Ruth of Wrestling" came under fire when a sex tape scandal revealed an ugly side of the man many wrestling fans once adored.

Chapter Fifteen: The Fall of Hulk Hogan

Originally published 2019

It's difficult to imagine a successful WWF without the presence of Terry Bollea (aka Hulk Hogan), a Superstar who helped take the WWF from a northeast territory into a national juggernaut as he played an All-American larger-than-life babyface. The following decade saw Hogan enjoy a career renaissance in WCW when he took a villainous turn, playing "Hollywood" Hulk Hogan. Hogan's fame made him into one of not only wrestling's most iconic figures but one of entertainment's most iconic figures. Sadly however, Hulk Hogan's last few years have seen his fame transform into infamy as one scandal followed another.

More Money, More Problems

As amazing as Terry Bollea's rise to stardom was, his early years saw him struggle like many young wrestlers, even quitting the sport in frustration over long travel hours and low payouts. Nonetheless, Terry Bollea rose to stardom when he took on the Hulk Hogan persona, initially working as a heel before enjoying incredible popularity in the American Wrestling Association (AWA). As sometimes happens with those who find fame and fortune, family members show up with outstretched hands. As Hogan's fame increased, one of his siblings seemed to take advantage of him.

That person was Hogan's much-older half-brother Kenny. Hogan had had little contact with Kenny until the two reunited during Hogan's first run in the WWF. The two reconnected and things seemed to be going well until Kenny asked to borrow five thousand dollars. According to the Hogan, he loaned Kenny the money only for Kenny to disappear without paying. The two have barely talked since.

Hogan's attempt to reconnect with his brother Alan proved even more tragic. Hogan's brother, a hard-living bruiser who Hogan had parted ways due to Alan's habit of getting into violent fights that endangered everyone around him. When the two brothers met up again, Alan was reportedly the vice-president of the Hell's Angels motorcycle club's San Francisco chapter (Hogan, "My Life" 98). However, Alan seemed to settle down when he got married and Hogan felt like his brother was back in his life. Sadly, it was clear that Alan was still using drugs as he would ask the Hulkster for pain pills, something Hogan claims he provided him with through his connection with Dr. George Zahorian, the WWF's "Dr. Feelgood." Subsequently, Hogan ran into his brother at a house show where Alan and his wife begged Hogan for money—his brother and wife's carpet company was in financial ruin and they were in desperate need of money. Hogan recalls giving them around 5-10 thousand dollars. What happened next devastated Hogan when Alan's wife called him later and informed him Alan had been found dead in a hotel room Hogan recalls, "Apparently Alan took all the money I gave him and rather than paying off his bills or getting a handle on all the shit in his life, he went out and bought a boatload of whatever his drug of choice was…I guess I'll never know if it was on purpose or not…My big-time wrestling career and big fat wallet made it possible for my brother Alan to die that night" (Hogan, "My Life Outside the Ring" 116). The only good thing that seems to have come out of the tragedy is that Hogan claims he stopped using cocaine, a drug he'd been increasingly using, like many other celebrities during the 1980's.

Steroid Scandal

In 1988, the U.S. government criminalized the distribution of anabolic steroids, a law which began a domino effect beginning with Dr. Andrew Zahorian, continuing with Hulk Hogan, and resulting in a federal criminal trial against Vince McMahon. This was the first real blemish on Hogan's reputation as the hero who said his prayers, took his vitamins, and did his training.

An investigation into Dr. Zahorian by the feds "...discovered a regular pattern of shipments to Vince McMahon, Terry Bollea, Roddy Piper, and dozens of other wrestlers on Vince's payroll. Many of the packages were shipped to hotels in cities where the WWF was touring" (Assael 91). Subsequently, a grand jury indicted Zahorian on 15 counts of distributing steroids, a serious charge that hit close to the WWF when Zahorian's lawyer leaked Hogan and Piper's names as clients (Assael 91). A *USA Today* headline "Hulk: Bulk from a Bottle" hit the front page (Assael 92), forcing Vince McMahon to work to save Hogan's reputation.

While WWF attorney Jerry McDevitt successfully argued that Hogan's testimony was unnecessary at Zahorian's trial, Vince McMahon knew he had to spin things in his favor in order to preserve Hogan's reputation. McDevitt wrote up a press release stating, "Hulk Hogan did nothing illegal and is not charged with any illegality" (qtd.

in Assael 92). McMahon held a press conference where it was revealed Hogan had taken steroids once during the late 80's, but Hogan himself wanted to come clean and speak with the American public. Hogan's move would only worsen matters.

Hogan's role as the WWF's top star and his all but undeniable chemically enhanced physique made him an easy target, something he felt he had to address. Unfortunately for Hogan, he chose to lie, rather than admit the truth. Against Vince McMahon's advice, Hogan appeared on the *Arsenio Hall Show* to discuss the allegations he used steroids. As detailed in the book, *Sex, Lies, and Headlocks:*

> Looking dewy-eyed at his host, Hogan made a concession: He'd taken a synthetic hormone three times, but just to get over a shoulder injury. Incredulous that anyone might question his integrity, he took out a picture of himself as a twelve-year-old Little Leaguer. "I trained twenty years, two hours a day to look like I do, Arsenio," he said. "I am not a steroids abuser and I do not use steroids." (97)

According to Hogan's first memoir, *Hollywood Hulk Hogan*, he had his reasons for downplaying his steroid use:

> "If it was just my reputation I had been concerned about, I might have been a little more honest. But I was worried about destroying all the good I had done with the Hulk Hogan character. Because of me, kids were living by the code of training, prayers, and vitamins, and I didn't want them to think that I'd given them bad advice."

In his followup memoir, *My Life Outside the Ring*, Hogan elaborates:

> "I told the truth—but I wasn't being honest. I told the truth so far as I wasn't using anabolic steroids at that moment. I might have been using them three weeks ago, but I wasn't using them right then. I was playing with words…But it wasn't being honest. There's a big difference. And it only made my problems worse. And I should have told the whole story. I should have apologized for making a mistake. Instead, I was calculated and deceptive, and it came back to bite me." (144)

Hogan goes on in the book to claim, "In 1992 I stopped using steroids entirely. It just wasn't worth it anymore" (144). This and Hogan's earlier claim that he had hid out in Vince McMahon's home for two months during the federal government's investigation against McMahon are dubious, something to consider whenever evaluating Hogan's honesty.

Hogan's comments would resurface during the steroid trial when the U.S. government called him to testify against Vince McMahon. Hogan was anxious at the trial, concerned that "…Vince was somehow going to try and flip the whole case and blame it on me" (Hogan, "My Life" 162). Hogan testified that he and McMahon did share steroids but denied that Vince ever injected him with steroids, stating that their mutual steroid sharing was the extent of things. McMahon was later acquitted of all charges, but Hogan claims he left New York for five years, "fearful that the Feds would find a way to arrest me or put a hit on me, or something" (Hogan, "My Life" 153). Hogan's testimony had not been the grand slam that federal prosecutors had imagined, and Hogan now had to deal with the fallout from his admitted steroid use. Wherever he wrestled, Hogan faced the scorn of fans who jeered him and brought signs mocking his steroid use.

Pastamania and a Lawsuit

Ever ready to diversify his earnings, Hulk Hogan bought in to Pastamania, a Hulk Hogan-themed pasta restaurant located in Minnesota's Mall of America. Despite some heavy promotion on *Monday Nitro*, Pastamania ultimately failed. As bad as the restaurant closing was, something worse happened when Hogan was sued by one of the company's employees.

According to Hogan, he was served with a letter on Christmas Day 1994 that rocked his personal life. The letter was written by Kate Kennedy, who managed the merchandise area of Pastamania. According to Hogan, Kennedy demanded three things, "That I write an apology and publish it in *USA Today;* that I complete some sort of sexual rehabilitation class; and that I pay her one million dollars" (157). Hogan claims he kept the matter from his wife for two years but also claims the matter was brought up in the Minneapolis area with Hogan claiming Jesse Ventura recycled Kennedy's claim during Ventura's radio show.

So, what was Kennedy's case about? According to Kennedy, Hogan sexually assaulted her:

> "The alleged assault occurred just two days before the launch of WCW's Monday Nitro program in September of 1995. Kennedy was a publicist for Hogan's failed restaurant endeavor called 'Pastamania.' She alleged that she met Hulk at the Marriott Hotel in Bloomington, Minnesota to talk

business. During the course of their meeting, Hogan allegedly became rough with Kate Kennedy and allegedly forced his penis into her mouth." (Damage)

Hogan refused Kennedy's demand and Hogan's attorney filed a lawsuit against Kennedy and her attorney, arguing the two were trying to extort his client. Once the lawsuit was filed, Kennedy and her attorney made her claims public.

At some point Hogan told his wife about the case (which was settled out of court for an unknown figure due to both parties signing a nondisclosure agreement). Hogan claims in his book that the lawsuit caused a rift in his marriage with Linda threatening divorce, despite the Hulkster pleading he was innocent.

The Auto Crash

With daughter Brooke looking to break into the music industry, the Hulkster agreed to star in a VH1 reality series titled *Hogan Knows Best*, a tongue-in-cheek look at the daily lives of Hulk Hogan, wife Linda, and their two children Brooke and Nick. Nick Hogan was a racing enthusiast and drove on racing courses in order to satiate his need for speed. Rumor has it Nick's friend John Graziano came from a troubled home and became close not only to Nick but the entire family. Then tragedy struck when the two were involved in a horrific auto accident. While Nick escaped without serious injuries, Graziano was not as fortunate, suffering serious injuries including brain damage (Graziano was not wearing his seat belt during the accident). The Graziano family ultimately sued and the police charged Nick with reckless endangerment, claiming he was driving at an unsafe speed. Nick pled no contest, receiving an eight-month sentence and five years' probation.

In a 2010 interview, Nick spoke about the accident:

> "John's my brother, we practically lived together and I just remember finding out about how bad everything was. It's still hard for me to think about it.' 'I pray every day that I will be able to deal with it. It's still at this point it's too much to think about. It's something that I carry with me every day.'" ("'There are days I can't get out of bed')

Because Nick was a minor at the time of the accident, Hulk Hogan was liable for the accident and the Graziano family sued him. The case was eventually settled in 2010 for an undisclosed amount.

The Divorce

Hulk Hogan's personal life continued to crumble when his wife filed for divorce during the

Graziano accident. According to Hogan, the couple had been fighting for years with Hogan claiming Linda put him through emotional abuse including verbal abuse towards him and his children. Hogan claims Linda spent millions of dollars buying new homes and furnishing them as well as excessive spending that included lavish gift giving to her friends, family, and even hired help. As often happens in matrimonial matters, both sides exchanged accusations and the case became both very public and very scandalous. Hogan discovered Linda was having an affair with 19-year-old Charlie Hill (Linda was 48-years-old at the time) while Linda later learned Hogan had had an affair with Brooke's 34-year-old assistant Christiane Plante. According to the Hulkster, Linda had frequently accused him of cheating but Hogan denies any extramarital affairs except the one with Plante.

The combination of his son's criminal case and his wife's divorce sent Hogan to the brink. In his memoir *My Life Outside the Ring*, Hogan details his downward spiral including a moment where he nearly committed suicide:

> A big bottle of Captain Morgan's and an open bottle of Xanax found their way to the counter. The gun found its way to the counter too. I can't tell you how. I can't tell you if I sat down with

the intent to kill myself. I don't know the answer…I just sat there, popping half a Xanax at a time—not the little pills, but those big horse-pill Xanax and washing them down with rum. There were times when I thought the whole bottle of pills would go down easy. A bunch of those pills with the rest of that bottle. I'd heard it wasn't a painful death—that you'd just go to sleep and that's it. Then I noticed the gun in my hand" (231-232).

Despite his deep depression and impaired state, Hogan did not kill himself (although he believes it was nothing short of a miracle that he didn't). Instead, he began the road to recovery when his *American Gladiators* co-host Laila Ali (daughter of Muhammad Ali) called to see how she was doing. This led to Hogan eventually attending Ali's church and finding the spiritual help he credits with turning his life around.

As acrimonious as the Hogan divorce became, Linda and Hulk Hogan eventually settled out of court, resolving their differences without a very public and potentially messy trial. The divorce was settled in 2009 with an agreement that would "…give Linda 70% of the couple's liquid assets plus properties worth $3 million. Additionally, she was to receive 40% of any future revenues in his businesses" (Lamare).

The Sex Tape

Although Hogan was not going to continue in the WWE as an in-ring performer, his prestige allowed him to serve as a WWE ambassador, appearing at events such as *WrestleMania*—that is until a sex tape surfaced of Hogan and Heather Clem, wife of disc jockey Bubba the Love Sponge. The tape was shocking on several levels as it revealed an unsavory side of Hogan's persona as well as a racist one.

In 2016, transcripts of the sex tapes were released during Hogan's trial against the website *Gawker* (which aired the second tape and who Hogan subsequently sued for invasion of privacy). It's believed Hogan and Clem made three sex tapes, two in 2007 and the third at an unknown date (Hogan was estranged from his wife at the time). The tape contains an interesting look into Hogan's mindset as revealed in a 2016 story by the *Daily Mail* documenting some of Hogan's discussions with Clem:

> Hogan also talks about his son's teenage girlfriend, saying; 'Nick's girlfriend is only 17. She has a killer f****** body.' He continues; 'The other night Nick is out and his dogs are playing tug of war with Nick's and

his girl's underwear. Then Nick has another girl who is even hotter in Orlando. Then she wants to be the first to get me if I'm divorced. Hot commodity.'" (Spargo)

As bad as the tape's release was for Hogan's reputation as a family man, it paled to the racist language contained in the tape. During the tape Hogan shared pillow talk with Clem that showed a vile side of his character:

"So it gets to the point where…I dunno if (daughter) Brooke was f-----g the black guy's son, or they've been hanging out, I caught them holding hands together on the tour. "They were getting close to kind of (INAUDIBLE) the f-----g (INAUDIBLE). I'm not a double-standard type of guy," he continued. "I'm a racist to a point, y'know, f-----g n-----s — but then, when it comes to nice people..." (qtd. in Blau)

Hogan's comments continued with him saying, ""I don't give a f--k if she (INAUDIBLE) an 8-foot tall basketball player," he says on the recording. "If we're gonna f--k with n-----s, let's get a rich one!" (qtd. in Blau).

The WWE took immediate action, removing Hogan from its Hall of Fame and releasing him.

While some fans questioned the WWE's actions in light of Vince McMahon's racist language (see our video "Is the WWE Racist" for further details), Hogan's expulsion stood for years.

Hogan had his share of defenders as well as people who assailed his comments. Some African-American wrestlers who had worked alongside Hogan reported never seeing any racism in Hogan's character. Others were unwilling to give him the benefit of the doubt. Hogan's attempt to apologize included some questionable comments such as the following:

> "I'm not a racist but I never should have said what I said. It was wrong. I'm embarrassed by it. People need to realize that you inherit things from your environment. And where I grew up was south Tampa, Port Tampa, and it was a really rough neighborhood, very low income. And all my friends, we greeted each other saying that word." (Blau)

The Apology Tour

On 15 July 2018 the WWE announced on *Instagram* that, "After a three-year suspension, @hulkhogan has been reinstated into the WWE Hall of Fame" (wwe). The WWE also stated:

> "This second chance follows Hogan's numerous public apologies and

volunteering to work with young people, where he is helping them learn from his mistake. "These efforts led to a recent induction into the Boys & Girls Clubs of America Alumni Hall of Fame." (qtd. in "Hulk Hogan Back")

A happy Hulkster took to *Instagram* and boasted of his experience reuniting with the WWE locker room:

> "Just met with the WWE Superstars and on all levels the volume of love and support was overwhelming. I've been praying for this day and I finally feel like I made it back home. Only Love 4 the #WWEUNIVERSE brother HH." (qtd. in "Hulk Hogan Back")

The WWE decided to reinstate Hogan into its Hall of Fame, feeling he had made substantial efforts to atone for his words. The New Day issued a statement concerning Hogan's reinstatement, a sign that Hogan's remarks continued to affect persons of color:

> "When someone makes racist and hateful comments about any race or group of people, especially to the degree that Hogan made about our people, we find it difficult to simply forget - regardless of how long ago it

was, or the situation in which those comments were made… Perhaps if we see him make a genuine effort to change, then maybe our opinion will change with him. Time will tell." (BBC News "Hulk Hogan: Black Stars Weigh In")

Hogan's return to the WWE also included an apology he made to the entire WWE locker room at the 15 July 2018 Extreme *Rules* pay-per-view. The apology became public when Hogan spoke with Bill Apter, recalling what he had said:

"Thank you guys for the time. The first thing I want to do is tell you guys, 12 years ago I said something. About three years ago it just came to light. And I want to apologize for everything I said. 'I could give you the 'woe is me' story, I could tell you all the things, all the reasons why I was in this space I was in — a very dark, dark space. But everybody's got a 'woe is me' story, everybody's got an excuse. But the truth is, I said these things 12 years ago and I didn't even know they were said until three years ago because that's when they came out. I can't remember what I said last weekend let alone 12 years ago. Maybe you guys can but I can't. And when I said it was in a fit of anger. But I did say it, I'm accountable, that's not who I am. That's not how I feel, that's not how I believe. But the one thing I will tell you is when I said it I was very, very mad. Very, very mad at a situation. But I did say it. It was inappropriate, it was out of context, it was hurtful, it was unacceptable and I did it. I apologize, if you guys could ever forgive me I would be forever grateful. Now, I want to let you guys know that this is the biggest spotlight in the world. The WWE's the biggest spotlight in the world. And if you're a little, teeny star, don't even slip on a banana peel when you're a little star here, because you're in the spotlight. Try not to make any mistakes like I made. But when you're a big star here and you make a mistake, the whole world is gonna know. You'll be on the front page of every newspaper, of every magazine — just like it happened to me. I made a mistake and this machine was so big — the WWE's made me such a big star — that everybody knows what's going on. So please be careful because people have cell phones and cameras — so just be careful," (qtd. in Seddon)." (qtd. in Seddon)

Not everyone was satisfied with the apology. For example, Titus O'Neil commented:

> "As to the reinstatement of Mr. Bollea, I can only communicate that I am a proponent of second and even third chances for individuals that show true remorse, acknowledgement of wrongdoing, fulfill their punishment, if applicable, and otherwise put forth sincere efforts to correct the issues. Unfortunately, I must echo the sentiment and dissatisfaction expressed by many of my fellow contemporaries concerning Mr. Bollea's apology and its lack of true contrition, remorse and a desire to change. Mr. Bollea's apology 'that he didn't know he was being recorded' is not remorse for the hateful and violent utterances he made which reprise language that has caused violence against blacks and minorities for centuries." (qtd. in Currier)

O'Neil wasn't the only Superstar who found fault with what he saw as Hogan focusing on the presence of cameras rather than true remorse for his words.

Hogan addressed this criticism afterwards, stating:

> "A lot of people accepted my apology. And a lot of people heard what they wanted to hear and a lot of the narrative that came out of the meeting was on point. A lot of the narrative was really different because I was surprised to hear some people interpreted what I said that I was just sorry I got caught on camera, whatever they interpreted, but I never said that. But I guess sometimes the media and people go with the most negative narrative that can come out of there."
> (qtd. in Rueter)

Despite his setbacks, the Hulkster seems committed to personal redemption. Only time will tell how history judges both Hulk Hogan the man, and Hulk Hogan the legendary wrestler. In the meantime, Hogan's personal life continues to have its ups and downs with ex-wife Linda suing Hogan, claiming he has hidden assets from their divorce agreement. Furthermore, she is seeking part of Hogan's proceeds from the lawsuit settlement against *Gawker,* her legal argument being that "Technically, due to the divorce settlement, Hulk doesn't own 100% of his image.

He owns 60% of his image. Linda owns the other 40%" (Lamare).

Works Cited

Assael, Shaun and Mike Mooneyham. *Sex, Lies, and Headlocks: The Real Story of Vince McMahon and World Wrestling Entertainment.* Three Rivers Press, 2004.

Blau, Reuven. "Hulk Hogan's bigoted rant revealed in newly-released audio from sex tape: 'If we're gonna f--k with n-----s, let's get a rich one' (WARNING: GRAPHIC LANGUAGE)." *Daily News.* U.S. 14 Apr. 2016. https://www.nydailynews.com/news/national/hulk-hogan-bigoted-rant-revealed-new-sex-tape-audio-article-1.2601524. Accessed 24 May 2019.

Currier, Joseph. "TITUS O'NEIL COMMENTS ON HULK HOGAN'S APOLOGY TO WWE ROSTER." *Wrestling Observer Figure Four Online.* 19 July 2018. https://www.f4wonline.com/wwe-news/titus-oneil-comments-hulk-hogans-apology-wwe-roster-262006. Accessed 24 May 2019.

Damage, Brian. "When It Comes Crashing Down: The Hulk Hogan Family Tragedy." *Ring the*

Damn Bell. Home. 8 Dec. 2017. https://ringthedamnbell.wordpress.com/2017/12/08/when-it-comes-crashing-down-the-hulk-hogan-family-tragedy. Accessed 24 May 2019.

Damage, Brian. "Wrestling with Sin: 170." *Ring the Damn Bell.* Home. 28 May 2018. https://ringthedamnbell.wordpress.com/2018/05/28/wrestling-with-sin-170. Accessed 24 May 2019.

Hogan, Hulk. *Hollywood Hulk Hogan.* World Wrestling Entertainment, 2002.

Hogan, Hulk and Marc Dagostino. *My Life Outside the Ring: A Memoir.* St. Martin's Press, 2009.

"Hulk Hogan back into WWE Hall of Fame after racism." *BBC News.* Newsbeat. 16 July 2018. https://www.bbc.com/news/newsbeat-44846142. Accessed 21 May 2019.

"Hulk Hogan: Black WWE stars weigh in on his Hall of Fame reinstatement." *BBC News.* Newsbeat. 19 July 2019. https://www.bbc.com/news/newsbeat-44884853. Accessed 21 May 2019.

Konuwa, Alfred. "Hulkamania Apology Tour Runs Wild as Hulk Hogan's WWE Return Appears Likely." *Forbes.* Sports Money. 5 May 2018. https://www.forbes.com/sites/alfredkonuw

a/2018/05/05/hulkamania-apology-tour-runs-wild-as-hulk-hogans-wwe-return-appears-likely. Accessed 21 May 2019.

Lamare, Amy. "Hulk Hogan and Ex-Wife Linda Still Battling in Court More Than a Decade Later." *Celebrity Net Worth*. 30 Jan. 2019. https://www.celebritynetworth.com/articles/entertainment-articles/hulk-hogan-and-ex-wife-linda-still-battling-in-court-more-than-a-decade-later. Accessed 24 May 2019.

Rouse, Mick. "Hulk Hogan Is Getting the Redemption Story He Never Earned." *GQ*. Culture. 26 Feb. 2019. https://www.gq.com/story/hulk-hogan-is-getting-the-redemption-story-he-never-earned. Accessed 21 May 2019.

Rueter, Sean. "Hulk Hogan says WWE stars who didn't accept his apology for saying he's a racist 'don't understand the brotherhood of wrestling'" *Cageside Seats*. WWE. 17 Aug. 2018. https://www.cagesideseats.com/wwe/2018/8/17/17720182/hulk-hogan-wwe-stars-who-didnt-accept-apology-dont-understand-the-brotherhood-of-wrestling. Accessed 24 May 2019.

Seddon, Dan. "Hulk Hogan shares his apology to WWE superstars over N-word controversy."

Digital Spy. 18 Aug. 2018.
https://www.digitalspy.com/tv/ustv/a8642
52/hulk-hogan-apologises-wwe-superstars-n-
word-controversy. Accessed 24 May 2019.

Spargo, Chris. "Unsealed Hulk Hogan sex tape
transcripts reveal lurid details of wrestler's
three encounters with best friend's wife." *The
Daily Mail*. 20 March 2016.
https://www.dailymail.co.uk/news/article-
3499500/Unsealed-Hulk-Hogan-sex-tape-
transcripts-reveal-lurid-details-wrestler-s-
three-encounters-best-friend-s-wife.html.
Accessed 24 May 2019.

"'There are days I can't get out of bed': Nick
Hogan finally opens up about 2007 car crash
that left his best friend brain damaged." *Daily
Mail*. 8 Oct. 2010.
https://www.dailymail.co.uk/tvshowbiz/arti
cle-1318896/Nick-Hogan-finally-opens-
2007-car-crash-left-best-friend-brain-
damaged.html. Accessed 24 M

"Wrestler Hulk Hogan fired over race outburst
caught on tape." *The Guardian*. The
Observer. 25 July 2015.
https://www.theguardian.com/media/2015
/jul/26/hulk-hogan-wrestling-racism-
gawker. Accessed 24 May 2019.

Social media has allowed wrestling fans to share their mutual passion for the grappling game but as we'll see, it's also allowed them to speak out about alleged wrongdoing that should not be ignored. In 2018, the WWE's decision to honor a wrestler with a questionable past lead to a major change to the WWE's flagship event, "WrestleMania."

Chapter Sixteen: The Frightening Legacy of the Fabulous Moolah

Originally published 2018

The evil that men do lives after them;
The good is oft interrèd with their bones.
"Julius Caesar Act 3 Scene 2 74-75

In 2018, the WWE announced its first women's battle royal, christening it the Fabulous Moolah Battle Royal, hoping to honor the WWE Hall of Famer, much as it did with Andre the Giant and the Andre the Giant Memorial Battle Royal. However, a fan backlash led to the WWE dropping Moolah's name from the event. The question some fans are asking is why would the WWE drop the name of a woman it has seemed to embrace for decades? Although the WWE has lionized Moolah's accomplishments, rumors have persisted for decades about Moolah's practices towards her trainee wrestlers. What are these allegations and what if any impact should they have on Moolah's legacy?

Outnumbered in a Man's World

South Carolina native Mary Lillian Ellison was born on July 22, 1923. The youngest of 13 children, Mary was the only daughter in the Ellison brood and lost her mother to cancer when she was only eight years old. Growing up around males, Ellison easily adapted to life as a tomboy. She discovered her love for professional wrestling when her father took her to matches to spend quality time with her away from her brothers. Young Mary knew right then how she wanted to spend her life when she saw women's wrestling for the first time (legend has it women's icon Mildred Burke was one of the performers that night). However, her father disapproved so Lillian eventually ran off and eloped with one Walter Carroll. Their daughter Mary (who would become a wrestler) was born but the marriage was short-lived.

In her memoir, *The Fabulous Moolah: First Goddess of the Squared Circle,* Ellison recalled her disdain for the patriarchal system ruling society and with it, wrestling:

> "When I was coming up, it was unheard of for a lady wrestler to be strong and independent. We were the valets for the men stars, and we had

men—promoters, other wrestlers, husbands, or boyfriends—telling us exactly what to do. I did what I wanted to do, ever since I was a little girl and defied my dear daddy's wishes by entering the ring." (qtd. in Laprade and Murphy 80)

Ellison's wrestling career would show her disdain for the system, with Ellison often refusing to "go along to get along." Ellison approached promoter Billy Wolfe, who controlled women's wrestling with an iron grip, but didn't last long when she rebuffed his sexual advances. Ellison was dating wrestler Johnny Long who introduced her to Jack Pfefer, a New York promoter. Legend has it when Pfefer asked Ellison why she was wrestling and her response was, "For the money! I want to wrestle for the moolah!" (Laprade and Murphy 82). Thus, was Ellison's ring name created.

Her first break came when she worked as "Nature Boy" Buddy Rogers' valet, under the stage name "Slave Girl Moolah." Ellison provided help for Rogers when called upon in the ring, but in her autobiography, Ellison claims Rogers' constant propositions for a sexual relationship led to her ending their business relationship. Moolah had burnt two important bridges, leaving her wrestling career in doubt.

Despite her setbacks, Ellison persevered and on September 18, 1956, Moolah won her first world championship when she overcame 12 other women in a battle royal, eliminating Judy Grable to become the World Women's Championship. As was standard for the time, there were multiple claimants to the world's title, and while not everyone recognized her as champion, this would change over time. However, promoter Vince McMahon Sr. rechristened her the Fabulous Moolah, launching his family's long business relationship with Moolah.

The NWA eventually recognized Moolah as its world women's champion and she began a long run as champion, defending the title internationally. Like many wrestling claims, Moolah's reign was exaggerated with her listed as never have been defeated for the championship. While that was not true, Moolah did hold the belt for extended periods and her grip was akin to a stranglehold.

1983 saw Vince McMahon approach Moolah about selling her championship to the WWF. At the time, Vince was intent on expanding his father's promotion into a national one and he had ambitious plans for women's wrestling. One such plan involved utilizing pop singer Cyndi Lauper in an angle where her proxy wrestler would take on Captain Lou Albano's proxy. This led to the July

23, 1984 "Brawl to End it All" where Lauper's wrestler Wendi Richter defeated Albano's wrestler Moolah for the WWF Women's Championship. Ironically, Moolah would be called upon to shoot on Richter and get the title back when McMahon's clash with Richter called for what is now known as "The Original Screwjob," a match where Moolah (disguised as the masked Spider Lady) won the WWF Women's Championship from Richter.

A Wrestling Resurgence

During the Attitude Era, Moolah's career enjoyed a resurgence when she began appearing in comedy segments, often alongside fellow women's wrestler Mae Young. These segments led to a new generation of fans being introduced to Moolah's work. Along the way, Moolah won the WWF Women's Championship at the young age of 76, with her last match occurring on September 15, 2003, when she defeated Victoria on *RAW*.

In their book, *Sisterhood of the Squared Circle: The History and Rise of Women's Wrestling*, Pat Laprade and Dan Murphy's chapter on Moolah sums up her career:

> Respected by her allies and feared by her enemies, Ellison was a master politician and a shrewd, calculating businesswoman. As an in-ring competitor, she was widely considered the most well-known female wrestler in

the game for 30 years. Her career as a
trainer and promoter extended even
further." (80)

While we know of Moolah's wrestling legacy, what
of her legacy behind the scenes?

A Not So Fabulous Experience

Moolah's longevity in the ring and her
reputation as someone able to hold her own in an
industry driven by men inspired respect. The
WWE Hall of Famer always seemed to be
welcome by the McMahon family. However, at the
same time, she has drawn criticism for using the
same exploitative tactics used by men with her
own wrestlers. These questionable practices
towards students and wrestlers in her employ
range from financial exploitation to sexual
exploitation including prostitution and
pornography.

A year after Moolah's death in 2007, famed
women's wrestler Penny Banner blasted Moolah's
legacy after she felt the wrestling star was being
prepared for sainthood:

Let's get this out of way first, so I don't
have to dance around the subject –
Moolah was a pimp…Moolah would
send out her half-trained underage
female-wrestlers to "photo shoots"
that would by the standards of today
be considered pedophilia and

pornography…Renting them out to promoters in bulk, with the understanding that the girls would have sex with the promoter and all the wrestlers on the roster who wanted them. Promoters liked free sex, but what they also liked is for boys not to go outside looking for it and possibly running into trouble. Sex on a road with a steady and pliant group of semi-attractive women in return for money, that is what Moolah offered. The women that were sent out on these tours were not told of this 'arrangement' ahead of time. They found out about it on the road. Those that refused to have sex with promoters and wrestlers, were raped." (qtd. in Greer)

Although the Fabulous Moolah ran a well-known wrestling school, there were always questions raised about how much she taught. Critics have argued that Moolah had others do the training while she collected the proceeds. To be certain, a number of successful wrestlers trained at Moolah's school, but how much they learned from Moolah remains in doubt.

Through the years, Moolah developed a reputation as someone quick to financially exploit wrestlers and sabotage their careers if they looked to threaten her spot at the top of the mountain. When 6'2" journalist Jeannine Mjoseth met a wrestler at a party, he caught her attention by regaling her with the easy life of a wrestler. Mjoseth ditched her reporter's notebook and began training with Moolah. With her height, colorful mohawk, and imposing figure, Mjoseth's character Mad Maxine had potential. At one point, Maxine was considered for a spot on the WWF's Saturday morning cartoon, *Hulk Hogan's Rock-n-Wrestling,* but according to Mjoseth, Moolah maneuvered her way onto the show instead. When Maxine learned Moolah was taking 50% of her pay, she left the WWF.

African-American wrestler Susie Mae McCoy was allegedly exploited as well, earning only a portion of what she earned as the successful African-American grappler Sweet Georgia Brown. In a 2006 interview, a family member recalled, "She thought that's what you've got to do to survive," Barbara says now. "She knew she was being used; she knew from the beginning that she was being lied to, but she was a black woman in the '50s" (Faulk). McCoy's story is just one of several allegations against Moolah.

As bad as Moolah's alleged financial exploitation was, Mjoseth supports the other stories of Moolah allegedly pimping her female wrestlers:

> "Moolah did send girls out to this guy in Arizona and pimped them out. I actually spoke to him on the phone and asked him what he was looking for. He said, 'If I'm spending all this money, you know what I want.' That was part of Moolah's way of making money. She was just a bad person. Moolah didn't have a good bone in her body." (Fernow)

In the film documentary *Lipstick and Dynamite,* wrestler Judy Grable said, "She was trained by him [Wolfe] so I guess you know she got it from him. What goes around comes around. She got it done to her and she was doing it to everyone else" (qtd. in Laprade and Murphy).

A common theme to the allegation is a combination of financial and sexual exploitation. Moolah's female charges were allegedly kept in debt, making it easier for other exploitation. For example, women's wrestler Ida Mae Martinez alleged some women would not get paid until they slept with promoters (Laprade and Murphy 86). Although Moolah was not directly involved, the correlation between the women wrestlers' financial straits and their exploitation is easy to see.

Wrestler Sandy Parker trained at Moolah's camp and noted:

> "Everybody knew that if you weren't on Lillian's good side, you got crappy bookings," comments Parker. "I wasn't on her good side because I wouldn't do what she wanted me to do. That was one of the reasons I never worked Madison Square Garden because every time the bookings came up, I'd be on her bad side. As far as I am concerned, I could wrestle just as good as Toni Rose, Donna Christenello or anyone of those girls (who were on Ellison's good side)." (Kreiser)

The tag team of Leilani Kai and Judy Martin (aka "The Glamour Girls") would later claim Moolah sabotaged their momentum in the WWF during their much-acclaimed program with the Japanese tag team, "The Jumping Bomb Angels."

Defending Moolah

Not everyone has vilified Lillian Ellison. Retired Hall of Fame wrestler Joyce Grable (not to be confused with the aforementioned Judy Grable) discussed her time with Moolah. "Well, Moolah trained me in 71' and I wrestled for her until 1984, and I was a four-time world tag team champion, so I've been around a long time." Grable was interviewed about the allegations and had this to say:

> "Well no, I never experienced that and all of the ones you named they're dead so how could they be saying anything. Maybe the family, or just making it up, but as far as I was concerned, she never sent me to nobody, and hey, I had a good body, back then. I was kind of pretty, long blonde hair. Especially when I went to Puerto Rico, Mexico; if she was gonna pimp somebody out, I would've been number one on the list." (Paglino)

In regard to the allegations about Moolah providing drugs to her wrestlers:

> "I never recall anything on that…. Moolah was 110% against any types of drugs. If she found out you smoked marijuana, she would X you off; told you 'You can't do that'. She told you how to dress when you went to arenas, how to act like a lady, and as far as I'm concerned, you know, I mean, she was a little stiff on some things, but she was my boss. I had to do what she told me to do. I had to go places; Japan, Australia, New Zealand. But

hey, this is what the business is
about…" (Paglino).

Grable would go on to comment about the
allegations Moolah pimped out her wrestlers to
men:

> "In fact, she wanted us to stay away
> from the guy wrestlers. She
> was…when one of us were dating one
> of the guys, she was so afraid we were
> gonna marry em', go off with them,
> and then she would lose a top girl. And
> so, she never promoted the girls and
> the guys getting together, or anyone.
> She was like, 'You're on your own in
> that situation, but this is what I'd like
> for you to do.'" (Paglino)

Did Moolah exploit her wrestlers or was it a
case of disgruntled wrestlers blaming her for their
shortcomings?

Moolah's Motivation?

What could motivate Moolah to allegedly
exploit women the same way she'd been exploited?
Consider these two opinions. The first, from
author Tim Hornbaker, "Moolah, however, could
have changed things by running an honest
syndicate, training and booking women on the
level. She could have broken the patterns
established by Wolfe. She chose not to. Maybe it
was just too deeply ingrained" (Laprade and

Murphy 86). The second from former wrestler Mad Maxine, who believes she knows Ellison's motivation, ""She was an evil person. I understand why. She came from nothing. Her mother died when she was just eight and she was never going to be poor again" (Fernow).

Assessing Moolah's Legacy

While Moolah's treatment of her wrestlers may never be known, there are questions about her legacy as a performer as well, with some believing the long-time women's champion was a limited worker who hurt the business.

Dave Meltzer feels women's wrestling suffered during Moolah's dominance, "During the period Moolah controlled women's wrestling, the popularity and the product didn't evolve. The women in the 1940's and the 1950's, even the late 1950's in some places like Florida, they were headlining the show" (Laprade and Murphy 87). Meltzer is not alone in this criticism.

Before her 2008 death, former AWA Women's World Champion Penny Banner agreed, arguing:

> "The reason women's pro-wrestling in North America was and still in large part today considered a joke and just an opportunity to ogle at tits and asses is largely in part thanks to the way Moolah trained her girls and how

Moolah wrestled... Those that argue that women's wrestling was always like that and Moolah did nothing to change it are ignorant. In the '30s and '40s, female wrestling employed shooters and they wrestled in the traditional sense of the term. Tits and asses were used to advertise and get them in the building, but the girls worked longer and more technically sound matches than today...The reason Japanese women's wrestling was light years ahead of North American's is because of one person and one person only – Moolah. Mildred Burke, the original women's champion, popularized female wrestling in the world in the '30s. Japan, Canada, Mexico and America can trace women's wrestling directly to her. She used a hard hitting style and outside of being an attractive woman, her matches were no different from the men's matches of her day." (qtd. in Greer)

Mary Lillian Ellison's legacy remains controversial to say the least. Whether her reputation is fabulous, frightful, or something in between, the WWE relented when its *WrestleMania XXXIV* sponsor Snickers issued the statement:

> "We were recently made aware of the World Wrestling Entertainment Inc's (WWE) decision to honor a former wrestler during the upcoming WrestleMania 34 event. As a principle-based business that has long championed creating inclusive environments that encourage and empower everyone to reach their full potential, this is unacceptable. We are engaging with the WWE to express our disappointment." (Currier)

The WWE's quest for mainstream corporate sponsors such as Snickers makes it obvious the company will avoid even the appearance of controversy. Whether wrestling's Fabulous Moolah is worthy of condemnation is for you to decide.

Works Cited

Ahmed, Tufauel. "WWE Announces Fabulous Moolah Memorial Battle Royal, but the Wrestler Has a Troubling Legacy." *Newsweek.* 13 Mar. 2018. http://www.newsweek.com/wwe-fabulous-moolah-memorial-battle-royal-842789. Accessed 21 Mar. 2018.

Bixenspan, David. "WWE's Revisionist History

Doesn't Take a Break During Women's History Month." *Paste*. Wrestling. 23 Mar. 2017. https://www.pastemagazine.com/articles/2017/03/wwe-and-mae-young-womens-revisionist-history-month.html. Accessed 21 Mar. 2018.

Burke, Tom. "The Fabulous Moolah." *The Professional Wrestling Hall of Fame and Museum*. Hall of Famers. https://web.archive.org/web/20090303135218/http://www.pwhf.org/halloffamers/bios/moolah.asp. Accessed 21 Mar. 2018

Collins, Elle. "WWE Is Right to Not Memorialize The Fabulous Moolah." *Uproxx*. WWE. 16 Mar. 2018. https://uproxx.com/prowrestling/what-did-fabulous-moolah-do-wwe-allegations-controversy-explained. Accessed 17 Mar. 2018.

Currier, Joseph. "WWE Changes Name of Fabulous Moolah Battle Royal." *Wrestling Observer Figure Four Online*. 15 Mar. 2018. https://www.f4wonline.com/wwe-news/wwe-changes-name-fabulous-moolah-battle-royal-253621. Accessed 21 Mar. 2018.

Dilbert, Ryan. "Fabulous Moolah, Ultimate Warrior and WWE's Wrestling with Its Own History." *Bleacher Report*. WWE. 16 Mar.

2018. http://bleacherreport.com/articles/2764715-fabulous-moolah-ultimate-warrior-and-wwe-wrestling-with-its-own-history. Accessed 17 Mar. 2018.

Fannin, Pat. "Fans React Negatively to Fabulous Moolah Memorial Battle Royal." *Fightful.* 13 Mar. 2018. https://www.fightful.com/wrestling/fans-react-negatively-fabulous-moolah-memorial-battle-royal. Accessed 21 Mar. 2018.

Faulk, Murfee. "Baby of Sweet Georgia Brown." *Free Times.* 20 Dec. 2006. https://www.free-times.com/archives/baby-of-sweet-georgia-brown/article_e82fe915-fb49-5d12-8848-42750f5dc785.html. Accessed 21 Mar. 2018.

Fernow, Bill. "Mad Maxine has quite a story to tell." *SLAM! Sports.* SLAM! Wrestling. 21 Mar. 2018. http://slam.canoe.com/Slam/Wrestling/2014/08/30/21908686.html. Accessed 21 Mar. 2018.

Greer, Jamie. "The Brutal History of Fabulous Moolah." *Last Word on Pro Wrestling.* WWE Universe 13 Mar. 2018. http://lastwordonprowrestling.com/2018/03/13/the-brutal-history-of-fabulous-moolah. Accessed 21 Mar. 2018.

Konuwa, Alfred. "WWE Changes Name Of

Fabulous Moolah Memorial Battle Royal Amid Pressure from Fans, Sponsor." *Forbes.* In the Ring. 15 Mar. 2018. https://www.forbes.com/sites/alfredkonuwa/2018/03/15/wwe-changes-name-of-fabulous-moolah-memorial-battle-royal-amid-pressure-from-fans-sponsor/#389315e7afd6. Accessed 17 Mar. 2018.

Krieser, Jamie Melissa. "Sandy Parker: Addicted to wrestling." *SLAM! Sports.* SLAM! Wrestling. 21 Mar. 2018. http://slam.canoe.com/Slam/Wrestling/2008/03/14/5009196.html. Accessed 21 Mar. 2018.

Laprade, Pat and Dan Murphy. *Sisterhood of the Squared Circle: The History and Rise of Women's Wrestling.* ECW Press, 2017.

Leen, Jeff. *The Queen of the Ring: Sex, Muscles, Diamonds, and the Making of an American Legend.* Grove Press, 2010.

Mooneyham, Mike. "Penny Banner Was Original Diva." *The Wrestling Gospel According to Mike Mooneyham.* Columns. 25 July 2004. http://www.mikemooneyham.com/2004/07/25/penny-banner-was-original-diva. Accessed 21 Mar. 2018.

Paglino, Nick. "Fabulous Moolah Performer Joyce

Grable Speaks Out in Defense of Moolah." *Pro Wrestling.com.* 17 Mar. 2018. https://www.prowrestling.com/fabulous-moolah-performer-joyce-grable-speaks-out-in-defense-of-moolah. Accessed 21 Mar. 2018.

Rickard, Michael. *Wrestling's Greatest Moments.* ECW Press, 2008.

Shields, Brian. *Main Event: WWE in the Raging 80's.* World Wrestling Entertainment, 2006.

Solomon, Brian. *WWE Legends.* World Wrestling Entertainment, 2006.

Thompson, Andrew. "Joyce Grable Goes to Bat For The Fabulous Moolah, Says If Moolah Would've "Pimped" Anyone Out It Would've Been Her." *Fightful.* https://www.fightful.com/wrestling/joyce-grable-goes-bat-fabulous-moolah-says-if-moolah-would-ve-pimped-anyone-out-it-would-ve-been-her. Accessed 21 Mar. 2018.

What's the worst that could happen with giving wrestlers an open bar on a trans-Atlantic flight? As we'll see, plenty, and like our previous story, it can be difficult to bury the past.

Chapter Seventeen: The Plane Ride from Hell

Originally published 2017

Back in the 1970's, Hollywood made a string of disaster movies including four films based on airline catastrophes, beginning with *Airport* in 1970 and ending with *The Concorde…Airport '79*. In May 2002, the WWE had an airline disaster of its own, leading to wrestlers' terminations, lawsuits, and reportedly, a close brush with death.

On May 5, 2002, the WWE chartered a commercial flight to take its wrestlers home after a tour of England, including its May 4, 2002, *Insurrrextion* pay-per-view (for trivia buffs, this was the last pay-per-view under the WWF name, as the company would begin using the WWE name on May 5, 2002). By most accounts, a tremendous amount of booze was consumed and a one-hour take-off delay didn't help. Wrestlers consumed drugs as well so by the time the flight was in the air, there was a plane full of wrestlers flying high in the friendly sky. What happened next became immortalized as "The Plane Ride from Hell," and it was no laughing matter. The "Plane Ride from Hell" exemplifies professional wrestling's ugly side and although such behavior is certainly not limited to wrestling, it does not excuse it.

A Recipe for Disaster

According to Justin Credible, the flight was a business-as-usual situation for WWF Superstars returning home. However, that quickly changed:

> Vince at the time was chartering flights. We weren't on commercial flights – we'd rent a whole plane. We had a 747 – all ours. Meaning [not only] all the wrestlers [but also] the TV crew. So we have every cameraman, all the girls that make the costumes, tour managers, everybody – a full plane of WWE people. Now with that comes – and I bet you Vince has not done it since – a full and open bar. And what I mean by that is…a plane filled with alcoholic wrestlers at the end of a grueling tour. So think about it…it's like the last day of school… ("Planes, Pills, and Spinning Dicks").

X-Pac, no stranger to the wild side, discusses the atmosphere onboard the flight, "It was brewing…everybody had their different little deals they were doing…some people were doing GHB [Gamma-Hydroxybutyric acid], getting pilled-up – whatever, you know…You could buy [GHB] in the health food store. It was legal, so that was the reason everyone was doing it. But it…fucked…you…up…" ("Planes, Pills, and Spinning Dicks"). GHB or Gamma Hydroxybutyrate is a central nervous system depressant that is commonly referred to as a "club drug" or "date rape" drug…Euphoria, increased sex drive, and tranquility are reported positive effects of GHB abuse." ("GHB or Gamma-Hydroxybutyrate")

Given the known effects of alcohol, GHB, and the presence of WWE Superstars (some of whom were abusing performance enhancing drugs), what's the worst that could happen?

The Usual Suspects:

Scott Hall

Scott Hall's personal demons are well documented and when he returned to the WWF in 2002, they were stronger than ever. When Vince McMahon brought the original members of the New World Order back (Hulk Hogan, Kevin Nash, and Scott Hall), it took little time to see Hall was out of control. Scott Hall was observed to be the first wrestler to hit the plane's open bar, setting the stage for "The Plane Ride from Hell." Before long, he and Mr. Perfect took cans of shaving cream and began spraying it on various passengers. This behavior was tame compared to what would happen later.

Michael Hayes

Former wrestler turned WWF front officer worker Michael Hayes was seated next to wrestler JBL (aka John Bradshaw Layfield). Hayes, a notorious boozer at the time was harassing JBL, who had suffered a nasty cut to his head during the overseas tour. For whatever reason, Hayes made the mistake of punching JBL in the head and JBL returned fire. Depending on whom you believe, JBL either knocked Hayes' out with one punch or the punch eased Hayes into unconsciousness with some help from the copious amounts of alcohol in Hayes' bloodstream. To add insult to injury, someone cut Hayes' ponytail while he slept, then posted the picture in the *RAW* dressing room the next night (X-Pac is believed to be the culprit). One story has it that Hayes almost urinated on Linda McMahon during the flight. Hayes' alcohol problems are well known. "He also got obscenely drunk at Triple H and Stephanie McMahon's wedding and made a fool of himself with his inebriated karaoke singing, so much so that Linda McMahon had to put him in his place by going on stage and taking the mic away from him" (Harris). Another lowlight involving Hayes and alcohol include a tirade at *WrestleMania*

XXIV's afterparty where he told Mark Henry, "I'm more of a ni**er than you are" (Harris). Hayes was also reportedly suspended in 2013 for having drinks with Rosa Mendes when Mendes had just returned from dealing with alcohol-related problems. The fact that Hayes has kept his job AND his teeth is nothing short of a miracle.

Ric Flair

Flair is known for living up the "Nature Boy" image not only in terms of a lavish lifestyle but in parading around in nothing more than his ring robe and birthday suit. The fifty-three-year-old star allegedly began flashing flight attendants and performing his own aerial maneuver, the famous "Helicopter Dick." Flair allegedly crossed the line with the flight attendants claiming he sexually assaulted them. According to a September 6, 2011, article at *Grantland.com*:

> Two flight attendants, Taralyn Cappellano and Heidi Doyle, would compile their allegations into a 2004 lawsuit. Chief among the chronicled misdeeds was Fliehr's sexual aggression. He wore nothing but a jeweled cape, the flight attendants said, and "flashed his nakedness, spinning his penis around." He separately grabbed each woman's hand and placed it on his crotch, and then

"forcibly detained and restrained" Doyle "from leaving the back of the galley of the airplane while he sexually assaulted her."

The allegations didn't end there. Wrestler Scott Hall was also accused of licking "Doyle's face" and telling her, "he wanted to 'lick her pussy,'" (Ryan). Jim Ross, who was head of talent relations at the time denied Hall did anything. Wrestler Goldust (aka Dustin Runnels) was also accused of telling Cappellano, "You and me are gonna fuck" (Ryan).

Goldust's Crazy Karaoke

Dustin Runnels' harassment did not end there. Dustin's ex-wife Terri Runnels was aboard the plane and Dustin reportedly began serenading his wife over the plane's intercom. Fortunately for Terri, Jim Ross exercised his authority and ordered Rhodes off of the intercom. Even more unfortunate is that Dustin was less than a year away from doing his Tourette's gimmick. Had he done a stuttering serenade, he might have calmed down the tortured souls on the tumultuous flight.

An Eight Miles High Match

Arguably the flight's most terrifying incident (although the sight of a naked Ric Flair comes close) involved an amateur wrestling contest between Curt Hennig and Brock Lesnar when the two decided to test their grappling skills against one another. Lesnar took Hennig down but the overmatched Hennig refused to back down. According to passenger Justin Credible:

> They weren't fighting…at first. But they're very competitive so they're just scraping along, like messing around – then something happened where it got serious. It didn't come to blows – but you know the opening that they have on planes – those openings are the emergency exit rows. Now Brock's a wrestling shooter – and Curt's a shooter kind'a too – so they took it seriously. They didn't wanna give in to each other. They went at it so hard [Lesnar shot in and drove Hennig so hard into the side] that they almost popped open the emergency exit – twenty-five, thirty thousand feet in the air…people [among them: Dave Finley, Triple H, and Paul Heyman] had to separate them."

While the incident has been sensationalized as one where certain death was somehow avoided, X-Pac notes. "Obviously [WWE management] made a big deal out of it…the fuckin' door – it's impossible for it to open at that altitude So it was real stupid ("Planes, Pills, and Spinning Dicks"). When a commercial airline is in-flight, the cabin is pressurized which makes it extremely difficult, if not impossible to open a hatch (short of a bomb). Lesnar and Perfect's take-down contest wasn't the first time one had been held during a WWF flight. As X-Pac recalls, "(The flight before) Vince and Kurt Angle had a take-down tournament in the aisle – but as soon as it happened with (Hennig and Lesnar), they made a big deal out of it…" ("Planes, Pills, and Spinning Dicks").

Fortune Favors the Foolish

It's been said that fortune favors the bold, but it also favors the foolish as seen by the incredible amount of luck expended on the flight from hell. Vince McMahon was wise in chartering a commercial jet as it's difficult to envision any scenarios where wrestlers would have escaped criminal charges had they been on a regular passenger flight during "The Plane Ride from Hell." While the Brock vs. Perfect battle has been blown out of proportion in that there was little chance of the door coming off, it had to be a scary situation for people onboard.

The Aftermath

The "Plane Ride from Hell" did not end well for Scott Hall and Mr. Perfect, with both wrestlers being fired. Hall's drunken behavior on the England tour was seen as the main reason for Hall's firing and any activities that occurred on "The Flight from Hell" were icing on the cake.

The WWE fired Hennig after his antics and the former "Mr. Perfect" worked in TNA for several months before passing away in 2003. Goldust found himself in hot water with the WWE over his sky-high serenade but he was not fired. Brock Lesnar escaped unscathed as did Michael Hayes except for the justice dealt out by WWE wrestlers. As for the sexual assault allegations, while no criminal charges were filed, the WWE did settle out of court. Ric Flair denies the allegations.

Well guys, there you have it, a flight that could have gone down literally and figuratively, but one which thankfully fell short of a Hindenburg-like disaster.

Nearly two decades later, "The Plane Ride from Hell" would come back to haunt the WWE as Vice's "Dark Side of the Ring" documentary series covered the story, leading to some sponsors dropping Ric Flair as their spokesperson. The controversy died down however and Flair is bigger than ever, showing how even some of the most disturbing allegations can be glossed over with the passage of time.

Works Cited

"GHB or Gamma-Hydroxybutyrate." *Drugs.com.* https://www.drugs.com/illicit/ghb.html. Accessed 3 Apr. 2017.

Harris, Keith. "WWE Suspends Michael Hayes for

Getting Rosa Mendes Back on the Booze." *Cageside Seats.* 9 Oct. 2013. http://www.cagesideseats.com/wwe/2013/10/9/4821974/wwe-suspends-michael-hayes-for-getting-rosa-mendes-back-on-the-booze. Accessed 3 Apr. 2017.

Konwuwa, Alfred. "Real Life Heat: Top 5 (Legit) Backstage Fights in WWE History." 25 June 2010. http://bleacherreport.com/articles/411180-real-life-heat-top-5-legit-backstage-brawls-in-wwe-history. Accessed 3 Apr. 2017.

Oxley, Dr. Robert. "6 Occurrences on the Plane Ride from Hell." *WWF Old School.* 29 May 2015. http://wwfoldschool.com/6-occurrences-on-the-plane-ride-from-hell. Accessed 3 Apr. 2017.

"Planes, Pills, and Spinning Dicks." *Pro Wrestling Stories.* http://prowrestlingstories.com/pro-wrestling-stories/vol24/2. Accessed 3 Apr. 2017.

"The Plane Ride from Hell." *Pro Wrestling Wikia.* http://prowrestling.wikia.com/wiki/The_Plane_Ride_From_Hell. Accessed 3 Apr. 2017.

Ryan, Shane. "The Wrestler in Real Life: Ric Flair's Long, Steady Decline." *Grantland.* 6 Sept. 2011. http://grantland.com/features/the-wrestler-real-life. Accessed 3 Apr. 2017.

"WWE: 10 Hushed Scandals That Rocked

Wrestling." *Whatculture.*
http://whatculture.com/wwe/wwe-10-hushed-scandals-rocked-wrestling?page=2.
Accessed 3 Apr. 2017.

The WWE's willingness to overlook an individual's questionable comments and/or behavior is epitomized by its treatment of The Ultimate Warrior. The Ultimate Warrior went from WWE pariah to patron saint, despite comments that would likely see him canceled today.

Chapter Eighteen Warrior Wackiness: The Twisted History of The Ultimate Warrior

Originally published 2018

A Twisted History

Known for his superhero-like musculature and bizarre promos, James Helliwig entered professional wrestling at a time when spectacular physiques could translate into spectacular success. Although Hellwig was short on wrestling ability, his phenomenal build and exotic personality transformed him into one of the icons of the Rock-n-Wrestling Era where he worked as the Ultimate Warrior. However, as surreal as Hellwig's promos were on the microphone, they paled to the reality of Jim Hellwig's personal life and opinions. Hellwig would have a love/hate relationship with the WWF, eventually changing his name to "Warrior" to stymie Vince McMahon's efforts to keep him from working under the name he became legendary for. Over time, Hellwig would reconcile with the WWE, but he never withdrew any of his outrageous statements or beliefs, leading fans to wonder how the WWE keeps him in the Hall of Fame despite homophobic and other hateful comments.

A Reason to Analyze

It may seem petty to examine the bizarre and hurtful comments made by a deceased wrestler, but the WWE's placement of the Warrior in its Hall of Fame coupled with it naming an annual award after him warrants examination of the individual, much as the WWE has ostracized WWE Legends who they feel have tainted the promotion. As fans know, Hulk Hogan was expelled from the WWE Hall of Fame for racist comments he made while Jimmy "Superfly" Snuka was expelled for a murder charge (although the case was never adjudicated due to Snuka's dementia). If these Superstars deserve banishment, what of the Warrior? While the Ultimate Warrior was never charged with any crimes, his racist and homophobic comments pose the question why he remains such a prominent and revered figure in the WWE Universe.

A Sanitized Past

The Ultimate Warrior made numerous tasteless remarks through the years, both in public and online. Curiously, many of his former blog posts and other rants have disappeared from the Internet, including the Internet Wayback Machine.

However, his remarks have been repeated on several websites which allow people a chance to experience them. Has there been an active campaign to remove the Warrior's outrageous comments? It certainly appears so, suggesting someone does not want them kept in the public eye.

A Cornucopia of Contemptuousness

During his public life, the Ultimate Warrior said so many bigoted and mean-spirited things that it's difficult to include them all in one video. While words such as racist and homophobic may be overused, there's no question the spirit that drove the Warrior's comments. While they are repugnant, they need to be repeated to show how truly awful the Warrior's comments were.

Hurricane Katrina

Hurricane Katrina devastated not only New Orleans, but many areas around it, with its aftermath being felt even today. While the natural disaster helped unify many people in aiding Katrina's victims, some such as religious zealot Pat Robertson used it to advance an agenda (As detailed by *Time* magazine's website, "…Robertson blamed Hurricane Katrina on the issue of abortion in John Roberts' Supreme Court nomination"). The Warrior proved equally heinous in using the disaster to spread his opinion:

> "If we could be shown what general conditions they lived in before the hurricane, we would see that had little respect for what they did have. We would see just how unorganized, unclean and dysfunctionally they lived. They never gave a care for order, cleanliness or function before, but now that they can get someone's attention who will possibly take over the responsibility of their life for them, they go on these tirades about how their life has been ruined. Their lives were already in ruin — self ruin. Ruined by the bad choices they made over and over." (qtd. in Rousseau)

That was only the beginning. The Warrior's rant continued:

> "And they are fat. Have you ever seen so many fat people? Poverty? Poverty of what? Having enough to buy so much food to eat that you become obese — this is poverty? Only one TV? This is poverty? A house with a roof over your head? This is Poverty? Indoor plumbing? Electric appliances? Refrigeration? Phones? Cell phones? Computers? Designer clothes made by rap stars? $200 Nikes? Free medicine

and medical care if you really need it?
Is having all this poverty? What the
hell, then, do we call the scenes they
shoot out of Africa that they use to lay
guilt trips down on all of us?" (qtd. in
Rousseau)

Taking the Warrior's remark about "the scenes
they shoot out of Africa" in context with New
Orleans' large African-American population, it's
difficult to ignore who he is discussing.,

The Warrior continued standing on his soapbox,
proclaiming:

They claim New Orleans was (is) a
great city. Maybe once it was, I don't
know. Too, maybe it's just always been
corrupt as it has been for years and
years. Truth is, today, it was nothing
more than a pornographic cesspool of
decadence and depravity. You know,
an East Coast version of that Las
Vegas take on vacation time — "what
you do there stays there." You go
there, drink and drink and drink and
behave like a pervert, reprobate and
degenerate, take a huge dose of
antibiotics and a nice extra long shower
before you hop on the plane back
home, and, "Hey, who knows any
better?" You go back to the church,

PTA, and local council and "squarely" fit right back in. One thing is for sure, IF New Orleans ever was a great city, it certainly was not because it had leaders and citizenry like the leaders and citizenry it has today." (qtd. in Rousseau)

Dr. Martin Luther King, Jr.

While an ardent Warrior fan (or the WWE's legal department) might argue the Warrior's rants on New Orleans had nothing to do with ethnicity, his comments on Dr. Martin Luther King, Jr. do him no favors as he vilifies the revered civil rights leader:

> Martin Luther King can have his own self-titled birthday recognized as a National Holiday, but not our country's First President? Should I go on? Should I have to? Do I want to? Will I? You bet your ass I will.
> Let's see if I understand this correctly. Or should I say, let's see if I can get to anywhere near a "correct understanding" of this piece of nonsense by, first, understanding it sensically using political-incorrectness? Martin marched a few times from Selma, AL to Montgomery, AL. It's only about 40 miles and he walked

along paved roads with security escorts and modern comforts and conveniences. He wrote a few jailhouse letters, plagiarized a great many speeches, and played up his last name "King" as if he was ONE. He led his best rally amid the monuments of Washington, DC. He preached proper, righteous behavior while he at the same time committed adultery many publicly verifiable times — oh, and he had "a dream." (qtd. in Petchesky)

Homophobia

After leaving wrestling, the Ultimate Warrior turned his attention to motivational speaking, proclaiming ultra-conservative views including his notorious speech where he proclaimed, "Queering doesn't work." The Warrior's contempt for homosexuals was repeated, including the following comments he made at DePaul University:

One of the premises that I put forward in my speech being that the fundamental difference between the ideological sides is "thinking vs feeling," the most enlivening emotional outbursts erupted when homosexuals were offended by my use of the word "queer." One guy without his husband and two physically-repulsive butch-dykes slurping on one another's tongues (really) on the front row had a real hard time cozying up to my principled heterosexual obstinacy. So, in an act of pure selfish pleasure the guy got himself physically thrown out by the masculine security guard, unmistakably loving every single masochistic, man-handled moment of it. And the dykes, well, they ran out screaming and yelling like speared wild boars that I was a homophobe for making my remarks. Rumor has it that they decided to exit more because I was not getting stimulated by watching their poorly performed two-nightcrawlers-in-heat act. (qtd. in Petchesky)

The Warrior would clarify his statement that "queering doesn't work," claiming the human race would die out in a homosexual world.

However, the event (hosted by the DePaul Conservative Alliance) featured more lowlights from the Warrior as reported in the *Wrestling Observer*:

- Gay and lesbian couples (or "queers", for brevity) have the same disease as pedophile priests in the Catholic

Church. That must have gone over well at a Catholic university.

- Israelis are "sub-human" because they fight with rocks.

- That his five-year-old daughter would grow up feminine "in every sense of the word."

- Told a lecture attendee to "go masturbate at home" when the attendee complimented Hellwig on his wrestling accomplishments.

- Responding to hard questions with the stock answer "your question doesn't make any sense." (qtd. in Sudo)

A Disdain for Others

The Ultimate Warrior repeatedly showed a complete lack of sympathy for the suffering of others. After the death of actor Heath Ledger, the Warrior went off on the star of *Brokeback Mountain, The Dark Knight,* and other films, spewing the following venom:

> In the interest of full disclosure, I must tell you I have watched *Brokeback Mountain* no less than 45 times and I own the Limited Edition DVD, signed by Willie Nelson a short time after he wrote that queer cowboy song as a tribute to the courage of the producers and actors who broke such incredible

creative ground when they made their agenda-less movie. Serious. Until I saw Bendover Brokeback, *Braveheart* was my favorite movie. But the love scenes of Brokeback sucked me right in and I had no choice but to give myself over to the passion of its wide open range, if you get my drift. Such courage this young man and his colleagues have. Reminds me of the courage of classic movie stars, where during the War they enlisted and flew bomber planes and fought on frontlines, then came back and picked up their lives and careers right where they left off, without anti-American sentiment, whining and complaining, or self-destructive self indulgence. I'm equally inspired... (qtd. in Bryce)

Not to be outdone, the Warrior praised Ledger for killing himself:

By today's standard, though, I do have to agree that he was a great father. Perhaps even greater than the father of the year, Hulk Hogan. After all, Leather Hedger did what it took to kill himself. His kid is without a father, yes, but the negative influence is now removed and his own child has the chance for a full recovery. (qtd. in Bryce)

The Ultimate Warrior's comments on Ledger's suicide were no isolated incident. Consider his remarks following the death of Davey Boy Smith:

> "Davey committed a slow, sure, suicide. He was eternally blaming his 'falling of the horse' again and again on nothing more than circumstances of his life. Circumstances he kept creating for himself. I read over and over: I was involved with the Harts for 20 years. It was the worst 20 years I've ever had. I have no intention of having anything to do with them. Why then was he banging his ex-brother-in-law's bimbo ex-wife?" (qtd. in Brosnahan)

The late British Bulldog wasn't the only wrestling figure targeted by the Warrior, who had this to say about legendary wrestling manager Bobby "The Brain" Heenan:

> "As for you, Booby Heenan, it's just too difficult to keep a straight face talking about the pure two-faced bag of sh– you are (and have always been), what, with you also actually wearing one as a piece of body jewelry. You are dying, dis-eased on the inside, and no

more time is left to get back any of the integrity that matters the most on death's bed. Imagine what it will be like, lying there taking in your last breaths, knowing you whored yourself out your whole life, and had to, in your final years, be faced with emptying your own personal sh— bag affirming to you the true value of what you achieved in your life. Not even Vince could come up with a better finish than this. Karma is just a beautiful thing to behold." (qtd. in Doric)

In a 2004 interview with James Flynn, Warrior discussed wrestlers' deaths further:

"Ultimately each individual is solely responsible for destroying their own life. I think there are always tell-tale signs one gets warning them that 'Hey, you better take a hard look at what you are doing.' Typically, self-destruction happens in stages and each person is given ample opportunity to get their act together. You can't keep tempting fate without there eventually being a serious, negative consequence."

Shit, the autopsies came back and a lot of those guys died from street drugs. Hennig died from a coke overdose.

Rick Rude died from [liquid] ecstasy. Davey Boy Smith was doing cocaine and ungodly amounts of growth hormone and all kinds of different steroids." ("Interview with the Ultimate Warrior Part 3")

The Warrior would defend his remarks concerning figures such as Davey Boy Smith, telling Daniel Flynn:

"People have criticized me about what I wrote in some posts when some of those guys died—like I didn't have any sympathy. Anybody who wants to can read them. Frankly, I'm sick of all the sympathetic praise we throw around adults who screw up their lives. Life is about finding the strength day in and day out to make it work. Most people do. I'd rather praise them than people who don't. We are a society, today, where we pathetically place praise of vice above praise of virtue and, as an adult, I'm not okay with it. My kids, if no one else, deserve better out of me, deserve better out of the world they will have to grow up in." ("Interview with the Ultimate Warrior Part 3")

A Cause for Concern

Considering the Warrior's undeniable history of racist, homophobic, and hurtful remarks how does the WWE continue to use the Warrior to exemplify its recognition of people who have overcome personal adversity. Consider that the WWE created its Warrior Award in 2015 to, "exhibited unwavering strength and perseverance, and who lives life with the courage and compassion that embodies the indomitable spirit of the Ultimate Warrior." In 2018, Dana Warrior, widow to the Ultimate Warrior commented on the award, "I think the award allows Warrior's legacy to run forever, I care for these people (the recipients). They're sewn into the history and the legacy of my husband. But also the new life the girls and I have moved forward with, that's equally important" ("Spirit of WWE's"). While the award recipients have undoubtedly shown admirable traits, it is a disservice for them to be associated with someone who showed no compassion for others and looked down upon people based on ethnicity and sexual orientation.

The WWE also continues to work closely with the Susan G. Komen Foundation, a breast cancer organization it has partnered with in its #UnleashYourWarrior campaign which uses the Ultimate Warrior's image to promote awareness of breast cancer. Last year, the WWE honored three breast cancer survivors during an episode of

RAW, bestowing them with WWE championship belts. The women were joined by the WWE's women division with everyone wearing "Unleash Your Warrior" t-shirts. These t-shirts were available on WWE.com with the proceeds going to fight breast cancer.

In 2017, *Vice Sports* published an article, "The WWE is Whitewashing the Ultimate Warrior's Bigoted Past," chronicling many of the Warrior's outrageous statements. When asked to respond to the article, the WWE commented:

> "WWE's 'Unleash Your Warrior' breast cancer awareness campaign and annual 'Warrior Award' recognize individuals that exhibit the strength and courage of WWE's legendary character The Ultimate Warrior. Any attempt to distract from the mission of these initiatives and take the spotlight away from the honorees is unfortunately misguided." (qtd. in Rousseau)

Dana Warrior also responded to the article, defending her husband by saying:

> "I will not be disloyal to my husband's memory or speak ill of a man who is not here to defend himself…I can, however, tell you his heart was changed by conversations with his two daughters. The true testament of the

man behind the character is his ability to evolve. My husband did just that." (qtd. in Doric)

However, no record exists of the Warrior disavowing any of the statements mentioned here. Considering their venomous and hurtful nature, it's arguable he would have made a statement to refute them had he experienced a change of heart.

Admitted Steroid Use

According to author Daniel Flynn (who interviewed the Warrior in 2004 and knew him personally), the Ultimate Warrior made no secret of his steroid use, "He acknowledged using steroids as a body builder and as a professional wrestler in our conversations" ("What the Ultimate Warrior Taught Me"). In an interview with James Flynn, the Warrior discussed steroids:

> "Steroids. Talking about them is always a Catch-22. They aren't all bad and they aren't all good. Athletes are going to do them—or whatever else—to be the best at what they do. But, let's face it, bodybuilding and wrestling is more circus like—people want to see the freaks. The guys today are definitely gassed to the max. Wrestlers and bodybuilders." ("Interview with the Ultimate Warrior Part 3")

The Warrior's comments on steroids are unlikely to shock anyone who follows wrestling, but it's likely they make the McMahon family and other figures at Titan Tower uneasy. So why has the WWE turned what can only be called a blind eye to these comments?

The Ignorance is Bliss Policy

The WWE has worked fast to avoid bad publicity such as when it dropped The Fabulous Moolah's name from its *WrestleMania* Women's Battle Royal last April. Considering the considerable controversy surrounding the Ultimate Warrior, it's curious why the WWE continues to use him prominently in both its annual Hall of Fame and its charitable campaigns. Should the Warrior's comments be exposed on a national level, it would do damage to the WWE's reputation as well as any charity associated with it. For the time being, the Warrior's remarks remain ignored by the WWE, leading some to wonder how long his dark past can be kept secret.

Works Cited

Assael, Shaun and Mike Mooneyham. *Sex, Lies, and Headlocks: The Real Story of Vince McMahon and World Wrestling Entertainment.* Three Rivers Press, 2004.

Brosnahan, Chris. "WWF Legend The Ultimate

Warrior Returns: Racist, Homophobe, Hall of Famer." *Sabotage Times*. Sport. 2 Mar. 2014. https://sabotagetimes.com/sport/wwf-legend-the-ultimate-warrior-returns-racist-homophobe-hall-of-famer. Accessed 30 June 2018.

Bryce, Ronnie. "The Ultimate Warrior: The Ultimate Hypocrite." *Bleacher Report*. WWE. 11 Oct. 2008. https://bleacherreport.com/articles/67597-the-ultimate-warrior-the-ultimate-hypocrite. Accessed 30 June 2018.

Crugnale, James. "Feud Over Ultimate Warrior's Death: WWE Star Diamond Dallas Page Slams Nancy Grace." *The Wrap*. TV. 10 Apr. 2014. https://www.thewrap.com/wwe-wrestler-diamond-dallas-page-strikes-back-hlns-nancy-grace. Accessed 2 July 2018.

Flynn, Daniel. "INTERVIEW WITH THE ULTIMATE WARRIOR - PART 1 OF 4." *Sporttaco.com* 14 June 2004. http://www.sporttaco.com/rec.sport.pro-wrestling/Flynn_Files_Ultimate_Warrior_Interview_Part_1_3281.html. Accessed 2 July 2018.

Flynn, Daniel. "INTERVIEW WITH THE

ULTIMATE WARRIOR - PART 3 OF 4."
Flynn Files. 2004.
http://archive.is/hffST#selection-81.0-
81.49. Accessed 2 July 2018.

Flynn, Daniel J. "What the Ultimate Warrior
Taught Me About Life While Lifting
Weights." *Breitbart.com.* 9 Apr. 2014.
https://www.breitbart.com/Sports/2014/04
/09/Ultimate-Warrior-RIP/. Accessed 2 July
2018.

Friedman, Megan. "God's Wrath Caused Katrina."
Time. Prickly Pat. 16 Sept. 2011.
http://content.time.com/time/specials/pac
kages/article/0,28804,1953778_1953776_19
53771,00.html. Accessed 2 July 2018.

Kyanka, Rich. "Something Awful vs. THE
ULTIMATE WARRIOR." *Something Awful.*
Legal Threats. 11 Apr. 2005.
https://www.somethingawful.com/legal-
threats/legal-threat-ultimate/1. Accessed 1
July 2018.

Pang, Kevin. "On Raw, WWE continues rewriting
Ultimate Warrior's hateful past." *AV Club.*
For Our Consideration. 3 Oct. 2017.
https://www.avclub.com/on-raw-wwe-
continues-rewriting-ultimate-warriors-hatef-
1819106332. Accessed 1 July 2018.

Petchesky, Barry. "The Ultimate Warrior Was An
Insane Dick." *Deadspin.* Ultimate Warrior. 9

Apr. 2014. https://deadspin.com/the-ultimate-warrior-was-an-insane-dick-1561275496.
Accessed 30 June 2018.

Rousseau, Rob. "WWE Is Whitewashing The Ultimate Warrior's Bigoted Past." *Vice Sports.* WWE. 27 Oct. 2017. https://sports.vice.com/en_ca/article/59y3nb/wwe-is-whitewashing-the-ultimate-warriors-bigoted-past. Accessed 30 June 2018.

Doric, Sam. "Media Outlet Looks at Ultimate Warrior's Past Controversial Comments, WWE And Dana Warrior Respond." *Wrestling Inc.* 30 Oct. 2017. http://www.wrestlinginc.com/wi/news/2017/1030/633576/media-outlet-looks-at-ultimate-warrior-past-controversial. Accessed 1 July 2018.

The Self-Destruction of the Ultimate Warrior. Directed by Kevin Dunn, performances by Jim Hellwig, Adnan Al-Kaissy, and Andre the Giant, World Wrestling Entertainment, 2005.

"Spirit of WWE's Ultimate Warrior lives on through Warrior award." *The Times Picayune.* New Orleans Entertainment News. 26 Feb. 2018. https://www.nola.com/entertainment/index

.ssf/2018/02/the_ultimate_warriors_spirit_1. html. Accessed 1 July 2018.

Sudo, Chuck. "Deep Thinking: Thine Scion is Warrior." *Chicagoist.* Arts and Entertainment. 6 Apr. 2006. http://chicagoist.com/2006/04/06/deep_th inking_thine_scion_is_warrior.php. Accessed 2 July 2018.

"Ultimate Warrior: The Controversial UCONN Speech – April 5, 2005." *YouTube* uploaded by The Three Horsemen, 24 June 2017, https://www.youtube.com/watch?v=tttKYd CLjl8.

Warrell, Richard. "WWE News: The Ultimate Warrior Opens "Warrior University" *Bleacher Report.* WWE. 19 July 2012. https://bleacherreport.com/articles/126440 7-wwe-news-the-ultimate-warrior-opens-warriors-university. Accessed 2 July 2018.

"WWE® and Susan G. Komen® Encourage You to "Unleash Your Warrior" in the Fight against Breast Cancer." *Business Wire.* 3 Oct. 2017. https://www.businesswire.com/news/home /20171003005874/en/WWE%C2%AE-Susan-G.-Komen%C2%AE-Encourage-%E2%80%9CUnleash-Warrior%E2%80%9D. Accessed 1 July 2018.

290

Part Five:
McMahon And Super-McMahon

What's Vince McMahon really like? There's Vince McMahon the business person and there's Mr. McMahon, the character he plays on TV that is supposedly an exaggerated version of his personality. Fans continue to speculate if there's any difference between the two, a valid question when you read the following anecdotes about the WWE's big man.

We've seen stories about Vince McMahon's past and his incredible approach to doing business but what about the man himself? Here are some stories that provide an insight into Vince's personality and his eccentricities. These stories are based on anecdotes told by people close to McMahon (or confirmed by people in the know).

Chapter Nineteen: A McMahon for All Seasons

Originally published 2018

He's Incredibly Isolated from the Outside World

Vince McMahon lives and breathes (we'd say sleep but as we'll see, sleep is the enemy) wrestling, which means he doesn't have time for going to the movies or even watching TV. Sound odd? In 1992, wrestler Scott Hall went to work for the WWF and sat down with Vince McMahon to discuss the character that would help him become a successful wrestler. Hall's initial meeting wasn't as promising as he'd hoped. When McMahon learned Hall's dad had served in the military, he suggested Hall become a G.I. Joe type character. According to Hall:

> "I said 'Vince, if you want me to be G.I. Joe, I'll be the best G.I. Joe I can be.'...I said, 'Did you ever see

Scarface?' He said 'No.' I went 'Say hello to the bad guy.' I just started doing that schtick and he loved it and he thought I was a genius. I'm ripping off the movie and he thinks I'm a genius. Of course I never corrected him about the genius part," Hall quipped. "But that's how it all came about." (Murphy)

Not everyone has seen *Scarface* but what about common food items?

Baffled by a Burrito

Is this a Vince McMahon world and we're just living in it? You might be doubtful but not after you hear this story from former WWE writer Dan Madigan, who told *Pro Wrestling Torch's* Wade Keller. Madigan discussed how the WWE's creative team wanted to incorporate a storyline with the wrestler The Big Show and a bad burrito:

"I think they were going to poison Big Show and give him a spiked burrito. The whole concept was: 'We're going to spike his food, spike the burrito, you cut to a vignette before that showing him eating it, and then he passes out in the ring.' So, Vince goes, 'Burrito?! Who the hell knows what a burrito is?' It was such a far concept. And everyone in the room goes, 'Well, we know what a burrito is.' And Vince goes, 'Well, where the hell have I been?'

He Loves Snow Cones

According to one tale, Vince McMahon once had a snow cone party and proclaimed his love for snow cones in the voice of his "Mr. McMahon" character. Wrestling legend has it that McMahon, who normally eats a very healthy diet, downed ten snow cones.

Hold It In: When it comes to sneezes, rumor has it that Vince will yell at someone for sneezing as he apparently sees it as a lack of control. Vince supposedly has the same disdain for himself when he sneezes as one of his associates has discussed how Vince gets angry with himself if he sneezes. (Rift)

He Should Have Held It In: If you've watched WWE TV for any significant amount of time, you'll find your fair share of toilet humor, which some fans think reflects Vince McMahon's sense of humor. This might explain this stinky situation. McMahon's former announcer and Head of Talent Relations Jim Ross farted while in a car with former WWE official Gerald Brisco. Brisco then gagged and barfed, a story which McMahon is said to have found amusing to no end. McMahon wanted to see if he could make Brisco puke so he farted. Regrettably for McMahon, he pooped his pants.

During an episode of his podcast, *Something to Wrestle With,* longtime WWE employee Bruce Prichard shared the disgusting details:

> "He was going to fart and he sh*t. And he walks up the stairs to 'gorilla' and says, 'Bruce, come here, pal.' And I went, 'yeah?' And he lifted his jacket up and he says, 'do you see anything?' And I said, 'yeah, you sh*t your pants.' 'G*ddamnit! How about now?' And he let his jacket down and I couldn't see it. And he said, 'do you think they'll be able to tell?' And I said, 'I think if you keep your jacket on, you'll be alright, buddy.'" (qtd. in Hanstock)

This awful accident occurred during a live episode of the WWE's *RAW* and McMahon was scheduled to cut a promo (make a speech) in the ring. McMahon's "the show must go on" attitude was readily apparent as he went to the ring and the camera crew were told to shoot McMahon above the waist for his entire appearance.

He Won't Let the Beard Win

Not only does Vince McMahon supposedly loathe sneezing but he won't let his beard win. Paul Heyman, who was worked in the WWE for many years once shared the story of how Vince has a thick beard but that he's constantly shaving because "I can't let it [the beard] win." (Rift)

He Once Suspended a Wrestler for Touching Him

Vince McMahon does not like to appear weak, which is why he never sneezes and tries to sleep as little as possible. He also likes to be perceived as a tough S.O.B. which is why Titus O'Neil found himself suspended for 3 months (the suspension was later reduced to 2 months) when he grabbed Mr. McMahon's arm during Daniel Bryan's retirement speech back in 2016. By one account, O'Neil grabbed Vince's arm so Stephanie McMahon could walk first (in a "ladies first" gesture) and by another, O'Neil was just being playful. According to some reports, Vince was going to fire O'Neil but changed his decision. McMahon's reaction is still talked about today with fans and writers wondering what led to McMahon changing his mind from firing O'Neil to suspending him.

Works Cited

Hanstock, Bill. "The Story of The Time Vince McMahon Crapped His Pants Before Going On TV." *Uproxx*. WWE. 13 Jan. 2017. https://uproxx.com/prowrestling/wwe-vince-mcmahon-shart-story. Accessed 15 June 2022.

Murphy, Jan. "Scott Hall once again the Bad Guy." *SLAM! Sports.* SLAM! Wrestling. 3 Apr. 2016. http://slam.canoe.com/Slam/Wrestling/2016/06/24/22646003.html. Accessed 19 Feb. 2018.

Rift, Aaron. "A compilation of 'crazy' stories about Vince McMahon that have been told over the years." *Nodq.com.* Features. 18 Dec. 2021. https://nodq.com/features/a-compilation-of-crazy-stories-about-vince-mcmahon-that-have-been-told-over-the-years. Accessed 15 June 2022.

Upton, Felix. "15 LEGENDARY VINCE MCMAHON STORIES CONFIRMED TO BE TRUE." *Ringside News.* WWE News. 5 May 2020. https://www.ringsidenews.com/2020/05/05/15-legendary-vince-mcmahon-stories-confirmed-to-be-true. Accessed 10 June 2022.

"Vince McMahon Stories That Will Make You Laugh." *IWNerd.com.* Hot Topics. https://www.iwnerd.com/10-hilarious-vince-mcmahon-stories-will-make-laugh. Accessed 25 June 2022.

Wilkinson, Matthew. "20 Recent Examples of

Vince McMahon Getting Upset Backstage." *The Sportster.* Wrestling. 24 Jan. 2019. https://www.thesportster.com/wrestling/wwe-recent-examples-vince-mcmahon-getting-backstage. Accessed 13 July 2019.

Chapter Twenty: McMahon's Gracious Giving: Helping Out Other Wrestlers

There are many stories and rumors that might make people think Vince McMahon tosses bags full of kittens into the Atlantic Ocean but as we'll see, while Vince McMahon is often vilified, there are several stories of the WWE kingpin helping out his wrestlers in need. McMahon doesn't broadcast his charity though and these stories have only emerged thanks to anecdotes from the wrestlers he helped or those close to the wrestlers.

Shawn Michaels: Shawn Michaels was one of the WWF's top stars of the 1990s and while Michaels was known for giving McMahon headaches due to his backstage antics, the wrestler was one of McMahon's favorites. In 1998, Michaels suffered what was believed to be a career-ending injury when he herniated two discs in his back during a match against The Undertaker. Although Michaels was under contract, the WWF could have released him. In 2021, Michaels revealed:

> "One hand, contractually I had a somewhat guaranteed contract, so to speak. But can they always refuse to do that? Yes they can. They chose not to. Vince chose not to. And if anybody wonders why my loyalty is what it is to the WWE, that's your answer."
> (Staszewski)

Harley Race: Wrestling legend Harley Race was one of wrestling's toughest men but when health problems finally caught up with "The greatest wrestler on God's green earth," he was in a bad way. According to former WWE star Trevor Murdoch, Vince helped Race out when no one else could:

> "Harley needed to be transferred from Atlanta to St. Louis. He needed to take a Med flight because he was in rough shape. Medicare wouldn't help him. A call was made to WWE and 10 mins later it was paid in full. Vince McMahon never blinked an eye. He wanted to make sure Harley was taken care of. Thank you, Vince, you gave me 2 more days with Harley." (Mendhe)

MVP: WWE star MVP (Montel Vontavious Porter) served nearly ten years in prison for armed robbery and kidnapping but he credits Vince McMahon with giving him a shot when he tried out for a job as a WWE Superstar:

> "Society wouldn't give me an opportunity to make minimum wage, Vince McMahon said. 'Yeah, you did some bad things, but everybody here gets an opportunity. You've earned an opportunity.'"

The Undertaker: The Undertaker (aka Mark Calaway) is one of the biggest stars in WWE history but there was point when he needed

McMahon's guidance. Calloway was going through personal problems that was affecting his work when Vince McMahon took him aside for a heart-to-heart talk:

> "Vince straight up pulled me into his office one day, and we started talking about it. He looked me straight in the eyes and he said, 'Mark, you need to quit feeling sorry for yourself. You need to quit feeling sorry for yourself. Then get your a** out there and do what you're supposed to do.' As I'm processing all that, I knew he [Vince] was right." (Mendhe)

This are just a handful of instances where McMahon has helped people financially and/or with personal advice.

Works Cited

Mendhe, Abilash. "5 WWE Superstars Vince McMahon helped in real life." *Sportskeeda*. 26 July 2020. https://www.sportskeeda.com/wwe/5-wwe-superstars-vince-mcmahon-helped-real-life. Accessed 24 June 2022.

Staszewski, Joseph. "This $750K Vince McMahon gesture helped earn Shawn Michaels' WWE loyalty." *The New York Post*. Sports. 18 Mar. 2021. https://nypost.com/2021/03/18/the-

750k-wwe-gesture-that-helped-earn-shawn-michaels-loyalty. Accessed 24 June 2022.

Chapter Twenty-One: McMahon's Sentimental Side

Originally published 2019

While Vince McMahon doesn't seem like the crying type, the WWE's head honcho can get emotional at times, showing his feelings by shedding some tears. Here are 12 times Vince McMahon got so emotional he cried.

1. **During the filming of the Andre the Giant documentary:** Vince McMahon shared a close bond with "The Eighth Wonder of the World," but sadly like some friendships, things soured towards the end between Vince and Andre the Giant. Documentary director Jason Hehir spent over a year looking into Andre's life and spent 45 minutes interviewing McMahon. During the documentary, McMahon choked up and fought off tears, an experience Hehir chose to show in the film. In a 2018 interview, the director explained:

    "Vince seemed to be trying to keep it together, and as an interviewer it's excruciating because your instinct is to turn the camera off, but you have a responsibility to the viewer to let them experience this feeling vicariously through the person who knows the subject well, so we included that in the film" ("Director of Andre")

Hehir reveals McMahon was even more emotional during their first encounter, "He got emotional when no cameras were there. The first meeting I had with him I mentioned that Andre had a really close relationship with his daughter, and he got pretty emotional there" ("Director of Andre").

2. **When Jerry "The King" Lawler Gave Him a Special Gift:** Sometimes the best gifts are the ones a person makes for someone. In this case, Jerry "The King" Lawler utilized his considerable talents as an artist to show the WWE kingpin how much he cared. As Jerry Lawler fans know, the once and future king of wrestling broke into the business by sending in cartoons of Memphis wrestlers to the local television station that carried wrestling. In 2018, "The King," recalled the gift and Vince's surprising reaction:

> "I can't tell you how many years ago it's been. I don't know where I got the idea from, but anyway I did a portrait,

a big nice portrait for Vince. It was like a triple portrait, a portrait where Vince was in the middle, on the left of Vince was his son Shane and on the right of Vince was his father Vince, Sr. and so I did this portrait, worked on it a long time. It really turned out great… a little bit later I saw Vince and I said, 'Vince, I've got something I want to give to you, if you've got a minute.' So I had him come into my room there and I opened the portrait up and he immediately looked at it and his hand came up and covered his mouth and he turned away like immediately. His hand came up. He turned away and walked over into a corner and he just stood there for maybe a couple of minutes and then he like slowly came back and looked at the picture again. I think it brought tears to his eyes. I was shocked and then he hugged me and said how much it meant to him and all that sort of stuff. That was like the one moment that I ever really saw from Vince that kind of emotion. I think it's still hanging in his office." (McCarthy)

3. **Shawn Michaels Entering the WWE Hall of Fame:** Shawn Michaels rightfully

entered the WWE Hall of Fame in 2011, a testament to his outstanding performances in the ring throughout the years. Behind the scenes, Michaels was a known troublemaker, something which caused fans and wrestlers to speculate as to how he kept his job, particularly during his tumultuous times during the 1990's. Nonetheless, Vince McMahon teared up when he greeted and hugged Michaels during "The Showstopper's" Hall of Fame ceremony. In 2012, Michaels discussed his relationship with McMahon, telling the *Miami Herald*:

> ...Vince McMahon, the guy I argued with more than anybody, understood it. He understood that it wasn't unprofessionalism or ego that was driving all that; It was a desire and a passion to be the guy and to be the absolute very best that I could be.... He tells people all the time the reason he didn't fire me is because he could see through all that. Ultimately, when it came down to his way or my way, he always knew when he said, 'This is what I want done, period.' He knew I'd do it, and I always did." (qtd. in Jalali)

Will fans see Mr. McMahon sobbing this year when Shawn Michaels is inducted again into the WWE Hall of Fame, this time for his time in D-Generation X?

4. **Discovering "Stone Cold" Steve Austin Needed Neck Surgery:** A botched piledriver at the hands of wrestler Owen Hart finally caught up with "Stone Cold" Steve Austin in 1999, forcing the WWF's biggest star at the time to undergo surgery and miss nearly a year of in-ring action. While Vince McMahon was likely concerned about the impact on the WWF's business, the loss was felt personally as well. In his 2004 memoir, Steve Austin discussed how, "J. R went into Vince's office and Vince's eyes were red, and he was wiping the tears from his eyes [...] he really cared" (qtd. in "10 Emotional Times").

5. **During the Freddie Blassie Tribute Video:** Despite working as a much-heated heel, "Classy" Freddie Blassie had an undeniable comedic aspect that won people over, including Vince McMahon. Blassie, a colorful character who was one of wrestling's earliest crossover stars appeared in the Andy Kaufman film *My Breakfast with Blassie* and the song, "Pencil

Neck Geek" as well as numerous humorous appearances with Vince McMahon on the WWF's *Tuesday Night Titans* show. Though confined to his wheelchair in later years, Blassie served as an elder statesman, famously appearing in the "Stand Up" hype video during the Invasion angle. When Blassie died in 2003, the WWE aired a poignant tribute video to the legendary star. During the video, Vince's fondness showed through and he remarked, "Even though there's a vast age difference, there's a tremendous camaraderie I have with Classy Freddie Blassie and I will miss that forever."

6. **After Eddie Guerrero Won the WWE Championship:** Eddie Guerrero's WWE Championship win at *No Way Out* was an emotional moment for WWE fans as well as the culmination of a long road back for "Latino Heat." Just a few years earlier, Guerrero's WWE career seemed finished thanks to his personal demons sabotaging his life. However, Eddie sobered up, proving he was ready to work through appearances on the indie circuit and this led to the WWE giving him a second chance, one he put to good use. Vince McMahon was a huge fan of Guerrero's

and Eddie's rise to the main event affirmed McMahon's belief in the Latino Superstar. Eddie's successful rehabilitation and in-ring comeback meant everything to Vince McMahon as well as the entire WWE locker room, as seen backstage when Guerrero's colleagues applauded his win. During an episode of his podcast, *Something to Wrestle With*, Bruce Prichard recalled, "It was a standing ovation. There were hugs and tears all around. Vince was crying. He was very emotional because it was magical. Everyone believed there was a happy ending" (qtd. in Stonehouse).

7. **The Eddie Guerrero Tribute Show:** Vince McMahon shared a friendship with Eddie Guerrero that saw McMahon watch with admiration as Eddie conquered his personal demons to become one of the most popular WWE stars of the early 2000's. The highly charismatic Guerrero eventually became WWE Champion in 2004 and *SmackDown's* biggest Superstar. Sadly, Guerrero's amazing second act was cut short when he died at age 38 from acute heart failure due to atherosclerotic cardiovascular disease. The WWE aired tribute shows to Eddie on November 14

and November 18th episodes of *RAW* and *SmackDown!* During a tribute video, an emotional Vince McMahon fought back the tears as he talked of his recently deceased friend, ""Eddie loved to perform…There's one thing Eddie loved more than performing, and that was his family. Eddie was a good man. A damn good man" (qtd. in "10 Emotional Times")

8. **During the Rock's Birthday:** Not every occasion where Vince McMahon cried was a sad one. On May 2, 2011, "The Most Electrifying Man in Sports Entertainment" returned to WWE television to celebrate his birthday, a joyful celebration as the Rock reflected on his WWE career and received birthday wishes from a number of individuals including the WWE's CEO, Vincent Kennedy McMahon. McMahon gushed with praise, thanking the Rock for his time in the company and for returning home to the WWE that night to celebrate his birthday. Although McMahon wasn't crying his eyes out, eagle-eyed fans could see him getting misty-eyed.

9. **After Shane O'Mac's *WrestleMania XXXII* Performance:** 2016 featured an

emotional on-air reunion as Shane McMahon returned to the WWE after several years pursuing business interests outside the WWE. Shane O'Mac didn't waste any time, staking his claim for storyline control of *RAW*. Vince McMahon agreed to his son's demand on one condition—he defeat the Undertaker in a Hell in a Cell Match at *WrestleMania XXXII*. The brutal match saw Shane miss a jump off the top of the Cell, plowing through an announcer's table and being stretchered out after dropping the match to "The Phenom." Backstage, Vince McMahon greeted his son and a jubilant Papa Vince began to tear up, undeniably proud at his son's performance and his contribution to the legacy of "The Showcase of the Immortals."

10. **Linda McMahon's Concession Speech?** While Linda McMahon is currently serving as Administrator for WWE Hall of Famer and U.S. President Trump's Small Business Administration, her political aspirations date back to two campaigns for the United States Senate. Linda, who had battled her husband in WWE storylines and even taken a piledriver from "The Big Red Machine"

Kane faced an even more daunting task when she entered Senate races in 2010 and 2012. Despite two spirited campaigns, Linda came up short both times and her 2012 concession speech to Chris Murphy was highlighted by a distraught Vince McMahon (likely so since he'd spent $100 million of the McMahon fortune to finance the campaign) standing in the background as Linda thanked him and told the audience her husband was a very shy person who didn't want to appear. One can only wonder what was going through Vinnie Mac's head as he watched Linda throw in the towel. Was he thinking he'd somehow doubled his losses from the XFL with Linda's campaign or was he considering sending in a troop of WWE Superstars to crash Linda's rival's celebration?

11. **During the Chris Benoit Tribute:** Although there is some question whether Vince McMahon knew Chris Benoit murdered his family when the WWE aired a tribute program to him on June 25, 2007 (see the chapter on the Benoit murders/suicide for more details), a teary-eyed Vince opened the show to announce Benoit's unexpected death before some of

Benoit's best matches aired. Just a day later, an angry McMahon would appear on ECW to announce:

"Last night on Monday night raw the WWE presented a tribute show recognizing the career of Chris Benoit. However, 26 hours later, the facts of this horrific tragedy are now apparent. Therefore, other than my comments there will be no mention of Mr. Benoit's name tonight. On the contrary, tonight's show will be dedicated to everyone who has been affected by this terrible incident. This evening marks the first step of the healing process. Tonight, WWE performers will do what they do better than anyone else in the world -- entertain you." (qtd. in Rovell)

12. **The Ultimate Warrior Tribute:** As we've seen, Vince McMahon has had some heated moments with his top stars, a situation exemplified by the hot and cold relationship between McMahon and the Ultimate Warrior. After the WWE released it's *The Self-Destruction of the Ultimate Warrior* DVD, few fans expected the Warrior to ever patch things up with the WWE. Inexplicably, that happened in

2013 when the two made peace. In 2014, the Ultimate Warrior was inducted into the WWE Hall of Fame, appearing at *WrestleMania XXX* and the next night on *RAW* where he gave an emotional speech. The wrestling world was shocked when the Warrior collapsed the next day, dying from a heart attack due to atherosclerotic cardiovascular disease. McMahon, an avid bodybuilder like the Warrior, had once been close friends with him and their reconciliation promised a chance to enjoy each other's friendship again. As shown in the WWE Network's Ultimate Warrior documentary, Vince McMahon was beyond devastated and the camera captures the WWE Chairman with tears in his eyes.

Works Cited

"Director of Andre the Giant film on making Vince McMahon cry and the truth about Samuel Beckett." *The 42*. 16 Apr. 2018. https://www.the42.ie/the-director-of-hbos-andre-the-giant-documentary-interview-3961526-Apr2018. Accessed 23 Feb. 2019.

Ghosh, Prayyay. "5 Emotional WWE moments when Vince McMahon cried." *Sporstkeeda*.

WWE. 22 Feb. 2019. https://www.sportskeeda.com/wwe/5-emotional-wwe-moments-when-vince-mcmahon-cried. Accessed 23 Feb. 2019.

Jalali, Imaan. "WWE News: Shawn Michaels on His Relationship with Vince McMahon." *Bleacher Report.* WWE. 24 May 2012. https://bleacherreport.com/articles/1195589-wwe-news-shawn-michaels-on-his-relationship-with-vince-mcmahon. Accessed 23 Feb. 2019.

"Linda McMahon Concession Speech Has Vince McMahon in Tears." *YouTube,* uploaded by Masked Tweeter, 7 Nov. 2012, https://www.youtube.com/watch?v=Pj9lUr3-pgE.

McCarthy, Alex. "Jerry 'The King' Lawler recalls the one time he saw Vince McMahon crying backstage in WWE." *Give Me Sport.* WWE. 23 Dec. 2018. https://www.givemesport.com/1425011-jerry-the-king-lawler-recalls-the-one-time-he-saw-vince-mcmahon-crying-backstage-in-wwe. Accessed 23 Feb. 2019.

Rovell, Darren. "WWE's McMahon Should Have Apologized." *CNBC.* Sports Biz with Darren Rovell. 26 June 2007. https://www.cnbc.com/id/19448064. Accessed 23 Feb. 2019.

Stonehouse, Gary. "'VERY EMOTIONAL' WWE boss Vince McMahon reduced to tears after Brock Lesnar lost title." *The Sun.* 23 Feb. 2019. https://www.thesun.co.uk/sport/8482901/wwe-vince-mcmahon-crying-brock-lesnar-eddie-guerrero. Accessed 23 Feb. 2019.

"10 Emotional Times Vince McMahon Cried His Eyes Out." *Whatculture.* WWE. http://whatculture.com/wwe/10-emotional-times-vince-mcmahon-cried-eyes. Accessed 23 Feb. 2019.

Chapter Twenty-Two: The Wit and Wisdom of Vince McMahon

Here are some words of wisdom from Vince McMahon that may provide some insight into who he is.

"There are just no excuses for anything. I read about some guy who has excuses for his behavior because he comes from a broken home or he was beaten or was sexually abused or got into the wrong crowd or whatever the case may be — all of which have occurred in my lifetime. But those are no excuses." (Sales)

"Oh my God! My dad was incredible. I wanted to be part of his world. I loved the promotion business. I'd hang with him at the wrestling; it was like being the kid in the candy store. I liked the roar of the crowd. I liked the charismatic people. I liked the entertainment. I liked all of it." (Drucker)

"When you feed the monster, the monster is happy. The problem with that is, the monster grows. And as the monster grows, then the monster wants more to eat. And as long as you do that, everything's great. And if you don't provide the food, then bad things start to happen." (Solomon)

"I like learning from my mistakes and bringing the values I've learned forward. But I'm not good at patting myself on the back. I'm not good at looking back." (Solomon)

Works Cited

Drucker, Joel. "King of the Ring." *Cigar Aficionado*. Celebrities. Nov/Dec. 1999. https://www.cigaraficionado.com/article/king-of-the-ring-6149. Accessed 24 June 2022.

Sales, Nancy Jo. "Beyond Fake." *New York Magazine*. 26 Oct. 1998. http://www.nancyjosales.com/wp-content/uploads/2015/05/Wrestling2.pdf. Accessed 24 June 2022.

Solomon, Michael. "Top Move: Why The Billionaire CEO Is Betting Big on The New WWE Network." *Forbes*. Lifestyle. 26 Mar. 2014. https://www.forbes.com/sites/msolomon/2014/03/26/vince-mcmahons-over-the-top-move-why-the-billionaire-ceo-is-betting-big-on-the-new-wwe-network/?sh=6e8d883239e2. Accessed 24 June 2022.

Chapter Twenty-Three: Stormy Weather or Blue Skies?

So, what's the forecast for Vincent Kennedy McMahon—stormy weather or blue skies? Although Vince McMahon's current crisis suggests the WWE's head honcho is headed for trouble, McMahon's history of surviving pitfalls and perils has some observers believing he'll find a way to either escape his latest problems or minimize the damage. While McMahon may pay some sort of penalty, he may easily weather the storm and land on his feet as he's done many times before. As we've seen, McMahon has experienced major failures but ultimately, he is a survivor—regardless of how people perceive him.

An important takeaway for people who don't follow the wrestling industry is that the scandals in wrestling are similar to scandals in sports and entertainment. For some reason, many people ignore wrestling's scandals, dismissing them because of wrestling's fictitious nature and/or it ranking low on the cultural food chain.

It doesn't help that the wrestling industry is built on a foundation of fooling the public (even today when it's well-known that wrestling matches are pre-determined). This means that it's essential to be skeptical when dealing with anyone from the industry whether it's a wrestler, a person lighting the ring, or a high-level executive.

Simply put, you need a strong bullshit-detector when dealing with the industry and you have to find a way through the industry's code of secrecy.

Former wrestler and WWE executive James J. Dillon recently shared his thoughts on the accusations against Vince McMahon, his former boss:

> "I was the Senior Vice President of Talent Relations for Vince Jr. and he took that brand and went global with it and stepped on a lot of toes doing it because all these other promoters that had their little things and produced their own TV, Vince had a vision of going global and used his money to do it and so, have I heard stories? Absolutely, and I've learned that a lot of times when you hear something, especially in this business, a lot of it's true, a lot of it's not true. People tell things on other people, whatever their thing is whether it's jealousy or thinking that they're gonna demean somebody and get even with them for something, whether they were slighted or what..." (qtd. in Thompson)

It's still unknown exactly what happened between the women who signed nondisclosure agreements and Vince McMahon and/or his Head of Talent Relations John Laurinaitis. Hopefully, the investigation will find a way to break through wrestling's code of secrecy and remember that while wrestling may be fictitious, what happens outside the ring is all too-real. All allegations of misconduct deserve to be heard and should not be dismissed because they happened in an environment some have likened to a mix of a circus and a sporting event.

Judgment Day for McMahon?

While McMahon's judgment day is still off and the penalties (if any) are unknown, there are some inescapable consequences ahead.

A Loss of Confidence

Even if Vince McMahon manages to avoid serious consequences in terms of any criminal charges and/or being expelled from the WWE, his leadership will be tenuous. Vince's handling of the alleged wrongdoing by John Laurinaitis stands out as McMahon being out of touch or perhaps indifferent to contemporary corporate values in light of the #MeToo movement.

One thing seems certain—John Laurinatis is finished. According to a report from *Fightful Select,* John Laurinatis (aka Johnny Ace) is likely on his way out:

> One higher up told Fightful "Johnny Ace's ninth life is about to be lost."

Around the time of the first Wall Street Journal story, we were quickly told that WWE talent and staff were briefed via memo about the story and investigation.

The *Fightful* report noted how McMahon's handling of Laurinaitis' situation was not well-received:

We're not told of any memo reflecting today's story. WWE talent have not been available to speak on the record about the allegations and reports, but have spoken with Fightful privately and expressed displeasure and extreme frustration with Vince McMahon's handling of it. Fightful's requests for comment went unreturned by WWE on this matter.

Regardless of any dissatisfaction from wrestlers and/or employees, it may not matter to Vince McMahon, which could result in a real-life situation that rivals any WWE storyline.

Will the Allegations Reach Vince McMahon's World?

There are serious allegations against Vince McMahon both in terms of a potential criminal offense and assorted instances of behavior that would get most corporate executives and CEOs thrown out on their asses. However, what is Vince McMahon's take on things?

The only way to try and understand McMahon's take on things is to look at his past remarks and actions. McMahon has admitted to extramarital affairs and canny observers of the grappling game have often pondered what difference there is between Vincent Kennedy McMahon and the Mr. McMahon character he portrays on TV.

Consider this. If one or more of the allegations involving the nondisclosure agreements are accurate, it suggests McMahon feels he can engage in questionable behavior (not only having extramarital affairs but doing so with employees and people with less authority) and solve any problem by paying people off to stay quiet. Perhaps I'm reading too much into things but it suggests McMahon feels his privilege makes him less accountable than other people.

If a report from *Fightful Select* is accurate, Vince's current take on things seems to reflect his past take on things i.e., that he does things his way:

> Fightful was contacted by multiple WWE staff, including some who had remained quiet in the past about McMahon's handling of the situation. One told Fightful they wished they'd spoken out sooner, and said that

McMahon's response would often go from "no selling the whole thing," to "being defiant." They also said that after Vince McMahon's "pointless" June 17 appearance, he returned to the Gorilla position and shouted "Fuck em!" seemingly in response to the allegations that caused his insistence to appear on television.

If McMahon's actions and the rumors of an indifferent attitude are more than speculation, Vince McMahon will do the bare minimum to resolve his problems. It's likely that he will fight tooth and nail to stay on in some capacity in the WWE and likely attempt to control the company through a proxy.

The Bottom Line

While Vince McMahon will likely fight any attempt to take control of his company, the WWE's success (particularly in making money when many other publicly traded companies are suffering) could keep him around in some capacity. This can be seen in the perception that Mr. McMahon is essential to the success of the WWE. Consider this comment from the *Wall Street Journal*:

> "The bar is going to be reasonably high to wrestle the business from family control," said Brandon Ross, a research

analyst at LightShed Partners who follows WWE. But he added that any outcome that would strip Mr. McMahon's creative responsibilities would materially change the company.

The *Journal* article also referenced WWE documents touting how essential Vince is to the WWE "WWE said in regulatory filings that losing Mr. McMahon would put its entire business at risk."

Ultimately, McMahon's future in the WWE is likely going to see him relieved of executive authority (at least on paper) while he remains in control of the company's creative end. Barring a criminal conviction (or plea to a criminal charge), Vince McMahon is likely staying in the WWE in the creative department. However, other allegations might be brought forward that are not covered by nondisclosure agreements and if these lead to lawsuits that decrease WWE stock, expect to see McMahon walk away from the company while maintaining a hidden role in its creative direction.

Work Cited

Thompson, Andrew. "POST NEWS UPDATE: JJ Dillon weighs in on Vince McMahon being investigated by WWE's Board, talks history with Vince." *POST Wrestling.* 28 June 2022. https://www.postwrestling.com/2022/06/28/post-news-update-jj-dillon-weighs-in-on-vince-mcmahon-being-investigated-by-wwes-board-talks-history-with-vince. Accessed 29 June 2022.

328

Appendix A

The World Bodybuilding Federation: Bigger Isn't Always Better

Originally Published 2017

Vince McMahon has always been a fan of larger-than-life wrestlers, as represented by main eventers like Hulk Hogan and the Ultimate Warrior in the past up through contemporary muscleheads such as Brock Lesnar, Roman Reigns, and Jinder Mahal. McMahon always preferred musclemen on his roster, so it was no surprise when he launched his own bodybuilding organization, the World Bodybuilding Federation. The WBF would last less than three years and become known for Lex Luger's first role in the WWF organization and as the venue that launched the much-maligned nutritional supplement, ICOPRO.

Body Building: A Monopoly Like Wrestling?

Professional wrestling was often accused of being a monopoly during the 1950's thanks to the stranglehold the National Wrestling Alliance exerted on would-be rivals. Such was the world of bodybuilding competition from the 1960's forward when an organization named the International

Federation of Bodybuilders rose to prominence over its rival the Amateur Athletic Union.

In his book *Wrestling Babylon*, Irv Muchnick described the rise of Canadian brothers Joe and Ben Weider:

> The bodybuilding world has its own history, older than the WWF's, and its McMahonish control-freak impresario: Joe Weider. Weider (pronounced "weeder"), the son of a Jewish pants-presser who emigrated from Poland to Montreal, has been in the muscle business since 1942, when at the age of nineteen he started mimeographing and circulating a newsletter called Your Physique. Along with his brother, Ben, with whom he co-founded the International Federation of Body-Builders (IFBB) in 1946.

The Weiders capitalized on bodybuilding's burgeoning popularity during the 1950's and 1960's, running a line of magazines and nutrition supplements for athletes, particularly those with aspirations of entering bodybuilding supplements. Over time, the Weiders' organization became the elite organization, hosting its annual Mr. Olympia contests. The 1970's was seen as a Golden Age of bodybuilding with larger-than-life competitors like

Arnold Schwarzenegger and Lee Haney. Rumors swirled that the competitions might be as worked as wrestling. According to Irv Muchnick's article "Pimping Iron," Joe Weider:

> ...practically admitted as much in 1970, when associates asked him why Schwarzenegger had won that year's Mr. Olympia title when Sergio Oliva, a black Cuban, had clearly had the better physique. Joe smiled and said, ..." I put Sergio on the cover, I sell x magazines. I put Arnold on the cover, I sell 3x magazines" (Muchnick).

However, by the 80's, things had slowed down and for whatever reason, media coverage had subsided (Salmon). The world of competitive bodybuilding was sagging faster than Hulk Hogan going off the juice.

By 1990, the Weiders controlled bodybuilding. However, a rival was waiting to try his hand at the market, a man who had defied a previous monopoly, using his ambition, ruthlessness, and marketing skills to build a professional wrestling juggernaut. That man was Vince McMahon, who looked to find success in another athletic endeavor.

McMahon's New Endeavor

As detailed in the article, "The Curious Case of the World Bodybuilding Federation," 1990 was an important year for Vince McMahon who:

> ...officially opened Titan Towers in Connecticut. The towers were a state-of-the-art television facility costing over 9 million dollars with production facilities comparable to anyone else in the business. The ribbon cutting was accompanied by the news that McMahon was henceforth president of Titan Sports Inc., a new business entity primarily concerned with wrestling but with an eye for new opportunities (Heffernan).

In 1990, Vince McMahon announced he was starting his own bodybuilding magazine, *Bodybuilding Lifestyles*. Given McMahon's dabbling in other areas such as music (*The Wrestling Album* and its follow-up *Piledriver*) and film (*No Holds Barred*), a bodybuilding magazine didn't seem like a stretch, particularly given the WWF's roster of musclemen. McMahon also announced the launch of his own nutritional supplement line, "The Integrated Conditioning Program" or "ICOPRO." Reportedly, Joe Weider was skeptical of McMahon's efforts.

McMahon brought in 1980's bodybuilding great Tom Platz as the consultant and talent scout for Bodybuilding Lifestyles. Platz had competed in a number of Mr. Olympia contests and while he never reached higher than third place, he was famous for his leg development, which earned him the nickname "The Quadfather." Platz would soon help McMahon launch a surprise attack on the IFBB.

A Shocking Announcement

On 15 September 1990, the IFBB held the 26th Mr. Olympia contest at the Arie Crown Theater in Chicago, Illinois. McMahon had secured a booth at the event for his bodybuilding magazine and he and Platz were on hand, shaking hands and signing autographs. The competition was surprisingly uneventful until rumors swirled McMahon was going to make a bold announcement about bodybuilding.

Platz would be the one making the announcement. In a move straight out of the McMahon hype playbook, Platz announced, "I have a very important announcement to make. We at Titan Sports are proud to announce the formation of the World Bodybuilding Federation. And we are going to kick the IFBB's ass!" (Heffernan). Platz' announcement was followed by a bevy of beauties with sashes bearing the WBG logo, who handed out literature on the new bodybuilding league. To no one's surprise, Joe and Ben Weider were not thrilled by McMahon's broadside. However, the announcement was just the beginning of McMahon's expansion plans.

As Platz made his announcement, McMahon's WBF workers put WBF contracts under the hotel room doors of every Mr. Olympia contestant. Like he'd done with his national wrestling expansion during the mid-80's, McMahon was willing to pay top dollar to steal the best of the best from his rivals—in this case, the IFBB.

Weider's Reaction

When asked about his reaction to the announcement, Ben Weider replied, "I'm not angry—you can quote me. I'm not even disappointed. But let's put it this way: It wasn't a very sophisticated or honorable thing to do" (Muchnick). Behind the scenes, Ben Weider promised anyone who signed with the WBF would be banned from the IFBB for life. Vince McMahon was ready to challenge the firmly entrenched Weider body-building empire, just as he'd done with the National Wrestling Alliance and the American Wrestling Association. A war was about to begin between the upstart looking to conquer new territory, and the long-dominant champion. Would history repeat itself?

Big Money for Big Bodies

Vince McMahon knew the allure of big money when it came to signing a rival's top stars.

Just as he'd done in signing away the crème de la crème from rival wrestling promotions such as the American Wrestling Association (AWA) and National Wrestling Alliance (NWA) during the 80s, McMahon did so when he signed away some of the WBF's top stars, promising salaries of $100,000 and more a year. This was a considerable pay boost as the winner of 1990's Mr. Olympia event brought in $70,000 in prize money. According to the article, "The Rise and Fall of the World Bodybuilding Federation," "Throughout that fall and winter, potential WBF candidates were flown first class to TitanSport's Connecticut headquarters and given VIP treatment." Speculation ran wild as to who the WBF would sign. It didn't take long before McMahon had his talent lined up. During a press conference at New York's Plaza Hotel, McMahon unveiled his 13 WBF musclemen. They were "Aaron Baker, Mike Quinn, Troy Zuccolotto, Danny Padilla, Tony Pearson, Jim Quinn, Berry Demey, Eddie Robinson, Mike Christian, Vince Comeford, David Dearth, Johnnie Morant, and Gary Strydom" (Heffernan). Just as McMahon called his WWF grapplers "Superstars" instead of wrestlers, he dubbed the WBF's bodybuilders "Bodystars." This would be but one of many changes in McMahon's vision of a new bodybuilding world.

McMahon chose a man who met his vision of what the WBF would be, just as he'd done in signing Hulk Hogan to lead his wrestling empire to victory. Gary Strydom was signed for a reported $400,000 a year (compared to the IFBB where $50,000 was the peak annual salary). Strydom was a charismatic and talented bodybuilder, who boasted a number of title wins in the IFBB during the 1980's. Signing the South African native was a coup for McMahon and his fledgling company. It was also announced the WBF would hold its first event on 15 June 1991 in the Trump Taj Mahal in Atlantic City. The event would be held on pay-per-view and crown the first-ever WBF champion.

The IFBB Responds

Despite Joe Weider's public comments, there was no arguing the IFBB's stance when they held their *Night of Champions* event in May 1991. The show began with thirteen tombstones on stage, each bearing the name of a WBF BodyStars. In a surreal moment out of a David Lynch film, the IFBB bodybuilders proceeded to destroy the tombstones on stage. The real evidence of the IFBB's concern was its announcement of a $100,000 prize at its 1991 Mr. Olympia event.

Musclemen the McMahon Way

Vince McMahon had a dream for revolutionizing the world of bodybuilding competition. In addition to dubbing his competitors BodyStars, he devised characters for each of the competitors, giving them more flash and hopefully, more marketability. For example, "Ditching his glasses for a black hood, Johnnie Morant became 'The Executioner.' Troy Zuccolotto employed a surfer gimmick and went as 'California Personified.' No longer just Aaron Baker, 'Dark Angel' donned a glittery red cape with a pointed collar ("Dilbert").

The WBF also had a relaxed policy towards the use of anabolic steroids and performance-enhancing drugs. The bodybuilding industry had come under scrutiny with allegations that the bigger-than-life bodies were made possible by an assist from a pharmacy rather than Mother Nature. Reportedly, the Weider Brothers were working to make bodybuilding an Olympic sport. That would prove easier if there were no allegations of better bodies through chemistry. Vince McMahon on the other hand seemed to have no qualms about how his wrestlers got big, much less his BodyStars. With no drug-testing in the WBF, the company's competitors had many tools to work. Over time however, this policy proved problematic to the WBF and Vince McMahon in general.

Although Tom Platz had stated there would be no overlap between the WBF and WWF, Vince McMahon saw no good reason why he shouldn't use his WWF Superstars to plug both the WBF and its nutrition supplement, ICOPRO. Randy "Macho Man" Savage and Miss Elizabeth were scheduled to appear at the first WBF pay-per-view while the Ultimate Warrior plugged the WBF in a hype video.

Vince McMahon's World Bodybuilding Federation had grabbed the attention of the bodybuilding world, signing some of its biggest stars to unheard of big-money contracts. With the WBF's first competition on the horizon, the bodybuilding world was anxious to see whether McMahon could succeed in the world of competitive bodybuilding, just as he had in wrestling. However, unknown to McMahon, his would-be bodybuilding empire had already reached its zenith, and was in for a fast road to the bottom.

The WBF's First Show

The WBF's pay-per-view was not bringing in the numbers Vince McMahon had counted on. This led to McMahon bringing in not only TV entertainer Regis Philbin to host the show, but an appearance by "Macho Man" Randy Savage and Miss Elizabeth. The June 15, show would also feature former bodybuilder Don Draper as a judge. McMahon was hoping this combination of various talent would help boost the show's buyrate.

With Vince McMahon orchestrating the show, there was lots of flash and pizazz onstage.

Not only was the pay-per-view held at the gorgeous Trump Taj Mahal, but it featured the production values the WWF was famous for. The show featured pyrotechnics, smoke, and a bevy of beauties. That was just the packaging though—how would the WBF do in its competitive events?

The bodybuilding competition consisted of various events. As Conor Heffernan explains:

> The WBF format was much the same as other competitions with the first two rounds comprising of the mandatory poses and the individual posing routines with the third round being where the magic happened. Called the 'Entertainment Round, it comprised of pre-taped themed videos that spilled onto the stage. Take Danny Padilla's routine which was inspired by Jack and the Beanstalk. It featured a pre-taped video of Danny as Jack being chased by the Giant, followed by Danny being chased around by the Giant on stage. Remarkably it wasn't the most bizarre routine in the Entertainment Round. Heck, check out Jim Quinn's futuristic posing routine

The event saw one BodyStar after another compete, until the WBF's top-paid star Gary Strydom entered the scene. When the announcer said, "You've seen the rest, now get ready for the best" (Heffernan), fans couldn't help but wonder if the fix was in, regardless of how talented Strydom was. After the judges reviewed their picks, Strydom was announced as the winner, bringing home a prize of $275,000, something unheard of in bodybuilding competition.

Although the pay-per-view did not attract the viewers the WBF had projected, the show itself drew a lot of talk—some positive and some negative. The much-larger payouts for WBF BodyStars were seen as a good thing, but some critics questioned the event's legitimacy, pointing out that the top five highest-paid BodyStars came in first through fifth place. Was the WBF as worked as the WWF?

Although the argument seemed to hold some weight, a closer analysis suggests this was coincidence as some analysts feel Gary Strydom's look and performance blew away his competitors. More important, many of the critics lambasting the WBF's integrity were allied with Joe Weider, a man who we mentioned earlier had all but admitted fixing his contests on at least one occasion.

Vince McMahon looked ahead as he planned for the WBF's second show the next year. He had considerable time to fix any mistakes and build the event into a must-see pay-per-view. To help familiarize viewers with his competitors,

McMahon created the weekly TV series *WBF BodyStars*. The eclectic show featured BodyStars giving fitness tips, performing in skits, and doing whatever McMahon hoped would form a bond with the public. However, circumstances beyond his control were about to affect not only the WBF, but McMahon's entire sports entertainment empire.

An Untimely Verdict

A mere twelve days after the WBF's pay-per-view, Dr. George Zahorian was found guilty of selling anabolic steroids to professional wrestlers, bodybuilders, and Vince McMahon (Heffernan). Zahorian, who served as a ringside physician for the WWF was found guilty on twelve out of fourteen counts. According to James Dixon's book *Titan Sinking* "Zahorian was the state athletic commission doctor in the state of Pennsylvania and was known among the boys as 'The Candy Man.' At shows in Hamburg and Allentown he would show up and set up shop, selling steroids ('candy') to members of the roster."

The fallout was inescapable and had an immediate effect. As Bret Hart recalls in his autobiography, *Hitman*:

> As soon as Zahorian was found guilty, Vince called a meeting to let his wrestlers know that starting in just a few weeks, he would voluntarily

implement a drug testing policy even stricter than the one used for Olympic athletes. Everyone had to get off the juice. He made it clear this time it would be impossible to cheat because there would be two people watching you piss in a cup" (269).

Obviously, this was a way to deflect attention away from his WWF Superstars. However, what of his WBF BodyStars, competitive bodybuilders who had no steroid policy? The Weider Brothers' IFBB had a short-lived steroid testing program but shelved it after fans complained of the competitors' smaller size. Rather than tackling the steroid problem directly, McMahon went with a gamma-irradiated distraction—the Incredible Hulk.

Hulkamania of a Different Stripe

In late 1991, rumors abounded that bodybuilding great Lou Ferrigno was considering a return to competitive bodybuilding. Ferrigno had famously played the Incredible Hulk in the CBS series of that name for its five seasons. His bodybuilding fame included his spot in the documentary *Pumping Iron*, where he appeared with Arnold Schwarzenegger. Ferrigno shocked the world when he signed with the WBF for an incredible two-year deal worth $900,000. Many expected Ferrigno to return to the Weiders who he'd competed for in the 1970's. However, as McMahon had shown in 1990, he was willing to spend whatever amount necessary to win the bodybuilding battle.

Ferrigno appeared in every conceivable marketing device available to the WBF. Whether it was pamphlets, posters, or promos, fans were told Ferrigno was headed for a pose-down with 1991 champion Gary Strydom. For a time, it seemed as if the WBF stood for "We Bought Ferrigno," with a different type of Hulkamania being called upon to save the day. There was no doubt a Ferrigno/Strydom showdown had potential if marketed right. However, the stigma of steroids threatened to let the air out of this version of Hulkamania.

No Puny Banner

By 1992, there was no escaping the intense scrutiny bearing down on the WBF to acknowledge its position on steroids. In March 1992, Vince McMahon announced the WBF would implement a steroid testing policy conducted by the highly respected Dr. Mauro Dipasquale. In addition, WBF BodyStars began airing snippets on the evils of steroid use.

Unfortunately, this created a serious issue for Lou Ferrigno. The former Mr. America and Mr. Universe had been out of competitive bodybuilding for some time, and only had three months to get into shape for the WBF's second pay-per-view. With no anabolic crutch to rely on, things may have seemed hopeless for Ferrigno as he envisioned his Hulk-like physique reduced on stage to that of a puny Bruce Banner. When the Weider Brothers offered him the opportunity to pose down at their Mr. Olympia event (with no drug testing of course), Ferrigno bailed on the WBF faster than WWE fans hitting the snack bar during a boring match.

"The Total Package" to the Rescue

With Lou Ferrigno gone, Vince McMahon brought in WCW's muscleman, "The Total Package" Lex Luger. According to Luger's memoir, he was going to ask WCW for a year off from wrestling. He called Vince McMahon and asked him, "What do you think about signing me to a one-year WBF bodybuilding contract if I can get out of the last year of my wrestling contract with the WCW?" (89). Luger claims he arranged a release from his contract (which had one year remaining). The WCW champion may have lacked for ring skills, but there was no denying his musculature. Although Luger couldn't wrestle in the WWF, he could skirt his no-compete clause by working in McMahon's WBF. WCW wasn't happy when they learned he was going to work in the WBF, but they had no legal recourse. This meant Luger was going to appear at the WBF event as a guest poser. Unfortunately, Luger was no substitute for Ferrigno, ruining any chance of a potential dream match.

Things worsened as BodyStars were heavily fined and suffered long suspensions for flunking out on their drug tests. As the WBF's second show neared, the drug tests were cancelled, calling into question the program's integrity. If that wasn't bad enough, Lex Luger suffered a motorcycle accident which knocked him out of the second pay-per-view. Things were looking grim for the WBF.

No "Show of Shows"

The WBF's second pay-per-view was a disaster. The show had the capacity to reach forty million viewers. Instead, 3,000 homes ordered the show, leading some cable outlets to give it a zero buyrate. Those who did see the show saw a parade of undersized bodybuilders who were clearly looked much different than the year before. BodyStar Mike Quinn was reportedly so out of shape that the bodybuilding community saw his appearance as one of the worst in the history of competitive bodybuilding. Quinn had no choice to appear as he was contractually obligated to go onstage. Mike Christian and Eddie Robinson weren't much better, looking like the before pictures in a bodybuilding advertisement.

Vince McMahon's number-one star Gary Strydom looked great though, blowing away the competition and walking away with his second consecutive WBF championship. With the show booked for the following year, Strydom might grab a third title, but there were doubts how much longer the WBF would be around. According to one report, the WBF magazine *Bodybuilding Lifestyles* magazine 'was losing as much as $200,000 a month'" (Dilbert). If true, how poorly was the rest of the federation faring?

An Over-Sized Liability

The WBF was clearly a failed experiment, but it was more than that—it had become a liability to Vince McMahon and his wrestling empire. As James Dixon suggests in Titan Sinking, McMahon was facing increasing pressure from the media and the federal government concerning the abuse of steroids. While McMahon had quietly begun shuffling out muscleheads from the WWF such as the Warlord, Davey Boy Smith, and the Ultimate Warrior, he still faced the glaring problem of a bodybuilding enterprise with huge stars and questionable drug testing.

Cheap Reps

In the weight-lifting world, "cheap reps" refers to when muscle fatigue begins to set in or the weight is too heavy, some athletes employ improper form to make a lift, using surrounding muscle groups or even momentum to assist in the movement" ("28 Gym Terms Explained"). By July 1992, Vince

McMahon was struggling to get the WBF off his shoulders.

On 15 July 1992, McMahon phoned the Weider Brothers, hoping to obtain their help. Given the audacity of McMahon's declaration of war on the Weider's IBFF, the Weiders had every right to tell McMahon where to go and what to do with his apology. Instead, they agreed to take the WBF BodyStars back into the IBFF with a remarkably light punishment of a $25,000 fine apiece. The Weiders even allowed McMahon to buy ads for ICOPRO in the Weider magazines. This act of graciousness was in stark contrast to Joe Weider's reputation for ruthlessness and it's unlikely McMahon would have acted similarly had the WBF triumphed over the IBFF.

Now that he'd found a venue to peddle his ICOPRO products, McMahon looked to cut ties with his BodyStars by any means possible. McMahon told the men he'd signed away from the IFBB that they were welcome to get gigs anywhere else. Since the BodyStars were still under contract to the WBF and entitled to payouts for a defunct organization, McMahon's offer was more a chance to escape their contracts than any generosity on his part.

As for the BodyStars, the 13 bodybuilders who risked a lifetime ban from the IBFF for signing with the WBF were welcomed back at the

IFBB's 22 May 1993 *Night of Champions* event. The show featured a bizarre segment where coffins and tombstones bearing the WBF Bodystars' names were arrayed onstage, with IFBB star Dorian Yates dressed up as a preacher. The WBF BodyStars burst out of their coffins as the song "Welcome Back" played. All had been forgiven and the IFBB was one big happy family again.

While Vince McMahon managed to ditch the WBF, he still faced mounting pressure from the federal government. In 1993, McMahon was indicted on charges of steroid distribution in federal court. However, he ultimately beat the charges, avoiding what could have been a lengthy prison sentence. In the meantime, he continued peddling ICOPRO, hyping it heavily on WWF television in banners conspicuously posted at TV tapings and in ads featuring WWF Superstars proclaiming the benefits of ICO-PRO. In the end, McMahon lost a reported $15 million on his bodybuilding gamble.

Despite his failure at launching a competitive bodybuilding league, Vince McMahon would try his hand at another sports venture. In 2000, Vince McMahon announced he was launching his own professional football league, the XFL. Like the WBF, the XFL would fail, suggesting Vince McMahon's energies are best utilized in the WWE.

Works Cited

Assael, Shaun and Mike Mooneyham. *Sex, Lies, and Headlocks: The Real Story of Vince McMahon and World Wrestling Entertainment.* Broadway Books, 2004.

Dilbert, Ryan. "Vince McMahon's Failed Attempt to Take over Bodybuilding." *Bleacher Report.* WWE. 27 Nov. 2015. http://bleacherreport.com/articles/2542941-vince-mcmahons-failed-attempt-to-take-over-bodybuilding. Accessed 21 Nov. 2017.

"Gary Strydom. IFBB & WBF Bodybuilding Champion." Gary Strydom IFBB Pro. About Gary. http://garystrydom.com/about-us. Accessed 23 Nov. 2017.

Hart, Bret. *Hitman: My Real Life in the Cartoon World of Wrestling.* Random House Canada, 2007.

Heffernan, Conor. "The Curious Case of the World Bodybuilding Federation." *Physical Culture Study.* Biographies. 8 Aug. 2015. https://physicalculturestudy.com/2015/08/08/the-curious-case-of-the-world-bodybuilding-federation. Accessed 21 Nov. 2017.

"International Federation of Bodybuilding and Fitness." *International Federation of Bodybuilding and Fitness.* https://www.ifbb.com. Accessed 21 Nov. 2017.

Luger, Lex and John D. Hollis. *Wrestling with the*

Devil: The True Story of a World Champion Professional Wrestler--His Reign, Ruin, and Redemption. Tyndale Momentum, 2013.

Muchnick, Irvin. *Wrestling Babylon: Piledriving Tales of Drugs, Sex, Death, and Scandal.* ECW Press, 2007.

"Rise and Fall of the World Bodybuilding Federation." *Getbig.com.* https://www.getbig.com/articles/faq-wbf.htm. Accessed 21 Nov. 2017.

Salmon, Jonathon. "The Rise and Fall of Vince McMahon's World Bodybuilding Federation." *Generation Iron.* https://generationiron.com/the-rise-and-fall-of-vince-mcmahons-world-bodybuilding-federation. Accessed 21 Nov. 2017.

"28 gym slang terms explained." *Coach Mag.* http://www.coachmag.co.uk/lifestyle/4234/28-gym-slang-terms-explained. Accessed 25 Nov. 2017.

"Tom's Bio." *Tom Platz.com.* 2008. http://www.tomplatz.com/goldeneagle/bio.htm . Accessed 21 Nov. 2017.

"WBF's wildest Bodystars!" *WWE.com.* http://www.wwe.com/classics/classic-lists/wbf-wildest-bodystars. Accessed 24 Nov. 2017.

Wilson, Craig. "Well That Didn't Work: World Bodybuilding Federation." *Ring the Damn Bell.* 20

Dec. 2013.
https://ringthedamnbell.wordpress.com/201
3/12/20/well-that-didnt-work-world-
bodybuilding-federation. Accessed 21 Nov.
2017.

"Wrestling Promoter Fights Steroid Charges." *The New York Times.* N.Y. Region. 28 Apr. 1994.
http://www.nytimes.com/1994/04/28/nyre
gion/wrestling-promoter-fights-steroid-
charges.html. Accessed 21 Nov. 2017.

352

Appendix B
Inglorious Bastards: The Story of the XFL

Originally Published 2017

It's become known as one of the biggest debacles in television history, but it began as an ambitious idea, mixing Americans' passion for football with the sports entertainment magic of the World Wrestling Federation. What became known as the XFL started under the auspices of entertainment Vince McMahon and Dick Ebersol, and featured a motley crew of football players, each with their own amazing stories. While the XFL failed miserably, costing the WWF and NBC each a reported $35 million loss, its legacy is still felt today.

Two Media Mavericks

The two men responsible for the XFL were media mavericks in their own right; Vince McMahon whose revolutionary transformation of the WWF from a regional business to a national one made him the king of professional wrestling; and Dick Ebersol, the wunderkind who co-created and developed Saturday Night Live with Lorne Michaels, becoming NBC's youngest executive in the process.

In 1985, Vince McMahon forged an unlikely business relationship with Ebersol, with NBC optioning the WWF's late-night wrestling special Saturday Night's Main Event. The show would air as an occasional substitute *for Saturday Night Live*. *Saturday Night's Main Event* became a hit for NBC, with Ebersol benefitting from yet another successful project, and the WWF learning much from Ebersol's production standards. McMahon and Ebersol became fast friends and the friendship would last even after Ebersol became president of NBC Sports in 1989, divesting his interest in *Saturday Night's Main Event*. Ebersol reportedly even named McMahon as the person he wanted to take care of his kids should he and his wife pass away ("This Was the XFL").

Two Parallel Paths Converge

Interestingly enough, both Vince McMahon and Dick Ebersol had toyed with the idea of getting into professional football. In McMahon's case, he'd sought ownership in the National Football League team the Minnesota Vikings, only to be frozen out by the NFL's owners. McMahon pursued the Washington Redskins next, only to have Dan Snyder buy the team. When McMahon learned the Canadian Football League team the Toronto Argonauts was up for sale, McMahon decided to buy the entire league. He would change the league rules and run games in the United States and Canada. However, the CFL owners were concerned about McMahon changing the CFL's longstanding traditions. The CFL chose not to sell, leaving McMahon to pursue something different. Dick Ebersol too wanted football on NBC, but not at the extortionary prices the NFL asked for. In Ebersol's view, NBC heightened the sport's popularity, with the NFL profiting from NBC's efforts, only to demand more money when rights came back up for renewal. Ebersol recognized the NFL's prestige, but felt the bottom line was more important, "The NFL is a great sports property, but there is no property we would go after that would lose at least $150 million a year" (Forrest 133). While the NFL was out, that didn't preclude Ebersol from looking into other football prospects.

Challenges to the NFL's dominance is nothing new. The World Football League existed briefly in the mid- 70s while the United States Football League lasted a few seasons in the mid-80s. Ebersol explored a partnership with Ted Turner, where the two would form their own football league and air games on Turner's TNT network. However, cost issues proved troublesome, particularly with Turner's wrestling company World Championship Wrestling (WCW) losing money during the Monday Night War. With the NFL gone and NBC's NBA deal coming up for renewal in two years, Ebersol concluded he needed sports programming to replace the NFL before NBC Sports lost the prestige he'd spent his career building up

Meanwhile, the CFL deal had fallen through, but Vince McMahon was determined to bring about his own football league. The WWE was branching out into more than wrestling, and McMahon perhaps felt he could take his Midas touch for wrestling and use it to promote football. McMahon held a press conference at the WWF's New York restaurant in Times Square on 3 February 2000, announcing his new football league, the XFL. McMahon ran down the NFL, calling it "The No-Fun League," promising to bring back the days of "smash mouth football" and appeal to fans of old-school football.

When Dick Ebersol found out about the XFL, he reached out to McMahon, certain the two old friends could combine their mutual goal into another successful partnership. Based on their past business relationship and friendship, Ebersol felt McMahon's football league was a good fit for NBC as there would be limited costs. NBC agreed to put up 50% of the cost, air the program on Saturday nights, and guarantee the product for two years. The deal seemed like a win-win with McMahon getting a trusted partner and the prestige of the NBC network. In addition, McMahon negotiated with UPN and TNN to air XFL games on Sundays.

Ebersol made sure to keep NBC's traditional sports broadcasters away from the XFL. Whether this was done surreptitiously to protect NBC's sports image, or just to further the XFL's image as an outlaw football league, Ebersol reached out to other broadcasters. NBC's top broadcaster Bob Costas was wary of the XFL:

> "Everything about it screamed to me schlock and crap. Everything that subsequently occurred validated that impression. In fairness, Dick Ebersol never asked me. None of the announcers who were associated with NBC were going to be used on this experiment, so there was never any danger of that" (Barrasso).

Instead, Ebersol hired Matt Vasgersian, who became a play-by-play announcer for the Milwaukee Brewers baseball team in 1997 at the age of 29. Vasgersian was paired with Jesse "The Body" Ventura (then sitting governor of Minnesota) on the main game, but Vasgersian was demoted to the "B" show after one week when he refused to follow Vince McMahon's orders to point out the cheerleaders on camera. Vasgersian was replaced by WWF announcer Jim Ross.

Overhyped?

McMahon began hyping the XFL right after he announced its creation. Would the XFL benefit from the man Dick Ebersol described as the "best marketer and promoter in America" ("This Was the XFL") and NBC's advanced marketing? The XFL was promoted heavily as a return to smash mouth football. The rules would be different and the players wouldn't be high-paid millionaires with bad attitudes. Instead, players would be paid $4,000 a game with a bonus of $3,300 for winning.

While there was considerable hype, there were no stadium agreements, no teams, no coaches, and no players signed. The XFL had little to present to advertisers other than the XFL logo and the concept. The XFL was slow in building up the infrastructure for a successful football organization. In hindsight, this was arguably the XFL's biggest mistake.

The XFL decided to get additional publicity during a January 6, 2001, playoff game between the NFL's Oakland Raiders and Miami Dolphins. In what many saw as an omen, the XFL blimp crashed days later during a practice run, flying into a seafood restaurant, only the beginning of the XFL's notoriety.

New League, New Rules

The XFL fielded two divisions, each consisting of four teams. The Eastern division consisted of; 1) The Orlando Rage; 2) The Chicago Enforcers; 3) The New York/New Jersey Hitman; and the Birmingham Thunderbolts; while the

Western division comprised four teams; 1) the Los Angeles Extreme; 2) the San Francisco Demons; 3) the Memphis Maniax; and 4) the Las Vegas Outlaws. The eight teams would compete with the top teams battling to see which two teams would compete in the season-ending finale which eventually became known as The Million Dollar Game (so named because the winning team split one million dollars).

The XFL featured rule changes designed to make for a more exciting and aggressive game. Instead of a coin toss to determine possession of the ball, the XFL held an opening scramble where a player from each team raced to see who could gain possession of the ball first. The XFL had no fair catch rule and extra points were based on rushing or passing, rather than kicking an extra point. Unfortunately, some of the rules such as the opening scramble proved dangerous (the first XFL injury occurred during an opening scramble with Orlando free safety Hassan Shamsid-Deen suffering an injury that sidelined him for the entire season).

Off the field, the XFL featured rules designed to make the game more like a reality show. While McMahon clarified the XFL would not be scripted, he and Ebersol hoped to capitalize on the wave of popular reality shows such as *Survivor*, by mixing sports with entertainment. For example, XFL cheerleaders were encouraged to date XFL players (whereas the NFL banned cheerleaders from dating players), reportedly hoping to create romantic storylines. The XFL also was aggressive with sideline reporters talking to players following big plays and filming events in the players' locker room during half-time. The league also allowed players to put nicknames on the back of jerseys rather than given names, with player Rod Smart gaining fame thanks to his nickname "He Hate Me." Not all nicknames got approved however as one player tried to sneak the name "Teabagger" onto his jersey.

Massive Success but Uncertainty

With a year's worth of hype, fans and industry insiders wondered how the new football league would do in its opening game. The XFL's debut game proved a wild ratings success as the Hitmen took on the Outlaws in a 19-0 blow-out. The ratings were double what the XFL predicted were needed to be a success with the XFL earning a 9.5 rating, over twice the 4.5 rating the XFL had guaranteed advertisers (Forrest 51). In spite of the first week success, there was a troubling sign. The ratings dropped from an opening high of 11.7 to a pronounced low rating of 8 (Forrest 53). In effect, the game had lost a third of its audience by the end of the night. The first game had not featured the level of football seen in the NFL, but viewers seemed willing to give the product a chance. The question was, would they return for the next week?

Any ratings surge was killed the following week in one of the biggest disasters in sports television history. Things started spectacularly, with the Rock introducing the game and the fans being treated to an exciting game between the Los Angeles Extreme and the Chicago Enforcers. Then, thirteen minutes into the game, things went black. For nearly two minutes, NBC aired a "please stand by" slide as the XFL's production team scrambled to discover why the power had gone out. NBC switched to a game between Orlando and San Francisco as technicians ran test after test, failing to restore power, despite the presence of back-up generators. Twenty-seven minutes later, the L.A. game resumed after technicians realized no one had bothered to fill the generators with gasoline.

"I wanted to break someone's neck," Vince McMahon recalled years later. Not only had the game been delayed by the power outage, but an injury to tackle Octavious Bishop kept him on the field another fifteen minutes while medical officials tended to him. The delays resulted in NBC delaying the airing of a much-hyped new episode of *Saturday Night Live*, with guest host Jennifer Lopez. The episode did not air until after midnight, reportedly enraging SNL's Lorne

Michael. However, that was only the beginning of the XFL's woes.

The ratings for week two had plunged to 4.6, a drop of over half the audience. The new-car smell was already off the XFL and viewers realized they'd bought a lemon. Over the next few weeks, the ratings continued to slide. Before long, the XFL was heading into record-breaking territory, but it wasn't anything one wanted to be known for. The XFL was on what seemed to be an inevitable course as the lowest rated sports program in network history.

Throwing a Hail Mary

Although an argument can be made the XFL improved its quality of play, NBC executives felt something drastic had to be done to draw an audience. If the play on the field couldn't be improved, perhaps Vince McMahon could up the league's entertainment aspects. At the end of week five's game, Jim Ross announced a game-changer for the next week and a blatant publicity stunt. Over the next week, fans learned the XFL was going to take viewers into the cheerleaders' locker room.

Naturally, anyone familiar with Standards and Practices knew NBC could show nothing more than eye-straining nudity. During half-time, the fans were treated to a boring bait-and-switch when the cameraman got knocked out and proceeded to dream of various encounters with the XFL cheerleaders. The segment was a disaster (other than a cameo by comedian Rodney Dangerfield) and did nothing to help the XFL.

As feared, March proved even worse with the NCAA "March Madness" tournament eating away at what little remained of the XFL's ratings. The XFL hit a new low as week seven's game scored a 1.6 rating, tying or breaking the record for the lowest-rated show in prime-time (depending on whom you believe). Since NBC had guaranteed a 4.5 rating to advertisers, the network lost more money as the season progressed.

By the end of the season, there was serious doubt about the XFL remaining on NBC. Although NBC had signed a contract to air the games for at least two seasons, forces were moving behind the scenes to get rid of the XFL albatross. Eventually, Dick Ebersol was able to persuade Vince McMahon there was nothing to be gained from continuing the show on Saturday nights, or NBC for that matter. McMahon agreed, but the XFL was not dead yet.

Vince McMahon still had a chance to air the XFL on UPN and TNN. However, McMahon became angry when TNN asked to renegotiate the contract, leading McMahon to end the agreement. There was still UPN, and while the network's clearance was low, McMahon was willing to rebuild the XFL from the ground up. According to Brett Forrest's book *Long Bomb: How the XFL Became TV's Biggest Fiasco*, UPN was happy with the XFL until the WB's show *Buffy the Vampire Hunter* became available, and UPN signed it away. Unfortunately, the cost of buying the show depleted any funds UPN had for the XFL. UPN offered to air the XFL if Vince McMahon cut *SmackDown!* (another popular weekly wrestling show that had spun off from the WWE's *RAW* wrestling program) by half an hour. Not wanting to cut into his biggest revenue draw, McMahon refused, effectively ending the XFL. Vince McMahon's dream of his own football league was officially dead.

Could the XFL Have Succeeded?

It's easy to play Monday morning quarterback but consider the following evidence whether or not the XFL might have succeeded. The XFL was not the first football league to challenge the NFL and the XFL had some things going for it, such as football fans' desire to watch the sport all year round and a network eager to feed this hunger. Sixteen years later, those involved with the XFL have their thoughts on why it failed, and whether it could have succeeded. XFL quarterback Charles Puleri thinks McMahon erred by attacking the NFL, "The first mistake they made was when they started knocking the NFL.

That's the first thing you don't do is try to knock the NFL. This league could have lasted. It could have been a spring version of football. People would have come out, as you saw in the first few weeks" (Crossman).

The XFL suffered from a bad timeslot as Saturday night often saw the much-desired younger demographic out on dates and/or partying. Vince McMahon wanted to air the games during traditional football times i.e., Sunday afternoons, but NBC Sports had paid over one billion dollars to air NASCAR on Sunday afternoons so the XFL was out. Although the XFL aired on Sundays on TNN and UPN, the two stations' audience was significantly smaller than what NBC could potentially draw, leaving Saturday night as the XFL's primary slot.

While the quality of play was initially lacking, some believe it improved over time. Even the most diehard XFL apologist would have to admit the team rosters weren't the crème de la crème of what was available. However, while the league consisted of NFL cast-offs and hopefuls, that didn't mean they lacked a desire to play. Many players saw the XFL as an opportunity to display their talents and get signed with the NFL. Players saw the XFL as fun. Football player Yo Murphy (who played in one Super Bowl and two Grey Cup games) commented:

When I got there, I was surprised about the money they were paying out. I think starting off, they made it so fun to play ... they could have sacrificed and not paid the players so much, and I think the league would have been around longer. Guys would have fought to play in that league because it was fun. That makes up for a lot. As long as you pay your bills and take care of your family, the opportunity to play and compete in professional football makes up for a lot (Crossman).

To be certain, the XFL players (much like the league itself) were works in progress, but as Mike Keller, the XFL's vice-president of football operations notes:

"The plain fact was that the product was very good. We had over 100 players go on to play in the National Football League. That's a large number. That's quality players" (Crossman).

One of the league's biggest stumbling blocks was the lack of preparation for team players. Mike Keller realizes it was a mistake:

"When you're a start-up league, the coaches who are coaching have never coached together before. The players had never played together before. One of the mistakes, and I will take credit for it, is we had a four-and-a-half-week training camp. And for a first-year league, it wasn't enough. We needed more time for those players who hadn't played together before and the coaches who hadn't coached together before to pull together so that when they took the field in the first game of the season we were in midseason form. We weren't" (Crossman).

Dick Ebersol was counting on the product to perform well:

> "I thought we were gonna deliver good football. I don't believe in my entire career in sports or show business I was ever more wrong. All of us were. We promised a lot. We didn't deliver" (This Was the XFL).

Some believe the XFL was doomed because of its ownership structure as there was no clear leader. Tom Viet, vice-president and general manager of the Orlando Rage said in a 2017 interview:

> "Our partnership with NBC was the greatest boon to launching the league and probably the greatest distraction

(that caused the league to fold)" (Crossman)

Steve Ehrhart, the first executive director of the USFL and vice-president and general manager of the Memphis Maniax argued "One of the lessons is it's never good to have a 50-50 partner. Somebody has to be in charge" (Crossman).

One last factor was Vince McMahon's adversarial attitude towards the media. After many in the sports media questioned the XFL (with some even questioning whether it would be scripted), McMahon gloated to the media after the success of week one. Consequently, things only worsened and it would not be until the end of the season that McMahon realized he needed all the help he could get. Sadly though, it was too late.

The XFL's Legacy

While the XFL was a failure, there were lessons to be learned. Today, the networks are experiencing the same sticker shock Dick Ebersol felt and avoided by turning down the chance to run NFL games at a premium. With NFL ratings down, some networks question whether or not it is worth paying to air the games. As for the NFL, they benefitted from the XFL, primarily in terms of production. The NFL has adopted some of the XFL's cutting edge presentation features such as the SkyCam, microphoning players, and providing more interaction on the sidelines. In a sense, the XFL served as a beta test for the NFL.

Dallas Cowboys team owner Jerry Jones feels the XFL helped the NFL, "I think these ideas have contributed to the success we have today" ("This Was the XFL"). XFL business consultant Rich Rose believes the XFL was revolutionary as well:

> "You look at the elements that came out of the XFL TV-wise. Skycam. You know how popular Skycam is. The interviews on the sideline and in the locker room and stuff, we had that access. That's commonplace now" (Crossman).

As for the XFL, could it ever return? On the documentary, *This Was the XFL*, Vince McMahon discusses the possibilities of the XFL or something similar. Charlie Ebersol, who directed the documentary (and who is the son of Dick Ebersol) commented in a 2017 interview:

> Look, when I interviewed Jerry Jones for the film, he brought it up. And when I interviewed Vince, he brought it up. My dad's not going to do it. He's really, really happily retired. Vince is still on the road three days a week producing 17 pay-per-views and 104 "Monday Night Raws" and

"Smackdowns" a year. He's a madman. If Vince has put enough thought into it, I never question the validity, because you never know when he's going to walk into the press room and announce that he's doing it.

This turned into a reality when the *New York Times* reported on January 25, 2018, that Vince McMahon's Alpha Entertainment Group would relaunch the XFL in early 2020. Since then, the XFL has established two divisions as before, with the Eastern division comprised of teams in Dallas, Houston, Los Angeles, and Seattle; and a Western division comprise of teams in New York, St. Louis, Tampa Bay, and Washington D.C.

Will the XFL and its eight teams be ready for football in 2020 or will the XFL be a sad replay of the original XFL?

Despite McMahon's efforts to learn from his past mistakes, the XFL 2.0 couldn't have come at a worst time as the coronavirus pandemic began to gather steam in the midst of the season. Once again, the XFL folded but this time it also led to a lawsuit as XFL Commissioner Oliver Luck sued Vince McMahon for terminating him. McMahon argued that Luck had violated his employment agreement and was not entitled to his remaining salary and bonuses. McMahon countersued. The case was settled out of court in June 2022.

The XFL refuses to die and a third incarnation is scheduled to begin in 2023. This version won't have McMahon's imprint on it but it will have one of his former Superstars Dwayne "The Rock" Johnson working alongside other business partners.

Works Cited

Barrasso, Justin. "Bob Costas discusses pro wrestling, the XFL, and that confrontation with Vince McMahon." *Sports Illustrated.* Extra Mustard. 10 May 2017. https://www.si.com/extra-mustard/2017/05/10/bob-costas-vince-mcmahon-pro-wrestling-XFL. Accessed 22 Sept. 2017.

"Blimp crashes into Oakland restaurant." *ESPN.* 31 Jan. 2001. http://www.espn.com/moresports/news/2001/0110/1005983.html. Accessed 22 Sept. 2017.

Carter, Bill. "XFL Game Intrusion on 'Saturday Night Live' Roils NBC Executives." *New York Times.* Business Day. 13 Feb. 2001. http://www.nytimes.com/2001/02/13/business/xfl-game-intrusion-on-saturday-night-live-roils-nbc-executives.html. Accessed 22 Sept. 2017.

Crossman, Matt. "A Beautiful Corpse: An Oral

History of the Fast Life and Quick Death of the XFL." *SB Nation*. 7 May 2014. https://www.sbnation.com/longform/2014/5/7/5683742/xfl-oral-history. Accessed 22 Sept. 2017.

Draper, Kevin. "Vince McMahon Says He Will Revive the XFL, With a Very Different Look." *The New York Times*. 25 Jan. 2018. https://www.nytimes.com/2018/01/25/sports/football/vince-mcmahon-xfl.html. Accessed 22 July 2019.

ESPN 30 for 30: This Was the XFL. Directed by Charlie Ebersol, performances by Vince McMahon and Dick Ebersol, ESPN Films, 2017.

Forrest, Matt. *Long Bomb: How the XFL Became TV's Biggest Fiasco*. Crown, 2002.

Halloway, Daniel. "'This Was the XFL' Director on Vince McMahon, Concussions and Whether League Could Make a Comeback." *Daily Variety*. 2 Feb. 2017. http://variety.com/2017/tv/news/xfl-espn-30-for-30-vince-mcmahon-dick-ebersol-1201976706. Accessed 22 Sept. 2017.

Wong, Alex. "What the Hell is 'He Hate Me' Doing Now?" *Complex*. 1 Feb. 2017. http://www.complex.com/sports/2017/02/what-the-hell-is-he-hate-me-doing-now. Accessed 22 Sept. 2017.

Ziemer, Tracy. "Where Did XFL Go Wrong?"
ABC News. 28 February 2001.
http://abcnews.go.com/Business/story?id=
88561&page=1/ Accessed 22 Sept. 2017.

374

Appendix C

Wrestling is scripted entertainment but what happens when creative differences arise? In 1997, the wrestling world found out when Vince McMahon showed why it's best not to cross the boss.

The Montreal Screwjob: Turning Chickenshit into Chicken Salad

Originally published 2017

On November 9, 1997, the WWF held its annual *Survivor Series* pay-per-view, main evented by a title match between Shawn Michaels and WWF Champion Bret Hart. Hart, who had worked in the WWF since 1984, was now leaving for the WWF's arch-rival WCW in less than a month. What was supposed to be a disqualification win for Bret Hart turned into a nightmare as he was bamboozled out of the WWF Championship- or was he? The night would become known as the Montreal Screwjob but there are many questions about what happened. While we may never know all the answers, one thing is clear—Vince McMahon took one of his biggest missteps and turned it into one of his greatest triumphs. **What's Past is Prologue.**

In order to understand the events of November 9, 1997, we need to see what led to so much animosity not only between Bret Hart and Shawn Michaels, but what led to Hart's abrupt send-off. Bret Hart was not only screwed at *Survivor Series but* screwed out of what was supposed to be a twenty-year contract.

Bret Hart to the Rescue

Bret Hart came to the WWF's rescue at a time when the company was facing trouble on multiple fronts. The steroid scandal involving allegations of wrestlers using steroids was hanging over Vince's head as well as a federal investigation against him into steroid distribution. In McMahon's mind, he had to take the company in a different direction. The days of roided out musclemen were over-at least until things settled down. The question was, who to take over as WWF Champion?

Enter Bret Hart. The second-generation star had evolved from a solid tag team wrestler into a solid singles competitor. Hart had held the Intercontinental Championship, seen as a belt to showcase technical wrestlers and an occasional stepping stone to the WWF Championship. Hart had proven himself as a reliable wrestler and he was known for staying out of trouble outside the ring.

Hart wasn't McMahon's only candidate to become WWF Champion though. WWF Superstars Tito Santana, Rick Martel, Randy Savage, and Shawn Michaels were all discussed but each posed challenges in McMahon's mind. Santana was too old and had spent too much time getting wrestlers over to seem like a world champion and Martel was out for the same reason. Like Santana, he was reliable and a skilled technician but his best days were behind him (although he still looked great, befitting his gimmick as "The Model"). While Randy Savage had held the WWF Championship twice, McMahon felt he too was past his prime, despite Savage still being a main event player. As for Michaels, McMahon felt "The Heartbreak Kid" still needed time working as a heel before he was ready for the big time.

On 12 October 1992, Bret Hart defeated "Nature Boy" Ric Flair for the WWF Championship in Saskatoon, Saskatchewan at a TV taping for *WWF Superstars*. The WWF chose not to air the match (which ran over 26 minutes), an omen of the way the company would treat Hart as champion, a convenience when needed, and an inconvenience when not.

Bret Hart: The WWF's Go-To Guy They Preferred Not to Go To

Bret Hart embraced his role as WWF Champion, but it's arguable Vince McMahon did not embrace him. Over time, it seemed as if the WWF was happy with Hart until something better came along. This began to become clear to Hart when Yokozuna defeated Hart at *WrestleMania IX* and Hulk Hogan swooped in at the pay-per-view's last moments, defeating Yokozuna in an impromptu match. According to Hart, Vince McMahon told Hart that Hogan would wrestle him, putting him over on his way out in a "passing of the torch." Hulk Hogan's account differs:

> Before we got to *King of the Ring* a month later, Bret Hart got in my face and said, "You son of a bitch, Vince McMahon told me you won't drop the belt to me." I said, "Brother, I'm dropping the belt to Yokozuna. That's the deal I made." And Bret said, "That's not what Vince told me. He said you wouldn't drop to belt to me because I'm not in your league and I couldn't lace your boots up." I said, "Well, how about you and me get in a room with Vince right now?" Finally, the three of us -Vince, Bret, and myself-wound up in a room together. Bret said to Vince, "Didn't you tell me that Hulk Hogan wouldn't drop the

belt to me?" And Vince said, "Bret, that's just what you *thought* you heard" (215-16).

In the end, Hogan faced Yokozuna at 1993's *King of the Ring,* dropping the WWF Championship to Yokozuna on his way out. Hart would win the *King of the Ring* tournament the same year, reportedly as a consolation prize for being a good employee.

With Hogan on his way out, *SummerSlam* seemed like a perfect venue for a rematch with Yokozuna. Instead, Hart saw Lex Luger positioned for a match with Yokozuna at *SummerSlam* after the WWF's huge "Lex Express Tour" saw Luger bussed around the United States to hype his new babyface character. Instead, Hart feuded with Jerry "The King" Lawler over the question of who the true king of wrestling was. As 1993 closed out, the WWF was building a feud between Bret and baby brother Owen.

Hart did as he was told, and when the WWF soured on Lex as a possible champion, Hart defeated Yokozuna at *WrestleMania X* for his second WWF Championship. "The Hitman" continued his feud with Owen throughout 1994, and once again, Vince McMahon decided to try someone else for the WWF Championship, putting the belt on Diesel after Bret lost to Bob Backlund at *Survivor Series.* However, McMahon's hope for Diesel to lead the company to new heights evaporated in the wake of dwindling house show attendance. As James Dixon details in his book *Titan Sinking,* "McMahon had actually made the decision to go with Hart back in August following a string of unsuccessful shows with Nash on top. The horrible *SummerSlam* number and the appalling *In Your House 4* the previous month in Winnipeg had only strengthened his resolve to switch the title" (199). Vince McMahon told Bret he would regain the belt at 1995's *Survivor Series,* but also informed him he would drop it to Shawn Michaels at *WrestleMania XII.* Any doubts Hart had about his importance in the company had to be clear. If not, his title defenses before 'Mania made it clear he was keeping the belt warm for Michaels. At *Royal Rumble,* Michaels won his second Rumble in a row while Hart kept the WWF Championship in a bout against Diesel when the Undertaker interfered ('Taker was feuding with Diesel, leading to their blow-off at *WrestleMania XIII*). At *In Your House 6,* Hart retained the belt against Diesel in a Steel Cage Match after Undertaker emerged from under the ring, attacking Diesel and allowing Hart to escape.

By now, Hart was questioning his position in the WWF, especially as it related to his growing rival, Shawn Michaels. What began as a friendly professional rivalry would transform into one of wrestling's bitterest personal rivalries in and out of the squared circle.

A Heated Rivalry Inside and Outside the Ring

No account of the Montreal Screwjob is complete without an examination of the real-life rivalry between Bret Hart and Shawn Michaels. Both men were tremendous Superstars in their own way but just as their style of wrestling differed, so did their lifestyle. Hart, a technical wrestler with an actual grounding in wrestling was more subdued than the show-stealing Shawn Michaels, whose high-flying and flashy style in the ring, mirrored his hard-living lifestyle outside the ring. While Michaels' partying lifestyle is well-known, Hart admits he passed time on the road with hook-ups, drinking, and even recreational drugs. However, whatever pleasures Hart enjoyed, they never seemed to spill over into his professional life, unlike Michaels.

In 1994, Hart was on tour in Europe when Shawn Michaels, Razor Ramon and Kevin Nash approached him. In his autobiography, *Hitman,* Hart remembers them:

> talking to me in Hamburg about the idea of forming a clique of top guys who strictly took care of their own. This was what Buddy Rogers did in the 1950's, working only with his selected clique to get him over, so he could

> monopolize the cash flow. These boys wanted me to be the leader, to voice concerns pertaining to the group as a whole. Even though they were my friends, I couldn't see it, and with the exception of Nash, their degree of pill popping was something I didn't want to be around" (356).

Hart passed on the idea but the Kliq formed, creating well-documented headaches in the WWF. By 1995, Hart's feelings were summed up in a remark he made to Davey Boy Smith about Shawn Michaels, "Shawn's a decent guy, but he's got his little hang-ups...Unfortunately, one of them is being an asshole" (Hart 363).

In his autobiography, *Heartbreak and Triumph: The Shawn Michaels Story,* Shawn Michaels is frank about the Kliq:

> Were we using our political clout to keep each other on top? Absolutely. What we did was no different than what Hogan, Savage, Piper, and Bob Orton Jr. had done before. If you are on top, you want to make sure you keep working with people on top. That's how you stay up there. The only difference between us and Hogan's and Savage's crew was that we actually liked each other. That's another reason why

we had heat. We didn't resent each other's success. We weren't bitter. There were five of us, and it didn't matter which one was on top...In addition, we were also smart enough to want to wrestle other top guys like Undertaker and Bret Hart. It would have been stupid of us to not want to wrestle people who were that good" (206).

Hart questioned Michaels' role as WWF Champion, "I knew that Shawn wasn't the guy to fill my shoes, and I was damn sure he wouldn't draw any better than I did. One big difference between me and Shawn, which would cost him, was that I appreciated my undercard" (Hart 369). Shawn's *WrestleMania XIII* win over Hart rubbed "The Hitman" wrong when according to Hart's autobiography, he told referee Earl Hebner, "tell him to get the fuck out of the ring! This is my moment!" (384). Whatever professional or personal respect Hart had for Michaels was quickly disappearing.

Michaels' opinion of Bret Hart, the wrestler? "I know this is going to sound offensive coming from me, but Bret was not a great wrestler. He was good-very good-but not great. He wasn't that versatile in the ring. The things he did, he did well, but he didn't do a lot of exciting stuff...Once Bret went into his routine, he wouldn't change it up" (Michaels 221).

Should I Stay or Should I Go?

By 1996, Vince McMahon had seen more top stars jump ship to WCW, forcing him to realize he had to lock up some of top talent. After WCW unveiled the New World Order at *Bash at the Beach,* Vince McMahon chartered a plane to see Bret Hart in July 1996. According to Hart, "He put a contract in front of me and told me to name my price. 'Whatever you want!' He told me Taker and Shawn were making around $700,000 a year" (Hart 392). Hart told McMahon he was in no hurry to sign but just two months later, he would face one of the biggest choices of his life.

Hart was in Los Angeles, making an appearance for *The Simpsons* when Eric Bischoff asked to meet with him. After discussing famous gunfighters, the two got down to business and Hart claims he told Bischoff he wanted the same deal as Hulk Hogan, "plus one penny" (Hart 394). Bischoff told Hart he couldn't do that but to give him a figure to take back to WCW. Hart told him $3 million a year and a lighter schedule. Days later, Bischoff countered with an offer of $2.8 million a year and a lighter schedule. Now, it was time to talk to Vince.

After hearing WCW's offer, McMahon reportedly told "The Hitman" there was no way he could match it. However, Hart told McMahon he wanted to stay in the WWF and asked him what he *could* offer. McMahon told Hart to give him some time and he would get back to him. McMahon flew to Calgary and made his offer:

> Vince said he had a better deal for me than WCW. He wanted to sign me for twenty years as a wrestler: $500,000 a year for the next seven years as one of his senior advisers; and then $250,000 a year for ten years thereafter, to be on standby as that Babe Ruth of the company Vince was always looking for. It was a satisfying feeling hearing him say, "I'll never give you a reason to ever want to leave (395).

Just a year later, Vince McMahon would come to Bret Hart and inform him he could no longer honor his deal, telling Hart to contact WCW about going to work for them. The events that followed would lead to one of wrestling's most treacherous acts and as we shall see, it never had to happen. Vince McMahon had the money to honor Hart's contract, but he no longer wanted to honor it.

I'll never give you a reason to ever want to leave

WWF kingpin Vince McMahon signed Bret Hart to an unprecedented 20-year contract, promising "The Hitman," "I'll never give you a reason to ever want to leave." However, that didn't mean others wouldn't give him a reason to leave; in this case, Hart's rival, Shawn Michaels.

Hart and Michaels' professional rivalry was turning personal as each wrestler felt the other was bad for the WWF. Hart was growing tired of Michaels' personal problems and what Hart perceived as a sexually provocative and morally degenerate act in the ring. Michaels felt Hart was too full of himself, overrated, and overpaid.

Michaels hit the roof when he learned of the sweet deal Hart had signed with the WWF. In his autobiography, *Heartbreak and Tragedy: The Shawn Michaels Story,* HBK recalls his meeting with Vince McMahon once he learned Hart was signed to $1.5 million a year. In 1996, McMahon signed HBK to a $750,000 a year deal. Supposedly, this was the biggest contract ever and Michaels told McMahon, "I'm just asking that you don't pay anyone, except Undertaker, any more than you pay me. That would be an insult" (241). When Michaels discovered Hart's new deal, he said, "You are paying Bret all that money that is b.s…I'm slaving up and down the road and you are paying him, twice as much as me. You think he is twice as good as me?" (241). According to Michaels, McMahon's response was, "I had to give him the big contract, Shawn. He had my back up against the wall. He was going to go to WCW, and now I have to get the money out of him" (242).

While Shawn was griping with McMahon, Hart continued having problems with Michaels. Hart and Michaels were set to meet at *WrestleMania XIII,* reportedly with Michaels set to drop the WWF Championship to Hart, just as Hart had done for Michaels at *WrestleMania XII.* With their series tied at two, Hart would give Michaels the victory in the third match, putting him over in a best of three series. However, behind the scenes, there was talk that Michaels didn't want to put Hart over which made some wrestlers and fans skeptical when Michaels announced his doctor had recommended he retire as he needed a knee replacement. Michaels' famous "I lost my smile" speech saw him drop the WWF Championship in the ring during an episode of *RAW.* Hart was doubtful and reportedly so was the Undertaker with both men reportedly saying they'd believe Michaels' story when they saw the scar from the surgery.

According to Michaels, he received fantastic news when he followed Vince McMahon's recommendation and went to "Stone Cold" Steve Austin's physician, Dr. Andrews for a second opinion. To Michaels' amazement, Andrews told him he could return to the ring with four to six weeks of therapy.

Sunny Days

Most fans are familiar with the infamous "Sunny Days" promo where Shawn Michaels implied Bret Hart (who was married) was having a relationship with the WWF's Sunny. Bret exploded backstage, reportedly attacking Michaels backstage and ripping out chunks of Michaels' hair. The incident seems to have come to a head after months of tension between Hart and Michaels. Both men were cutting promos on one another and they cut close to home. As might be expected, each man's story differed from the other's.

Shawn Michaels claims he had grown tired of Hart cutting personal attacks on him, then apologize for it, only to do it again. Michaels admits he intentionally made the "Sunny Days" comments but felt there was no denying Hart's affair with Sunny. Hart recalls not hearing the remarks when they happened but learning of them when he went home and his family was understandably upset by them. Hart's friend Jim Neidhart asked him not to physically attack Michaels. Some sources indicate Neidhart was concerned because he'd just been picked up by the WWF and he might be fired if Hart beat up Michaels. Neither man spoke to each other for weeks. In Hart's autobiography, he claims he tried to talk things out only for Michaels to swear at him, "Fuck you. You haven't fucking talked to me in a fucking month, what makes you think I'm gonna talk to you now?" (429).

It should come as no surprise that both men's recollections of the incident are different. Consider Michaels' account of the events. HBK remembers someone pushing him from behind. Then:

> I turned around and Bret asked, "What's your fucking problem?" "You!" I yelled. He tried to punch me, but I peeled back and he missed. He pushed me again, and this time I stood up. He swung again, and missed. The next thing I knew, he went for a double leg dive. I caught him around the upper body and we went straight back through a piece of paneling. We had each other in front face locks when Pat Patterson and Davey Boy came over and grabbed us. Pat was yelling, "Come on, you guys!" I let go and Bret yanked a handful of my hair off my head. That hurt like heck, but I didn't retaliate. The fight was over (Michaels 245).

Bret Hart's version is that he recalls Michaels disappeared, leading "The Hitman" to believe Michaels would return once he thought Hart was gone. Hart claims he hid until Michaels returned then walked up to him and said, "You got something to say to me?" (Hart 429). From there, things quickly escalated:

> He flicked a weak punch at me and missed. Balancing awkwardly on my good leg, I popped him on the chin, rocking him on his heels. He came for me, but I grabbed him by his long hair and pretended I was doing a hammer throw at the Olympics. I was dragging him around the room when a hysterical Pat and a frantic Lawler ran in and jumped on top of me. Unable to pry me off, Pat shouted for the other wrestlers to help, but Davey and Crush had no intention of saving Shawn. It was nothing but a scratch-fight really but when we were finally separated, clumps of Shawn's previous hair fell from my hands. I blasted him, "Don't fuck with me or my family, you little fucker" (Hart 429).

In *Titan Screwed,* Jim Cornette is quoted as saying, "'Bret was killing him. Shawn couldn't whip cream with an outboard motor in a real fight, much less Bret Hart." Finally, Gerald Brisco was able to pull Hart off of Michaels and as Michaels left…" (*Titan Screwed).* Fans can decide which account (if any) to believe.

Michaels reportedly stormed into Vince McMahon's office and told him, "Goddamn this bullshit...It's not safe to work here anymore. You've got a goddamn lunatic in there. You've obviously worked him into a frenzy or somebody has. Fuck this shit, Vince. I'll never work for you again" (Dixon *Titan Screwed*). Vince McMahon suspended Michaels without pay, claiming he was in breach of his contract. Michaels' lawyer Skip McCormick informed the WWF's counsel Jerry McDevitt Michaels had injured his neck and knee during the altercation, resulting in his inability to work. The WWF agreed to pay Michaels and Michaels returned to work after McCormick advised him he faced breach of contract if he refused to work (Dixon, *Titan Shattered*).

Bret Gets Replaced...Again

In *Wrestling with Shadows*, Bret talked about the realization that Michaels was turning heel at *Summer Slam,* something he wasn't happy about. Hart knew what that meant for his role as the WWF's number one heel. Hart had reluctantly agreed to a heel turn, alienating a large amount of his fans. Now, he faced becoming second banana to Shawn Michaels...again.

If that wasn't bad enough, Hart also felt he was falling from the main event, despite being WWF Champion. Hart became upset when the WWF informed him he would work a program with newcomer, The Patriot. Although Hart had no problems with the Patriot, he felt wrestling the masked man was a step down into the midcard.

The WWF is in Financial Peril

On 22 September 1997 at Madison Square Garden, Vince McMahon approached Bret Hart and told him in no uncertain terms he could no longer honor his contract. On the documentary *Wrestling with Shadows,* Hart recalls how McMahon told him the WWF was "in financial peril." McMahon told Hart to pursue negotiations with WCW, giving him his full blessing since Bret had always been loyal to him. Bret told McMahon he wanted to stay with the WWF and money wasn't an issue. In *Wrestling with Shadows,* Hart talks of how he saw Vince McMahon as a father figure, how he owed his success to McMahon, and how he felt he'd be walking out on his own father if he left the WWF. At the same time, Hart felt McMahon had painted him into a corner. Hart was a heel but Shawn Michaels was a heel now as well. Hart couldn't go back to being a babyface after insulting American fans, 95% of the people he performed before. By now, what choice did he have?

McMahon reportedly told Hart his economic woes meant he was scaling the WWF back to a regional promotion. He told Hart he'd help him get the best deal possible with WCW. Hart was understandably concerned WCW might not give him the same deal they'd done before if they knew Vince couldn't afford him. However, during a trip to Los Angeles to film an episode of *Mad TV*, Hart met with Eric Bischoff and told him he had a clause in his contract allowing him to leave the company thanks to the change in tone towards a racier product. Whether or not Bischoff bought the story, WCW was still eager to sign Hart, not only wanting to harm the WWF by robbing it of a top star, but to use Hart to help them with plans to expand into Canada. Hart told Bischoff to give him time to think the deal over. Hart wanted to remain in the WWF is possible.

However, unknown to "The Hitman," Vince McMahon was eager to dump him. What was McMahon's reasoning? Why would the WWF kingpin want to lose another one of his top stars to WCW? Were the WWF's finances that bad? The answer is clearly no.

Although the WWF would not go public until 1999, authors James Dixon and Justin Henry revealed in their book *Titan Screwed,* that Vince McMahon:

> had recently met with a Manhattan investment house for early talks about the possibility of taking the WWF public, a move he felt would help boost the company's coffers and allow

them to compete on a more even playing field with Turner. During the meeting, McMahon had been advised to limit or, if he could, remove any long-term obligation so as to make the company appear more profitable to potential investors.

Dixon and Henry also argue McMahon was unhappy with Hart's performance as champion and that he hadn't helped ratings or pay-per-view numbers. McMahon felt Michaels and Hart were bound to clash again and one of them had to go. Another story is McMahon wanted to focus on other stars and felt Bret Hart was no longer necessary, particularly with a 20-year commitment and the wrestler now 40 years old. Another factor against Hart was McMahon feared other stars like Steve Austin and the Undertaker would expect a comparable salary to Hart.

What is known is the WWF was not in the desperate financial straits McMahon painted to Bret. The WWF had raised its pay-per-view price from $19.95 to $29.95. According to *Titan Screwed,* the WWF was looking at bringing in an addition six million dollars income from the hike.

Give Me a Reason to Stay

Although Bret Hart negotiated a fantastic deal, he told Vince McMahon he wanted to stay with the company. With a deadline looming to sign the WCW contract, Hart reached out to McMahon several times. McMahon told him to follow his head and not his heart. Hart reached out again asking McMahon to give him a reason to stay. When McMahon reportedly told Hart he planned to have him lose three out of four matches to Shawn Michaels before putting Steve Austin over at *WrestleMania,* Hart knew the choice had been made for him and he signed the WCW deal.

Vince's Worst Nightmare

With Hart signed with WCW, McMahon knew he had to get the WWF Championship off him before 10 November 1997. That was the day when Eric Bischoff could announce Hart had signed with WCW. Vince McMahon's worst nightmare was for Bret Hart to show up on *Nitro* with the WWF Championship, similar to how WWF Women's Champion Alundra Blayze showed up on the 12/18/95 *Nitro* and threw the title in the garbage. It was bad enough the fans would see yet another WWF star jumping to *Nitro,* particularly the WWF Champion. What would happen if Bischoff announced they'd sign the reigning WWF Champion?

McMahon's quest to get the belt off Hart ran into a number of problems. First, Hart refused to lose to Shawn Michaels. Once again, Michaels had rubbed Hart the wrong way. Hart's memoir contains his recollection of how he tried to make peace with Michaels backstage, telling him, "Shawn, I just want you to know that despite any difference we've had this past year, I have no problem working with you. You can trust me in every way to be a professional. I want you to know that you are not in any danger and that I have no problem dropping the belt to you if that's what Vince wants" (443-444) Michaels replied, "I appreciate that, but I want you to know that I'm not willing to do the same for you" (444). This blatant disrespect in front of the boys, and Hart's feeling Michaels had never apologized for his "Sunny days" remarks made Hart decide he would never drop the WWF Championship to Michaels. Furthermore, Hart refused to drop the belt in Canada, particularly at the pay-per-view in Montreal. When McMahon suggested Hart drop the belt in Detroit before the pay-per-view, Hart refused, arguing he didn't want to let his fans down by going into the pay-per-view as challenger instead of champion. Hart offered to drop the belt the next week at a house show in Madison Square Garden but McMahon balked at the idea of having to pay $40,000 (the supposed cost of filming in the Garden) to record the title switch.

With Hart refusing to do the time-honored tradition, and McMahon facing the disgrace of WCW announcing it had signed the WWF Champion, Vince McMahon was running out of options until an off-hand remark led to McMahon devising one of the most controversial swerves in wrestling history.

"A Canadian Standoff"

Bret Hart and Vince McMahon had reached an impasse about Hart dropping the WWF Championship to Shawn Michaels at *Survivor Series* in Montreal, Canada. Bret was adamant about refusing to lay down for Michaels, especially after Michaels insulted him in the locker room when he told Hart he wouldn't lose to Hart. With Bret Hart having reasonable creative control for his last month in the WWF, there were limits to how the WWF could take the belt off Hart.

While McMahon was insisting Hart drop the WWF Championship before November 10, 1997 (Eric Bischoff had promised Hart he wouldn't announce his signing until the *Monday Night Nitro* on that date), Bret remarked in the documentary *Hitman Hart: Wrestling with Shadows* that he'd worked over 300 dates in 1997, considerably more than the 275 dates required by contract. If so, Hart was under no obligation to show up for *Survivor Series*. This seemed unlikely though as Hart's commitment to the WWF had always been solid. In his 14 years working for the company, he claimed he'd only missed two dates.

McMahon seemed confident that Hart wouldn't betray him by showing up on *Nitro* with the WWF Championship, but he was also confident WCW's Eric Bischoff would do whatever he could to capitalize on WCW signing "The Excellence of Execution." In an interview with *Kayfabe Commentaries*, Jim Cornette said Vince McMahon didn't trust Eric Bischoff after the Madusa incident (where the WWF's Women's Champion showed up on *Nitro* and dumped the title in the garbage). He said Vince put himself in a bad position when he kept the belt on Hart before Hart made his decision to go to WCW. When McMahon told Cornette Hart had suggested handing the WWF Championship to him on *RAW,* Cornette told him, "Why don't you lay down in the ring and let him piss in your mouth" ("Jim Cornette Explains the Montreal Screwjob"). In a shoot interview, Eric Bischoff recalls there was no way they would pull a stunt like that with Bret because WCW was buried in litigation following Kevin Nash and Scott Hall's jump to WCW. The WWF had sued WCW alleging they were using Nash and Hall's Diesel and Razor Ramon characters, implying they still worked for the WWF. In the interview, Bischoff said he couldn't have recreated the Alundra Blayze angle even if he wanted to. Whether or not Bischoff's remarks are true, Vince McMahon was growing more concerned, leading him to consider options he might not have considered before, such as a double cross.

Although the moment when Vince decided on a shoot are unknown, we do know this; things were looking grim when Jim Cornette jokingly suggested McMahon put Ken Shamrock in the ring with Bret and pull a shoot. Cornette said McMahon's options suddenly changed. According to the book *Titan Screwed,* it's arguable the seed had been planted in McMahon's mind and he was looking for someone else to suggest what he was now considering himself.

McMahon then met with Shawn Michaels and Hunter Hearst Helmsley to discuss Michaels' match. McMahon implied he was having problems getting the belt off of Hart when Helmsley chimed in. Michaels recalls in his autobiography *Heartbreak and Triumph* how he and Hunter spoke on the phone weekly with McMahon to discuss creative ideas. McMahon told the two of Hart's refusal to drop the belt in Canada, explaining his hands were tied due to Hart's creative control. It was at this point that Hunter Hearst Helmsley reportedly said:

> "I know I'm not supposed to be talking here," it was Hunter. "Maybe I'm out of line here, but what kind of business is this? Who in the world says. "I don't want to drop the belt? You helped him to get a better deal there

and he is leaving. That isn't right. That's b.s. How in the world can you trust him? This is the same guy who while he was off, after dropping the title to Shawn, went behind your back and negotiated a deal with WCW only to come back and renegotiate a twenty-year-way-out-of-bounds contract with you. He has not done good business since, and now he is leaving to get even more money, by you giving them the impression that you wanted to keep him" (266).

Helmsley's tirade may have been the impetus McMahon was looking for to suggest a double-cross. When McMahon restated his hands were tied, Michaels said, "I'll do whatever you want. We'll just take it off him. I'll just swerve him or whatever I have to. You tell me what needs to get done. You and this company have put up with so much from me. My loyalty is here with you. I will do whatever you want" (266). Michaels' reply led to McMahon reportedly saying, "That's pretty serious. That has to be a last resort. I still have until Saturday to talk to Bret. That may have to be a real option. This cannot be discussed with anyone. Pat can't know, nobody can know about this but the three of us right now. It's something we will have to talk about" (266).

By Saturday night, it was clear to Vince McMahon that Bret Hart wasn't going to drop the WWF Championship the next night at *Survivor Series*. McMahon met behind closed doors with Hunter, Michaels, and Gerald Brisco. McMahon announced his decision to proceed with the double-cross and told all three men no one else was to know about the coming action. While speculation has run rampant that Pat Patterson or Jim Ross knew, numerous parties have stated McMahon kept them out of the loop as Patterson (the head booker at the time) and Ross (in charge of talent relations) were too close to the boys for them to be tainted by such a scandal. After all, who would trust them after this if it was discovered they'd known about the double-cross?

Hart's Ace in the Hole

While Bret Hart was wary going into the match, he felt more confident when he talked with referee Earl Hebner to discuss his concerns about a double-cross. Hebner promised Hart there was no possibility he'd betray him, swearing to God and on his children's lives. Once Hart saw Hebner was refereeing the match, he was confident he could get out of any possible swerve. Unbeknownst to "The Hitman," Hebner was confronted by the WWF's Gerald Brisco on his way to the ring and told to call for the bell when Michaels put Hart in the Sharpshooter. Brisco warned Hebner he was microphoned and any attempt to alert Hart would lead to his firing.

Hart has been asked many times whether he suspected any treachery. He writes in his autobiography, "People still ask me, 'Didn't you see it coming?' The truth was, I'd been reasonable in every way, and with Earl watching my back, I thought I had nothing to worry about" (Hart 451).

The Trap is Set

November 9, 1997 saw Bret Hart meet with Vince McMahon to discuss Hart's upcoming match and Hart and McMahon's long relationship. Unknown to McMahon, Hart was wearing a hidden microphone (an idea reportedly suggested during the filming of Hart's documentary *Wrestling with Shadows*), so the conversation was recorded. McMahon and Hart went back and forth on the finish for Hart's match, Hart suggesting he retain the WWF Championship but forfeit it the next night on *RAW*. McMahon told Hart the match would end in a disqualification when DX interfered in the match. However, McMahon had something else planned for "The Hitman."

Hart met with Shawn before their match to have a final heart-to-heart. Shawn Michaels remembers Hart and him talking about putting things in the past and how Hart explained his reasoning for not wanting to drop the title. To Michaels, Hart's need to keep the title in Canada defied the understanding the business is a work. In his autobiography, Michaels recalls:

> I was thinking, "You take yourself pretty seriously, don't you?" He's dropping a title, but it's the same title someone else let him win. I know the first time you win it, it's real, but it always remained real for him. It was just a conversation that I couldn't believe I was having with a guy who had been in the business for twenty years and was forty-plus years old" (Michaels 270).

Despite Hart's refusal to drop the belt, Michaels claims he felt terrible when Hart asked him if he could trust him and he replied yes. According to Michaels, "Despite all our problems, I really felt bad for him because I knew this was the end and he had no idea what was coming" (271).

When Shawn Michaels went to the ring, he noticed a congregation near the Gorilla position. In his autobiography, Michaels noted:

> Hunter was there, so was Brisco, Vince started drifting to us and Pat was there as well. Then Davey Boy, Jim Neidhart, and Owen Hart came up next to us. The finish, as far as everyone else knew, was that Hunter

> was going to come down and interfere, and then those guys would come down, and there would be a big fight and a DQ. But when guys are going to do a run-in, they don't stand at gorilla before the match starts. It was very unusual for them to be there, and since I knew what was happening, I was thinking they were there in case something happens (274).

Vince McMahon's sudden appearance at ringside wasn't out of the ordinary as he'd been involved in a storyline with building tension between him and Bret Hart. McMahon was there supposedly for dramatic purposes as he'd try and get the match under control as Michaels and Hart battled in and out of the ring, including the crowd. McMahon's true purpose was to make sure the bell was rung before Hart had a chance to stop Michaels during the double-cross.

In his autobiography, Bret remembers Shawn applying the Sharpshooter but not getting it right. He then corrected Shawn, unaware he was pulling the trigger on the double-cross. Moments later, Earl Hebner motioned for the bell to be rung. As Michaels music played, Hart realized he'd been double-crossed. Hart held on to Michaels at first, but then got up, spitting in Vince McMahon's face.

Hart recalls his anger and emotion. "Looking out at the stunned crowd, I fought the tears that were swimming in my eyes and thought, Don't you dare give these backstabbers the satisfaction of seeing you cry over any of this" (453). Hart pantomimed the letters for WCW. While word was already out he was jumping ship to WCW, Hart wanted as many people to know as possible.

Backstage Confrontation

Triple H shuttled Shawn Michaels out of the ring. As Bret Hart remembers, the fans looked like they might riot. The thought of the fans attacking them had to be running through Shawn and Hunter's mind. What was going to happen backstage?

What was going on? The backstage was in chaos as wrestlers tried to piece together what happened. Bret Hart went to find Vince McMahon but McMahon was locked in his office. Hart went to the dressing room where he recalls, "walking inside only to see Shawn sitting in the corner. 'Shawn, you weren't in on that?' 'I swear to fucking God, I had nothing to do with it!'" (Hart 453). With the *Wrestling with Shadows* crew still filming everything, Hart debated whether or not to attack Michaels. "I wanted to rip Shawn to shreds-deep down I knew he was in on it all the way-but I didn't want to lose my cool in front of [Hart's son]

Blade" (Hart 453). Hart warned Michaels he'd judge him by what he did the next night on *RAW*.

In the meantime, the Undertaker reportedly stormed up to Vince McMahon's office and demanded that McMahon face Bret Hart. As the WWF's locker room leader, it's likely the Undertaker understood an explanation was due, not only to Hart but to the boys in general. Multiple sources state the Undertaker went to McMahon and told him he owed Hart an apology. Hart apparently had changed his mind when McMahon and his entourage showed up. Hart warned McMahon to leave or get hit. However, McMahon refused to leave. Hart says McMahon's group tried to clear out the dressing room, but Davey Boy Smith told Owen to stay, reminding him of what had happened to Bruiser Brody when promoter Jose Gonzales allegedly stabbed him to death in the dressing room showers.

According to Hart, McMahon told him, "It's the first time I ever had to lie to one of my talent" (454) but Hart wasn't buying it. Hart claims he replied, "Who are you kidding, you lying piece of shit?" (454). Hart warned McMahon to leave the dressing room but Hart states they continued arguing, with McMahon claiming he'd helped Hart get his WCW deal and Hart reminding McMahon he wanted to stay in the WWF, even if it meant less money. The war of words escalated and Hart knew things were going to escalate to physicality, even if it would be short-lived with everyone standing nearby, waiting to break things up. Hart recounts:

> I picked up my knee brace, thinking to smash Vince over the head with it, but I tossed it down, declaring, 'I won't need this!" and went straight for him. Cockily, Vince came back at me and we actually tied up, fourteen fuckin' years. I launched a rocket-launcher uppercut that connected with Vince's jaw. My right fist actually popped him like a cork off the ground, and he collapsed unconscious to the carpet.

Like many of the accounts here, there are conflicting reports of what happened. Shawn Michaels claims McMahon let Hart strike him, suggesting he even took a dive. In subsequent interviews, McMahon would claim he had given Hart a "free shot." While there's no conclusive proof of whether Vince took the punch or McMahon made the mistake of stepping to Hart, the footage from *Wrestling with Shadows* shows a dazed Vince McMahon walking out of the dressing room.

The WWF Championship was off Bret Hart and Hart was on his way to WCW. The fallout from the Montreal Screwjob saw the birth of the

Mr. McMahon character, one of the key moments in the Monday Night War. Initially, Vince McMahon tried to defend his actions but when it became clear the fans would not forgive him, he channeled their anger and vitriol into a revolutionary heel character—the owner of the WWF who manipulated his talent for his every whim. Authority figures were not new to wrestling, but the Mr. McMahon character took it to new heights, particularly when "Stone Cold" Steve Austin opposed him.

Eventually, Bret Hart, Shawn Michaels, and Vince McMahon reconciled over the Montreal Screwjob, after years of guilt and bitterness. The healing process was slow and scars likely remain, but it's a testament to the power of forgiveness that the three men reconciled.

Twenty years later, the Montreal Screwjob remains one of wrestling's most controversial incidents. Fans still argue whether the events of November 9, 1997, were an underhanded power play against Hart, or an elaborately worked scheme to draw controversy for both the WWF and Bret Hart on his way out of the company. Despite wrestlers and others alleging the Montreal Screwjob wasn't a double-cross but an angle, it's difficult to conceive of someone keeping a secret of this magnitude for twenty years. With wrestlers and backstage personnel coming and going in the

WWE, it defies the odds that someone wouldn't have presented evidence that the Montreal Screwjob was an elaborate work by Vince McMahon, Shawn Michaels, and Bret Hart. Thus far, that hasn't happened. It's even arguable Vince McMahon, known for his large ego, would want to take credit for it. The question seems to come down to one of whether something is possible or probable. Is it possible the Montreal Screwjob was a work? Of course. Does the evidence support it as being probable? That is something we will leave you to decide.

Works Cited

Assael, Shaun and Mike Mooneyham. *Sex, Lies, and Headlocks: The Real Story of Vince McMahon and World Wrestling Entertainment.* Three Rivers Press, 2004.

Barrasso, Justin. "Bret Hart Opens Up About the Montreal Screwjob." *Sports Illustrated."* 10 Nov. 2014. https://www.si.com/extra-mustard/2014/11/19/bret-hart-opens-about-infamous-montreal-screwjob. Accessed 1 May 2017.

"The Brothers Hebner Shooting on the Montreal Screwjob." *YouTube,* Pro Wrestling Clips, 21 Apr. 2015, https://www.youtube.com/watch?v=jDghO Oyl65M.

Dixon, James and Justin Henry. *Titan Screwed: Lost Smiles, Stunners, and Screwjobs.* Lulu.com, 2016.

Dixon, James. *Titan Shattered: Wrestling with Confidence and Paranoia.* 2015.

Dixon, James. *Titan Sinking: The Decline of the WWF in 1995.* Lulu.com, 2014.

"8 Things Everybody Gets Wrong About The Montreal Screwjob." *Whatculture.* http://whatculture.com/wwe/8-things-everybody-gets-wrong-about-the-montreal-screwjob. Accessed 1 May 2017.

"Eric Bischoff on Montreal Screwjob & Madusa dropping WWF title in trash." *YouTube,* Your Eternal Destiny1, 23 May 2014, https://www.youtube.com/watch?v=g8_Zf nKa3uo.

Hart, Bret. *Hitman: My Real Life in the Cartoon World of Wrestling.* Random House Canada, 2007.

Hitman Hart: Wrestling with Shadows. Directed by Paul Jay, performances by Bret Hart, Owen Hart, and Brian Pillman, High Road Productions, 1998.

Hogan, Hulk. *Hollywood Hulk Hogan.* World Wrestling Entertainment, 2002.

"Jim Cornette Explains the Montreal Screwjob." *YouTube,* uploaded by Wrestling Hut, 17 Feb. 2017, https://www.youtube.com/watch?v=1cOI7 1NH8SY.

Michaels, Shawn and Aaron Feigenbaum. *Heartbreak and Triumph: The Shawn Michaels Story.* World Wrestling Entertainment, 2006.

Reynolds, R.D. and Bryan Alvarez. *The Death of WCW: Wrestlecrap and Figure Four Weekly Present...*ECW Press, 2004.

Rickard, Michael. *Wrestling's Greatest Moments.* ECW Press, 2008.

WWE: Greatest Rivalries - Shawn Michaels vs. Bret Hart. Directed by Kevin Dunn, performances by Bret Hart, Shawn Michaels, and Jim Ross, World Wrestling Entertainment, 2011.

412

Acknowledgments

As a wise man in the operating room once said, "That surgery isn't as easy as it looks." While writing a book is less hazardous, it can be a daunting task which is why I want to thank my friends and family for their encouragement (and for my brother Dave for reading the manuscript). Thanks to my Dad for his great cover idea and my Mom and Dad for their encouragement.

Equally important is the encouragement I received when I was released from prison and people were willing to give me a second chance whether it was furthering my education or writing about wrestling again. Thanks to the great faculty at Buffalo State College for helping me navigate undergrad and graduate school (especially Dr. Lorna Perez who was my thesis adviser). Special thanks to Ryan from *Wrestlebotch*, Canadian Bulldog and the site *Wrestling Merchandise and Memories*, and of course, everyone at the *YouTube* channel *WrestleLamia*.

414

If you enjoyed this book, be sure to review it on Amazon and/or Goodreads. Even something as simple as a star-review will help! On the other hand, if you didn't enjoy the book, let's keep it our little secret.

416

Printed in Great Britain
by Amazon